MW00629514

THE KLEINMAN EDITION

לִימוּד יוֹמִי

A
Daily
Dose
of Torah

A Torah theme for every day of every week,
blending profound perspectives
from all areas of Torah literature –
Scripture, Mishnah, Jewish Law, Mussar/Ethics,
Tefillah/Prayer, and Hashkafah/Jewish Thought –
collected for daily study.

ArtScroll Series®

THE KLEINMAN EDITION

A TORAH THEME FOR EVERY DAY OF EVERY WEEK
FROM ALL AREAS OF TORAH LITERATURE —
COLLECTED FOR DAILY STUDY.

Rabbi Yosaif Asher Weiss
General Editor

לימוד
יומי

OF TORAH

VOLUME 1

DAILY STUDY FOR THE WEEKS OF
BEREISHIS-VAYEIRA

Published by
ArtScroll ❖ Mesorah Publications, ltd

FIRST EDITION
First Impression … September 2006

Published and Distributed by
MESORAH PUBLICATIONS, LTD.
4401 Second Avenue / Brooklyn, N.Y 11232

Distributed in Europe by
LEHMANNS
Unit E, Viking Business Park
Rolling Mill Road
Jarow, Tyne & Wear, NE32 3DP
England

Distributed in Australia and New Zealand by
GOLDS WORLDS OF JUDAICA
3-13 William Street
Balaclava, Melbourne 3183
Victoria, Australia

Distributed in Israel by
SIFRIATI / A. GITLER — BOOKS
6 Hayarkon Street
Bnei Brak 51127

Distributed in South Africa by
KOLLEL BOOKSHOP
Ivy Common
105 William Road
Norwood 2192, Johannesburg, South Africa

ARTSCROLL SERIES®
THE KLEINMAN EDITION — LIMUD YOMI / A DAILY DOSE OF TORAH
VOL. 1: BEREISHIS – VAYEIRA
© Copyright 2006, by MESORAH PUBLICATIONS, Ltd.
4401 Second Avenue / Brooklyn, N.Y. 11232 / (718) 921-9000 / www.artscroll.com

Typography by CompuScribe at ArtScroll Studios, Ltd.

Printed in the United States of America by Noble Book Press Corp.
Bound by Sefercraft, Quality Bookbinders, Ltd., Brooklyn N.Y. 11232

To our fathers and grandfathers, daily Torah study was the first priority.
It is fitting, therefore, that we dedicate this Limud Yomi Series in their memory

Avrohom Kleinman ז"ל
ר' אברהם אייזיק ב"ר אלכסנדר ז"ל
נפ' י"ב שבט תשנ"ט

After years of slave labor and concentration camps — years when he risked his life to put on *tefillin* every day! — he courageously rebuilt. Wherever he was — in DP camps, Poughkeepsie, Borough Park, or Forest Hills — he was a one-man *kiruv* movement, before "*kiruv rechokim*" was a familiar phrase. Everyone was drawn to his enthusiasm for Yiddishkeit.

His home was open to anyone in need, even when there was barely enough for family.

All his life he felt close to his Rebbe, the Nitra Rav, and to the father-in-law he never knew; their *sefarim*, *Naos Desheh* and *Lechem Abirim*, were part of our Shabbos table. He was a caring and gentle man whose life was defined by his love of learning Torah, *gemillas chasadim*, *kiruv* work, *hachnasas orchim*, *askanus*, and love for his family. He left a noble legacy that we are honored to perpetuate.

Mendel Indig ז"ל
ר' מנחם דוד ב"ר מרדכי שמואל ז"ל
נפ' ט' אדר ב' תשס"ג

"It was as if a *maloch* protected us," he used to say about the dark years of Churban Europa. He lost almost everything — even the *tefillin* that he put on every day until the very end — but he kept his spirit, his *emunah*, his dedication to Torah, and his resolve to rebuild.

He became a living legend of Torah, *chesed*, and service to his Bensonhurst community. His home was open to anyone in need, and there was always enough room for guests. His *succah* was the largest in the neighborhood, and he always found a way to bring endangered relatives to America and help them become established.

After he retired, he devoted himself to learning and bringing others close to Yiddishkeit, especially immigrants from the former Soviet Union, teaching them to put on *tefillin* and reuniting them with the Judaism of their ancestors. It is our privilege to carry on his glorious legacy.

We pay tribute to our mothers
Ethel Kleinman תחי'
Rose Indig תחי'

To us and our children and grandchildren — and to all who know them — they are role models of *emunah*, *chesed*, love and wisdom.

Our mothers שיחיו and our fathers ז"ל planted seeds of Torah in America and produced magnificent *doros* of children, grandchildren, and great-grandchildren following their example. May Hashem continue to bless our mothers with good health and many nachas-filled years.

Elly and Brochie Kleinman and their children
**Deenie and Yitzy Schuss   Yossie Kleinman   Aliza and Lavey Freedman
and families**

DEDICATION OPPORTUNITIES

We are gratified by the
very enthusiastic response to this
new program for daily Torah study.
It is yet another demonstration
of the strong and growing desire
to make Torah a part of every Jew's life,
seven days a week, fifty-two weeks a year.

Each volume of the

KLEINMAN EDITION
A DAILY DOSE OF TORAH

will carry individual dedications.
Many visionary families have already
undertaken to dedicate volumes
in memory or in honor of loved ones.
Additional dedication opportunities are available.

For further information, please call:
718-921-9000,
write to:

ARTSCROLL · Mesorah Publications, ltd

4401 Second Avenue · Brooklyn, NY 11232
or e-mail: DailyDose@artscroll.com

‎⪘ Publisher's Preface

King David said: גַּל עֵינַי וְאַבִּיטָה נִפְלָאוֹת מִתּוֹרָתֶךָ, *Unveil my eyes that I may perceive wonders from your Torah* (*Psalms* 119:18).

Shammai said: עֲשֵׂה תּוֹרָתְךָ קֶבַע, *Make your Torah study a fixed practice* (*Avos* 1:15).

Rav Saadiah Gaon said: The Jewish people is a nation only by virtue of the Torah.

The Torah is the essence of the Jewish people, and not a day should go by without Torah study. How much learning should there be? Just as the Torah itself is infinite, there is no limit to the effort to master its contents. The task does not end when one bids farewell to the academy and enters the world of work and business. All over the world, study halls are filled before dawn and after dark with men plumbing the depths of the Talmud and other works. Before and after their workdays, they overcome fatigue with a relentless desire to absorb more and more of God's word.

To such people, **The Kleinman Edition: Limud Yomi / A Daily Dose of Torah** will be a welcome supplement, an enrichment that offers glimpses of additional topics and a means of filling the day's spare minutes with nourishment for the mind and spirit.

To those who as yet have not been able to savor the beauty of immersion in the sea of study, this new series will be a vehicle to enrich their every day with an assortment of stimulating Torah content.

Each "Daily Dose of Torah" includes selections from a broad spectrum of Torah sources (see below); in combination they provide a multi-dimensional study program. Each selection can stand on its own, or, ideally, serve as a vehicle for further research and enrichment. These components are as follows:

❏ *A Torah Thought for the Day*, focusing on a verse in the weekly *parashah*. The discussion may revolve around various classic interpretations, or it may offer a selection of insights and lessons that are derived from the verse. This section will draw from a wide gamut of early and later commentators, and will enhance the reader's appreciation for the wealth of Torah interpretation and its lessons for life.

❑ *The Mishnah of the Day,* presenting a Mishnah selection every day, with text, translation, and concise commentary, adapted from the classic ArtScroll Mishnah Series and the Schottenstein Edition of the Talmud. This daily dose will begin with Tractate Shabbos, and continue through Seder Moed.

❑ *Gems from the Gemara,* presenting some of the Talmud's discussion of the daily Mishnah. Thus the reader will "join the academy" of the Talmud's question-and-answer clarification of the laws and underlying principles of the Mishnah.

❑ *A Mussar Thought for the Day,* building upon the theme of the *Torah Thought for the Day*, by presenting an ethical or moral lesson drawn from the masters of Mussar, Hashkafah, and Chassidus. This selection will stimulate thought and growth — and be a welcome source of uplifting ideas for times when the reader is called upon to speak at a *simchah.*

❑ *The Halachah of the Day,* presenting a practical, relevant halachic discussion, beginning with the thirty-nine forbidden categories of Shabbos labor. The selections are adapted from Rabbi Simcha Bunim Cohen's popular and authoritative works, which are part of the ArtScroll Series. [These brief discussions are not intended to be definitive. Questions should be directed to a qualified rav.]

❑ *A Closer Look at the Siddur,* broadening the reader's understanding of the rich tapestry of *tefillah*/prayer. The Shabbos Daily Dose will focus on the Shabbos prayers. And once a week, this section will discuss such universal themes as the Thirteen Principles of Faith or the Six Constant Commandments.

❑ *A Taste of Lomdus,* a special weekly feature that will present a brief but in-depth discussion of a Talmudic subject, in the tradition of the Torah giants whose reasoning and novellae are the basis of research and study in advanced yeshivas. Every day, there will be a challenging "Question of the Day," related to the theme of the day. The answers for the questions will come at the end of each week.

❧❀❧

Each volume of the Daily Dose of Torah Series will present a capsule study program for twenty-eight days. The annual cycle will be comprised of thirteen four-week volumes, covering all fifty-two weeks of the year, and a fourteenth volume devoted to Rosh Hashanah, Yom Kippur, and the festivals. We are confident that the complete series will bring the excitement of Torah study to countless people, and that many of them will use it as a springboard to further learning, both independently and by joining *shiurim*.

The Kleinman Edition: Limud Yomi / A Daily Dose of Torah is dedicated by ELLY AND BROCHIE KLEINMAN, in memory of their fathers ל"ז and in honor of their mothers שיחיו. The Kleinmans have long distinguished themselves as generous and imaginative supporters of Torah and *chesed* causes. With warmth and kindness, they have opened their home countless times to help institutions and individuals. They have richly earned the respect and affection of all who know them, and we are honored to count them not only as major supporters of our work, but as personal friends. They and their family bring honor to the legacy of their parents.

This inaugural volume is dedicated by Mr. and Mrs. Kleinman.

The editor of this new series is RABBI YOSAIF ASHER WEISS, Rosh Yeshivas Ohr Hadaas, Staten Island, who is also a distinguished editor of the Schottenstein Edition of the Talmud Bavli and Yerushalmi. Rabbi Weiss' reputation as a noted scholar and educator will be justly embellished by the Daily Dose Series.

We are grateful to RABBI RAPHAEL BUTLER, the dynamic and innovative founder and president of the Afikim Foundation, who conceived of this concept and had a significant role in its development. We are proud to enjoy his friendship.

We are grateful to the outstanding *talmidei chachamim* who are contributing to this series: RABBI YOSEF GAVRIEL BECHHOFER, RABBI REUVEN BUTLER, RABBI ELIYAHU COHEN, RABBI ASHER DICKER, RABBI MEYER GOLDSTEIN, RABBI BEREL SCHIFF, RABBI MORDECHAI SONNENSHEIN, RABBI MOSHE UNGAR, RABBI YISROEL DOV WEISS, AND RABBI ZEV ZIONS. The quality of their scholarship shines through every page.

The beauty and clarity of the book's design is yet another tribute to the graphics genius of our friend and colleague REB SHEAH BRANDER. As someone once said in a different context, "I can't put it into words, but I know it when I see it." It is hard to define good taste and graphics beauty in words, but when one sees Reb Sheah's work, one knows it.

ELI KROEN, a master of graphics in his own right, designed the cover with his typical creativity and good taste. MOSHE DEUTSCH had an important hand in the typesetting and general design. MRS. CHUMIE LIPSCHITZ, a key member of our staff, paginated the book. TOBY GOLDZWEIG, SURY REINHOLD, AND SARA RIFKA SPIRA typed and corrected the manuscript.

MRS. MINDY STERN proofread and made many important suggestions. AVROHOM BIDERMAN was involved in virtually every aspect of the work from its inception, and MENDY HERZBERG assisted in shepherding the project to completion.

We are grateful to them all. The contributions of ArtScroll/Mesorah to the cause of Jewish life and Torah study are possible because of the skill and dedication of the above staff members and their colleagues.

It is an enormous privilege to have been instrumental in bringing Torah knowledge to the people of Torah. There are no words to express our gratitude to Hashem Yisbarach for permitting us to disseminate His Word to His children.

Rabbi Meir Zlotowitz/Rabbi Nosson Scherman

Elul 5766 / September 2006

פרשת בראשית

Parashas Bereishis

SUNDAY

PARASHAS
BEREISHIS

בְּרֵאשִׁית בָּרָא אֱלֹהִים אֵת הַשָּׁמַיִם וְאֵת הָאָרֶץ
In the beginning of HASHEM'S creation
of the heavens and the earth . . .
(Bereishis 1:1).

This is the translation of the first verse of the Torah according to *Rashi.* He explains that if the Torah had meant to tell us the *sequence* of Creation (stating that the heavens and earth were created first), the verse would have used the word בָּרִאשׁוֹנָה, which means *in the beginning,* rather than the word בְּרֵאשִׁית, which means *in the beginning of.* Furthermore, *Rashi* notes, it is impossible to say that the verse is teaching that the heavens and the earth were created before anything else, because this is demonstrably not true! The very next verse states that before the earth was created, Hashem's Spirit hovered over the face of the waters. This proves that the waters existed *before* the earth. The heavens, too, could not have come into being before the waters, for the heavens — שָׁמַיִם — were created from a mixture of fire — אֵשׁ — and water — מַיִם (see *Rashi* to *Bereishis* 1:8). Thus, it is clear that the verse does *not* mean to say that the heavens and the earth were created first. Rather, this verse (as well as the verse that follows) should be understood as an introduction to the creation of light. Hence, the translation, *In the beginning of Hashem's creation of the heavens and the earth . . .*

Ramban defends the more familiar translation of the verse: *In the beginning, Hashem created the heavens and the earth.* He explains that while the word בְּרֵאשִׁית indeed means *in the beginning of,* in this verse it means that in the beginning of *all things,* Hashem created the heavens and the earth. However, *Ramban* elaborates, the verse does not refer literally to the actual heavens and earth, for these were *not* created first, as *Rashi* states. Rather, this verse refers to Hashem's creating, from utter nothingness, of the raw material (the potence of the elemental materials, which are fire, wind, water and dust — *Ramban* refers to this substance as חֹמֶר הַיּוּלִי, *primary matter*) that He later molded and fashioned into the elements that formed specific parts of the universe (referred to in the verse *as the heavens* — i.e., the heavenly bodies — and *the earth* — meaning the earth and all that is upon it). Thus, according to *Ramban,* the verse is stating that Hashem began the process of Creation by creating, from absolute nothingness, the primary matter that would be used to form the heavens and the earth.

This Mishnah discusses the the *melachah* (prohibited labor) of הוֹצָאָה (lit., *taking out*). One violates this *melachah* by transferring an object from a private domain[1] to a public domain[2] — or vice versa — on the Sabbath. The Mishnah illustrates the cases of forbidden transfer using the example of a house: The inside of the house is a private domain, and outside the house is the public domain.

יְצִיאוֹת הַשַּׁבָּת — The *transfers* that are prohibited *on the Sabbath* שְׁתַּיִם שֶׁהֵן אַרְבַּע — are of *two* types[3] forbidden by Torah law[4] *that are*

─────── NOTES ───────

1. With respect to the laws of the Sabbath, a private domain (רְשׁוּת הַיָּחִיד) is defined as an area that is at least 4 *tefachim* [handbreadths] square, and is confined by walls that are at least 10 *tefachim* high. It may be a ground-level area enclosed by a wall of requisite height, or a pit 10 *tefachim* deep. [For a full discussion of these parameters, see *Beur Halachah* to the beginning of *Orach Chaim* 363 ד״ה אסרו.] Private ownership is *not* a precondition for this type of domain.

2. A public domain (רְשׁוּת הָרַבִּים) is defined, with respect to the laws of the Sabbath, as a street or plaza that is at least 16 *amos* wide, and that is not covered by a roof or enclosed by walls. According to many authorities, the street or plaza must also serve as a thoroughfare for 600,000 people. [For further discussion of these parameters, see *Shulchan Aruch* 345:7.]

3. The Torah expressly forbids the transfer of objects from domain to domain on the Sabbath: אַל־יֵצֵא אִישׁ מִמְּקֹמוֹ בַּיּוֹם הַשְּׁבִיעִי, *let no man go out of his place on the seventh day* (*Exodus* 16:29). [The Rabbis (*Eruvin* 17b) explain that this verse was a commandment to the Jews, forbidding them to take a vessel out of their tents (a private domain) and bring it outside the camp (a public domain) to gather manna (*Tosafos*).] This Mishnah teaches that there are two types of prohibited transfers: (a) הוֹצָאָה — *hotzaah: taking out* an item from a private domain to a public domain; and (b) הַכְנָסָה — *hachnasah: bringing in* an item from a public domain to a private domain. As we shall see, a person can violate this prohibition by performing either of these types of transfer, regardless of whether he is standing in a private domain or a public domain.

4. A prohibited act of "transferring" must contain three components: (a) עֲקִירָה — *akirah* (lit., *uprooting*): removing the object from its place in one domain; (b) the transfer of the object from domain to domain; and (c) הַנָּחָה — *hanachah*: setting the object down in a place in another domain.

There is a rule that a person has desecrated the Sabbath on the Biblical level only if he carries out a forbidden *melachah* in its usual manner. Since it is unusual for a person to transfer an object from domain to domain without also doing an *akirah* and a *hanachah*, if a person's transfer of the object lacks either of these components, he is not in violation of a Torah prohibition (see *Rashi* to 3a). Nevertheless, the transfer is forbidden by Rabbinic decree. [The Mishnah will illustrate cases in which violations of Rabbinic decrees are involved.]

four types (if transfers forbidden by Rabbinic decree are also included in the count), בִּפְנִים — for a person standing *inside* a house, וּשְׁתַּיִם שֶׁהֵן אַרְבַּע — *and* also *of two* types forbidden by Torah law *that are four* types (if transfers forbidden by Rabbinic decree are included), בַּחוּץ — for a person standing *outside* the house.

The Mishnah illustrates the various cases, using a scenario in which a poor person receives food from a householder: כֵּיצַד — *How is this so?* הֶעָנִי עוֹמֵד בַּחוּץ וּבַעַל הַבַּיִת בִּפְנִים — When a *poor person is standing outside* a house, *while the householder* is standing *inside* the house.[5]

The Mishnah first illustrates the types of transfer prohibited by Torah law, beginning with those that apply to the poor person: פָּשַׁט הֶעָנִי אֶת יָדוֹ לִפְנִים — If *the poor person* holding an object in his hand *extended his hand into* the house וְנָתַן לְתוֹךְ יָדוֹ שֶׁל בַּעַל הַבַּיִת — *and* put the object *into the householder's hand,*[6] אוֹ שֶׁנָּטַל מִתּוֹכָה וְהוֹצִיא — *or* if the poor person *took* an object *from [the householder's hand] and took it out of* the house,[7] הֶעָנִי חַיָּיב וּבַעַל הַבַּיִת פָּטוּר — *the poor person is liable*[8] *and the householder is exempt.*[9]

The Mishnah next illustrates the two types of transfer prohibited by Torah law with respect to the householder: פָּשַׁט בַּעַל הַבַּיִת אֶת יָדוֹ לַחוּץ — If *the householder,* holding an object in

── NOTES ──

5. The Mishnah illustrates these laws using a case of a householder and a poor person to teach us that although it is a great mitzvah to give charity, nevertheless, this mitzvah does not take precedence over the laws of the Sabbath (*Rav*).

6. In this case, the poor person has completed an entire act of *bringing in*: He removed the object from its place in a public domain (*akirah*); transferred it to a private domain (*hachnasah*); and placed it down in the private domain (*hanachah*).

7. In this case, the poor person has completed an entire act of *taking out*: He removed the object from its place in a private domain (*akirah*); transferred it to a public domain (*hotzaah*); and placed it down in the public domain (*hanachah*).

8. Since in both of these cases the poor person's act includes all three necessary components (see above, note 4), he is in violation of a Torah prohibition. [Throughout this tractate, a violation of a Torah prohibition is identified by the use of the term חַיָּיב, *liable*. This is because a person in violation of a Torah prohibition on the Sabbath is liable to some consequence: If the violation was intentional, he is liable to execution; if the violation was unintentional, he must bring a *chatas* offering.]

9. The householder, on the other hand, is exempt. Moreover, since he was completely passive (he merely *allowed* the poor person to take an object from his hand or put an object in it, but he himself was not active in any way) he is not even in violation of a Rabbinic decree. [Below, the Mishnah will consider cases in which a Rabbinic decree *is* violated.]

his hand, *extended his hand out of* the house וְנָתַן — **לְתוֹךְ יָדוֹ שֶׁל עָנִי** *and put* the object *into the poor person's hand,*[10] **אוֹ שֶׁנָּטַל מִתּוֹכָהּ וְהִכְנִיס** — *or* if the householder *took* an object *from [the poor person's hand] and brought it into* the house,[11] **בַּעַל הַבַּיִת חַיָּיב** **וְהֶעָנִי פָּטוּר** — *the householder is liable*[12] *and the poor person is exempt.*[13]

PARASHAS
BEREISHIS

We will conclude the elucidation of this Mishnah tomorrow.

—————————————————— NOTES ——————————————————

10. In this case, the householder has completed an entire act of *taking out*: He removed the object from its place in a private domain (*akirah*); transferred it to a public domain (*hotzaah*); and placed it down in the public domain (*hanachah*).

11. In this case, the householder has completed an entire act of *bringing in*: He removed the object from its place in a public domain (*akirah*); transferred it to a private domain (*hachnasah*); and placed it down in the private domain (*hanachah*).

12. Since in both of these cases the householder's act includes all three necessary components, he is in violation of the Torah prohibition (see above, note 8).

13. The poor person, on the other hand, is exempt. Moreover, he is not even in violation of a Rabbinic decree (see above, note 9).

GEMS FROM THE GEMARA

We learned in the Mishnah that a prohibited act of transfer must contain three components:

❑ עֲקִירָה — *akirah* (literally, *uprooting*): removing the object from its place in one domain;

❑ transferring the object from one domain to another;

❑ הֲנָחָה — *hanachah*: setting the object down in another domain.

The Gemara (4a ff.) notes that the *akirah* and *hanachah* are considered legally significant acts that can result in liability only if the item has been removed from, and set down upon, an area whose surface measures at least 4 *tefachim* square. *Rambam* (*Commentary to the Mishnah*) and *Rashba* explain that since it is not customary to place anything other than very small objects upon an area that is smaller than 4 *tefachim* square (for the object will not sit there securely, and is in danger of falling), such an area is not legally significant enough to be regarded as the object's "resting place." Thus, removing an item from such an area is not considered an *akirah,* and placing it there is not considered a *hanachah*. [*Ramban* cites another view, according to which the 4-*tefach* minimum was known to the Sages via tradition.]

SUNDAY — PARASHAS BEREISHIS / 5

This requirement, however, makes it difficult to understand the Mishnah's rulings. For the Mishnah clearly states in several of its cases that removing an item from a person's hand is considered an *akirah,* and that placing an item into a person's hand is considered a *hanachah.* Now, a person's hand does not measure 4 *tefachim* square. Why, then, is it viewed as a legally acceptable "resting place"?

The Gemara advances several possible resolutions of this problem. In its final answer (on 5a), it cites the view of Rava, who says that a person's hand is as legally significant as an area 4 *tefachim* square, its smaller size notwithstanding. This can be well understood in light of the explanation of *Rambam* and *Rashba* cited above; for although it is true that one does not usually place items on surfaces smaller than 4 *tefachim* square, he will certainly grasp those items in his hand, for a hand can grasp the item securely. Accordingly, a hand serves as a repository for even large objects, and it therefore qualifies as a valid resting place with regard to *akirah* and *hanachah,* despite its small size (see *Rambam, Commentary to the Mishnah,* and *Rashba* to 8a).

A MUSSAR THOUGHT FOR THE DAY

*R*amchal, in *Derech Hashem* (1:2-3), discusses the age-old question: Why did Hashem create the world? He explains that it was the will of Hashem to bestow His goodness upon another. However, since Hashem Himself is the epitome of perfection, merely bestowing "good" would be insufficient; He wished to bestow upon His creation the highest possible level of beneficence attainable. And that ultimate level of good is found only in Hashem Himself! Therefore, the method of bestowing the highest level of goodness would be to create beings that could cleave to Him, thereby deriving enjoyment to the greatest degree possible from Hashem, the Source of ultimate good.

In His wisdom, Hashem saw that in order for His creations to derive the fullest enjoyment from their closeness to Him, it was necessary for them to have *earned* this closeness, for one who enjoys a well-earned reward has greater pleasure than one who receives it as a gift. Accordingly, Hashem created man, with the unique ability to perceive right and wrong, and to choose the path of righteousness or the path of sin (see also *Rambam, Hil. Teshuvah* 5:1). When man chooses the correct path, he is granted the ability to cleave to Hashem, and gain the greatest reward of all.

To achieve this end, Hashem created two environments for man to exist in — this world, in which he must struggle and strive to earn his place, and the World to Come, in which he enjoys his reward. In each world, he is given the tools that he requires to accomplish his task. But since, as a general rule, the attribute of good is greater than that of punishment, man remains in this world, in the presence of potential evil, only as long as necessary for him to achieve his purpose. The World to Come, on the other hand, is eternal, allowing man to enjoy his reward for all time.

HALACHAH OF THE DAY

The first of the ל"ט מְלָאכוֹת, the *thirty-nine categories of labor* forbidden on the Sabbath, is the *melachah* of *zorei'a,* planting. The act of planting was a necessary part of the activities that took place in the Mishkan. Herbs were planted in order to provide the raw materials needed for the production of dyes, which were used to color the various tapestries and curtains found in the Mishkan.

Additionally, flour was needed in the Mishkan, both for the *lechem hapanim* (the Showbread) that graced the *Shulchan* (Table) in the Mishkan, as well as for the meal-offerings that were brought upon the Altar. Indeed, for this reason the first eleven of the thirty-nine *melachos,* all of which deal with the production of wheat and the process of bread-making, are collectively referred to in the Talmud as the *Sedura D'Pas,* the Order of Bread. [Although logic would seem to dictate that the *melachah* of *plowing* should be listed prior to that of planting, the Gemara (*Shabbos* 73b) explains that in Eretz Yisrael, soil conditions mandated that plowing be performed after planting as well, in order to bring the seeds into proper contact with the soil. The Tanna who listed the *melachos* listed *plowing* after planting to teach that such plowing is included in the melachah as well.]

The *melachah* of *planting* is not limited to simply the sowing or planting of seeds. Rather, we may define the *melachah* as including any activity that initiates or promotes the growth of a plant. Additionally, acts that protect the growth of the plant may also be included, as we will discuss further on.

Some examples of forbidden activities that initiate growth are: scattering seeds over a field (as is done when planting grain); placing a seed or seedling into a hole in the ground; or the replanting of saplings, sprouts, bulbs or plants.

One transgresses the *melachah* of *planting* by planting or improving the growth of even the smallest seed or plant. It is therefore necessary to take great care when eating outdoors not to throw seeds or pits on the soil. Since these seeds or pits may germinate, such action may result in a violation of the *melachah* of *planting*.

The activities listed above are only forbidden, however, when performed in a manner that can produce growth. One may, therefore, insert a seed into the sand of a desert — for since such a seed will not germinate, no planting has taken place. Similarly, one may place seeds on a paved surface, because they cannot grow there.

A CLOSER LOOK AT THE SIDDUR

The Gemara (*Taanis* 2a) describes the mitzvah of *tefillah,* prayer, as "a service of the heart" (עֲבוֹדָה שֶׁבַּלֵּב). Although we are accustomed to think of prayer as the process we are instructed to follow when asking Hashem for our needs, in truth it is much more than merely a protocol for obtaining sustenance. A look at our *siddur* shows us that the vast majority of our prayers (especially *Shacharis,* the morning service) are not comprised of personal requests; rather, they are statements of praise for Hashem, and recognition of His wondrous deeds. Personal requests can be found mainly in the middle section of the *Shemoneh Esrei* Prayer; in all of the introductory prayers (*Pesukei D'Zimrah*), as well as the *Shema* and its blessings, the emphasis is on acknowledging Hashem's mastery over the earth and the heavens, and the multitude of kindnesses that He bestows upon His creations.

These two concepts, of course, are closely interwoven. Before we ask Hashem to provide for our needs, we must acknowledge that it is He — and He alone — Who has the power to supply them. Indeed, *Ramchal* states that this is one of the purposes of *tefillah.* Hashem directs us to pray for the things that we need, for this causes us to come to realize that He is the Source of all blessing (see *Derech Hashem* 4:5).

Most basic to our recognition that Hashem is the One to Whom we must turn with all our requests, is the belief that He created the world and all of its creatures. So central is this belief to proper *tefillah,* that its expression can be found at the beginning of each of the three major sections of *Shacharis.* We begin *Pesukei D'Zimrah,* the introductory section of praises, with the words בָּרוּךְ שֶׁאָמַר וְהָיָה הָעוֹלָם, *Blessed is He Who spoke, and the world came into being.* The section of the *Shema* and its blessings begins with: *Blessed are You, Hashem, our God, King of the universe, Who forms light and Who creates darkness, Who makes peace and creates everything.* And the first blessing of the *Shemoneh Esrei* contains the description of Hashem

as קוֹנֵה הַכֹּל, which means *He Who creates everything* (see *Rashi* to *Bereishis* 4:19, and *Yesod VeShoresh HaAvodah* 5:3).

Only when we are truly convinced that Hashem is our Creator and that He alone can grant our requests, can we approach Him with our prayers.

In addition, when approaching *tefillah* one must always bear in mind the tremendous kindness that Hashem shows us, by allowing us to approach Him — three times daily! — with all of our requests. The Gemara in *Bava Basra* (10a) notes a similar distinction between Hashem and a mortal ruler in the context of charity. A man can bring a large gift to the king; but it is not certain whether the king's servants will accept it or not. And even if they do accept it, there is no guarantee that the man will be granted a personal audience. But Hashem grants an audience to anyone who gives even a *perutah* (a small coin) to a pauper! [This Gemara is the source for the custom of many to give charity before praying.]

Prayer is a time of transformation. Before a person speaks to God, he is alone and frightened, weak and torn by worries that threaten to overwhelm him. When the moment of prayer arrives, man understands that there is a sympathetic listener. He turns to his Father in Heaven and admits his frailties; he allows the weighty burdens to slip from his shoulders, in the comforting realization that he is not alone in his troubles. As the verse states (*Tehillim* 55:23): *Cast upon Hashem your burden, and He will sustain you; He will never allow the righteous to falter.*

R' Yechezkel Levenstein writes in his work on *Emunah* (pp. 182-183) that one should stand in prayer like a beggar standing at a door with outstretched palm, asking for alms. The supplicant must fill himself with the awareness that his existence is entirely dependent upon Hashem. When one elevates his prayer to this level, his sustenance will truly become completely independent of the hands of men, as he will receive it as a direct gift from Hashem Himself.

QUESTION OF THE DAY:
On what calendar date was the world created?

For the answer, see page 52.

MONDAY

PARASHAS
BEREISHIS

וַיַּעַשׂ אֱלֹהִים אֶת־שְׁנֵי הַמְּאֹרֹת הַגְּדֹלִים

And HASHEM created the two great luminaries . . .
(Bereishis 1:16).

This verse speaks of the creation of the sun and the moon. Although the two are clearly not equal in size (indeed, the verse continues by stating that the greater luminary would dominate by day, while the lesser one would dominate at night), the verse refers to them as *the two great luminaries.* To resolve this seeming contradiction, *Rashi* cites the Gemara in *Chullin* (60b), which states that when first created, the sun and the moon were of equal size. However, the moon complained, arguing: "It is not possible for two kings to make use of the same crown!" Hashem replied: "If so, go and diminish yourself!"

Many commentators discuss why the moon was punished for advancing a seemingly valid argument. [Indeed, the Gemara in *Chullin* states that Hashem mentioned His Name in the Torah in connection with the he-goat offering brought every Rosh Chodesh (that is, at the beginning of every lunar month) in order to appease the moon — see *Shevuos* 9a.] *Rabbi Yosef Chaim Sonnenfeld* suggests that the root of the problem was not the moon's complaint per se, but the fact that it perceived itself as the sun's equal. True humility demands not only that we not consider ourselves greater than others, but that we actually view our fellows as *greater* than ourselves. One who considers himself to be equal to his fellow indeed deserves to be diminished!

Daas Zekeinim maintains that the diminishment of the moon was not a result of the moon deserving punishment, but a reward for the humility of the sun, which heard the moon's complaint and did not respond. He connects this to the Baraisa in Tractate *Shabbos* (88b) that states: "Those who suffer insult but do not insult in return, who hear their disgrace but do not reply . . . concerning them the verse states (*Judges* 5:31): *But they who love Him will be as the sun going forth in its might.*" Because the sun did not respond to the complaints of the moon, which could have resulted in the sun's diminishment, it merited to continue to go forth in all its glory, while the moon was made smaller. [For yet another interpretation, see *Rabbeinu Bachya* to *Numbers* 28:15.]

MISHNAH OF THE DAY: SHABBOS 1:1

The beginning of this Mishnah, which we studied yesterday, illustrated the four types of transfer forbidden by Biblical law — two performed by the poor man from outside the house, and two performed by the householder. The Mishnah next illustrates the types of transfer that are forbidden by Rabbinic decree, beginning with the two cases where the poor person does the transfer:[1]

פָּשַׁט הֶעָנִי אֶת יָדוֹ לִפְנִים — If *the poor person,* holding an object in his hand, *extended his hand into* the house **וְנָטַל בַּעַל הַבַּיִת מִתּוֹכָהּ** — *and the householder took* the object *from it,* [2] **אוֹ שֶׁנָּתַן לְתוֹכָהּ וְהוֹצִיא** — *or if [the householder],* holding an object, *put* the object *into [the poor person's extended hand] and [the poor person]* then retracted his hand and thereby *took* the object *out* of the house,[3] **שְׁנֵיהֶם פְּטוּרִין** — *they are both exempt* on the Biblical level, but these transfers are forbidden by Rabbinic decree.[4]

Finally, the Mishnah illustrates the two types of transfer that are forbidden by Rabbinic decree where the householder does the transfer: **פָּשַׁט בַּעַל הַבַּיִת אֶת יָדוֹ לַחוּץ** — If *the householder,* holding an object in

---------- NOTES ----------

1. In the next two cases of the Mishnah, neither the poor person nor the householder violates Torah prohibitions, but *both* violate Rabbinic decrees. Since we have already seen two cases for the poor person and two for the householder in which they would be in violation of Torah prohibitions, the following four cases complete the Mishnah's elucidation of its statement: "The *transfers* that are prohibited **on the Sabbath are of two** types forbidden by Torah law *that are four* types, for the person that is inside and the person that is outside."

2. In this case, the poor person removed the object from its place in a public domain (*akirah*) and transferred it to a private domain (*hachnasah*). However, he did not place it down. Rather, the householder who took the object from the poor person placed it down in the private domain (*hanachah*).

3. In this case, the poor person transferred the object from a private domain to a public domain (*hotzaah*), and placed it down in the public domain (*hanachah*). However, he did not remove the object from its place in the private domain. Rather, the householder who placed the object in the poor person's hand removed it from its place in the private domain (*akirah*).

4. Since neither the poor person nor the householder performed an act that included all three components of the Torah prohibition (see *Mishnah of the Day* for Sunday, note 4), they are not in violation of the Torah prohibition. Nevertheless, lest either one of them comes to perform an act that *does* include all three components, the Rabbis decreed that it is forbidden to perform an act that includes even one of the three components. Hence, both the poor person and the householder are in violation of a Rabbinic decree.

פרשת
בראשית

MONDAY

PARASHAS
BEREISHIS

his hand, *extended his hand out* of the house וְנָטַל
הֶעָנִי מִתּוֹכָהּ — *and the poor person took* the object
from it, [5] אוֹ שֶׁנָּתַן לְתוֹכָהּ וְהִכְנִיס — *or if [the poor
person],* [6] holding an object, *put* the object *into [the
householder's extended hand] and [the householder]*
retracted his hand and thereby *brought* the object *into*
the house, שְׁנֵיהֶם פְּטוּרִין — *they are both exempt* on
the Biblical level, but these transfers are forbidden by Rabbinic decree. [7]

——————————— NOTES ———————————

5. In this case, the householder removed the object from its place in a private domain (*akirah*) and transferred it to a public domain (*hotzaah*). However, he did not place it down. Rather, the poor person who took the object from the householder placed it down in the private domain (*hanachah*).

6. In this case, the householder transferred the object from a public domain to a private domain (*hachnasah*), and placed it down in the private domain (*hanachah*). However, he did not remove the object from its place in the public domain. Rather, the poor person who placed the object in the householder's hand removed it from its place in the public domain (*akirah*).

7. See above, note 4.

GEMS FROM THE GEMARA

The Mishnah listed four cases in which neither the poor man nor the householder committed a Biblical violation, because neither of them performed both the *akirah* and the *hanachah* in any of those cases; rather, one performed the *akirah,* and the other performed the *hanachah.* Nevertheless, Rabbinic decree forbids both the poor person and the householder from performing any of these four transfers.

The Gemara (2b) notes that this does not seem to fit with the opening statement of the Mishnah, that there are two types of transfers forbidden Biblically, and two more forbidden Rabbinically, both for the one who is inside (the householder) and for the one who is outside (the poor man). Seemingly, there are *four* cases that are forbidden Rabbinically to the householder (the last four cases of the Mishnah), and the very same four cases are forbidden to the poor man! Thus, the Gemara asks: Why does the Mishnah count only eight forbidden acts in all (four Biblical violations and four Rabbinic ones)? There are actually twelve!

The Gemara answers that although it is true that there are eight acts in the Mishnah that are Rabbinically forbidden, the Mishnah counts only those that have the potential to *possibly* result in a *Biblically* forbidden act — the acts of *akirah.* One who removes an item from its place *can* set it down in another domain and incur Biblical liability. By way of contrast, the second partner in the two-person transfer — the one who sets the item down and makes the *hanachah* — can never come to perform a complete act of transfer, since the *akirah* has already been performed by the first partner. Accordingly, although each of the final four cases of the Mishnah involves Rabbinical violations by *both* partners, the Mishnah reckons each case only for the one who performs the *akirah* (*Rashi's* preferred explanation).

MONDAY

PARASHAS
BEREISHIS

According to this, it emerges that according to the Gemara's conclusion, of the eight cases described in the Mishnah, the four that are ascribed to the poor person are the first two (Biblical violations), and the fifth and eighth (Rabbinical violations through *akirah*); while the third and fourth (Biblical violations) and the sixth and seventh (Rabbinical violations through *akirah)* are ascribed to the householder.

[This follows *Rashi's* preferred explanation. See there for another explanation that *Rashi* cites from his teachers; and *Ramban* and *Tos. HaRosh* for differing interpretations of that explanation.]

A MUSSAR THOUGHT FOR THE DAY

The classic work *Orchos Tzaddikim* lists six ways to recognize one who is truly humble:

(1) If a person is humiliated by his fellow through word or deed, and he has the opportunity to revenge himself upon his adversary, but he controls himself and forgives him for the sake of Hashem — this is a sign of true humility. [Of course, there are times when it is forbidden to forgive such humiliation, as when the honor of the Torah has been impugned.]

(2) If a person suffers a great loss, or his children or relatives pass away, God forbid, and he nevertheless accepts Hashem's judgment with love, as did Aharon, concerning whom it is stated [after the death of his two sons] *and Aharon was silent* (*Vayikra* 10:3), this is indicative of his great humility and submission to Hashem's will.

(3) If he hears people praising his wisdom and good deeds, and he does not rejoice over this, but rather is convinced that his deeds fall far short of what they should be, this is true humility. [It goes without saying that he does not take credit for good deeds attributed to him that he has not

MONDAY — PARASHAS BEREISHIS / 13

actually performed.] And if his faults are spoken of, he should not attempt to exonerate himself, but should admit his shortcoming, as did Yehudah in the matter of Tamar (see *Bereishis* 38:26).

(4) If Hashem grants him wealth, wisdom, and good children, and his response to this is to become even more convinced that he is undeserving of the good he has received, he has acted with humility. This was the path taken by our father Avraham: When Hashem accorded him the honor of wishing to advise him in advance of the destruction of Sodom [as the verse states (ibid. 18:17): *Shall I conceal from Avraham what I am about to do?*], he reacted by stating: *I am but dust and ashes* (ibid. v. 27).

(5) If he harms another through speech or action, and does not wait to be reproached, but instead comes of his own volition to redress the wrong and ask for forgiveness, this too is a sign of humility.

(6) The man who is truly humble does not pursue luxuries, nor does he seek beautiful clothing or adornments. His manner is gentle, and he speaks softly.

By striving to follow these guidelines, one can attain humility — the trait which *Orchos Tzaddikim* refers to as "the ladder by which one can ascend to emulate the ways of Hashem."

HALACHAH OF THE DAY

As we noted yesterday, the *melachah* of *planting* includes any activity that promotes the growth of a plant. The most basic example of this would be the watering of any growing thing. There are, however, activities that stimulate growth in a less obvious manner, which are also included in the *melachah,* such as the pruning of trees or the weeding of a garden or field. These actions, while not at all similar to planting seeds, are also forbidden as *planting,* since they promote the growth of the plant(s) that remain.

Watering plants is forbidden even if there is no intent to water the plants in question. For example, it is forbidden for a person to wash his hands over grass even if he has no intent at all to water the grass at his feet. Since it is inevitable that the grass will become wet, and by extension inevitable that he will promote the growth of the grass, to wash in such a location violates the *melachah* of *planting.* [This is in accordance with the rule of פְּסִיק רֵישֵׁיה, *the inevitable consequence,* which states that an act that would itself be permitted on the Sabbath is prohibited if it will inevitably result in a forbidden act being performed.]

פרשת
בראשית

MONDAY

PARASHAS
BEREISHIS

Liquids other than water will also promote plant growth. One must therefore take care not to pour or accidentally spill soda, juice, or the like onto grass or other growing plants.

Flowers or other plants that have been cut from their roots are no longer living, growing plants. There is therefore no Biblical prohibition against placing them into water on the Sabbath. However, depending on the specific situation, there may be Rabbinic prohibitions that forbid this. The following is a brief summary of the laws pertaining to placing cut plants into water on the Sabbath:

One may not fill a vase with water on the Sabbath to place flowers or plants into it. This is forbidden because it is deemed *undue exertion* (טִירְחָא יְתֵירָא), a category of activities that were forbidden by the Sages because they resemble weekday activities, and therefore detract from the special aura of the Sabbath day. Nor may one add water to a vase that had been filled prior to the onset of the Sabbath. [It is, however, permitted to add water to a vase on Yom Tov.]

Flowers that have not yet opened completely may not be placed into water on the Sabbath. Although causing flowers to bloom is not, strictly speaking, a violation of *planting,* the Sages prohibited this because of its strong resemblance to planting.

There is a dispute among the authorities concerning placing flowers that have already opened completely into a vase of water that was filled before the Sabbath. While neither of the two problems mentioned above would seem to apply (as the vase was filled before the Sabbath, and the flowers are completely open), there are nevertheless those who rule that one should not place flowers into water *for the first time* on the Sabbath. According to these authorities, it is preferable to place even fully opened flowers into water prior to the onset of the Sabbath. If, however, one forgot to do so, he may rely on those who rule leniently.

QUESTION OF THE DAY:

We know that the Jewish calendar is based on the lunar cycle.

Where do we find a halachah that is tied to the solar calendar?

For the answer, see page 52.

MONDAY — PARASHAS BEREISHIS / 15

In the prayer of *Keil Adon,* which is said during the *Shacharis* service on Sabbath mornings, we find the phrase: קָרָא לַשֶּׁמֶשׁ וַיִּזְרַח אוֹר רָאָה וְהִתְקִין צוּרַת הַלְּבָנָה — *He called out to the sun and it shone forth with light; He saw and He fashioned the form of the moon.* Simply understood, this phrase alludes to the creation of the sun and the moon, and notes that Hashem established the order of the phases of the moon so that they could be used as the basis of the Jewish (lunar) calendar.

Shiras David connects this phrase to the episode of the moon's diminishment. He cites the Gemara in *Rosh Hashanah* (23b) that expounds the verse in *Job* 25:2: *He makes peace in His heights.* How, asks the Gemara, has Hashem made peace in His heights? By arranging matters so that the sun never "sees" the missing part of the moon. [That is, the crescent of the moon always faces away from the sun. Of course, this is a natural result of the fact that the side of the moon facing the sun always reflects the sun's light; however, the verse finds a lesson in the fact that Hashem arranged the heavens in this way.] *Maharsha* explains: The sun was the cause of the moon's diminishment (see above, *A Torah Thought for the Day*). Thus, if the sun were to "see" the missing part of the moon, this would distress the moon greatly. Hashem therefore arranged the heavens so this could never happen, to spare the moon distress.

This, explains *Shiras David,* is the meaning of the *Keil Adon* prayer. Hashem called to the sun, and it shone forth with light; but He *fashioned the form of the moon* so that its deficiency would not be visible to the sun, sparing it distress.

Daas Zekeinim (to *Bereishis* 1:16) cites another text of *Keil Adon,* in which the reading of the second half of this phrase is רָאָה וְהִקְטִין צוּרַת הַלְּבָנָה, *He saw and He "diminished" the form of the moon.* According to this text, the prayer is referring directly to the episode that resulted in the moon's diminishment. *Daas Zekeinim* also offers an alternative interpretation of our reading of רָאָה וְהִתְקִין צוּרַת הַלְּבָנָה. He explains that the prayer is referring to the initial creation of the moon. Originally, Hashem created only the sun, and it shone forth with light. However, Hashem *saw* that the nations of the world would err, and come to believe that the sun was a deity. To show them that this was not the case, He *fashioned the form of the moon,* showing that the sun did not even possess total dominion over the heavens, and therefore it should not be viewed as a divine power.

A TORAH THOUGHT FOR THE DAY

וַיֹּאמֶר ה' אֱלֹהִים לֹא־טוֹב הֱיוֹת הָאָדָם לְבַדּוֹ
אֶעֱשֶׂה־לּוֹ עֵזֶר כְּנֶגְדּוֹ

And Hashem/Elohim said:"It is not good that man should be alone; I will make him a helper opposite him" (Bereishis 2:18).

The Torah describes the woman using the unusual term *eizer k'negdo,* which means *a helper opposite him.* How are we to understand this seemingly self-contradictory description? If the woman is opposing the man, how can she be a helper to him?

Rashi addresses this question by citing an exposition of R' Elazar from the Gemara in *Yevamos* (63a) that explains that the two parts of the description refer to two different situations. If the man is worthy, then his wife shall be a *helper* to him. But if he is not worthy, then she will *oppose* him.

Accordingly, the woman is described as *k'negdo, opposite* the man, in a purely negative sense, in a scenario to be realized only when the man is lacking. However, the Gemara there also cites a second version of R' Elazar's exposition: *If he is worthy, she will be "k'negdo"; if he is not worthy, she will whip him (m'nagdaso).* R' David Luria (*Radal*), in his commentary to *Pirkei D'Rabbi Eliezer* (§12), explains that according to this understanding of the verse, the meaning of the phrase *eizer k'negdo* is indeed a positive one, as it means *a helper who is always at his side.* It was this attribute, asserts *Radal,* for which Adam searched in vain among all the creatures of the world (see *Bereishis* 1:19-20). Most animals mate indiscriminately, without bonding; even those few species (such as doves) that mate for life do not remain together and live their lives as a couple. Humans are unique in that man and wife are true partners who stand united and work together, sharing challenges and triumphs. This is the true meaning of *eizer k'negdo.* However, if the husband is not worthy, his very closeness with his wife becomes a terrible liability; for instead of being his trustworthy, steadfast helpmate, she is the constant thorn in his side, always ready to provoke and anger him.

Many commentators have offered yet another way to understand the attribute of *k'negdo* in a positive light. It is axiomatic that the ideal marriage is not necessarily one that includes total agreement between husband and wife in all matters. Often it is the responsibility of the wife to oppose her husband and prevent him from acting rashly or incorrectly, helping him arrive at the proper course of action by questioning, discussing, or even criticizing. Thus, she acts as a *helper* to her husband when he pursues the correct path, and she stands *opposite him* when he would stray.

TUESDAY

The laws discussed in this next Mishnah apply to every day of the week:[1] לֹא יֵשֵׁב אָדָם לִפְנֵי הַסַּפָּר — *A person should not sit down before a barber* to have his hair cut סָמוּךְ לַמִּנְחָה — when it is *near* the time to pray *Minchah* [the afternoon service][2] עַד שֶׁיִּתְפַּלֵּל — *until he has prayed.* [3] לֹא יִכָּנֵס אָדָם לַמֶּרְחָץ וְלֹא לַבּוּרְסְקִי — Similarly, *a person should not enter a bathhouse*[4] *or a tannery,* [5] וְלֹא לֶאֱכוֹל — *nor* should he enter *to eat* a meal,[6] וְלֹא לָדִין — *nor* should he enter a court *for judgment,* if it is near the time for *Minchah* and he has not yet prayed.[7] וְאִם הִתְחִילוּ — *But if they* (i.e., any of these

─────────── NOTES ───────────

1. The laws taught in this Mishnah do not apply specifically to the Sabbath. They are taught here in contrast to the similar laws that are taught in the next Mishnah (1:3), which *do* apply specifically to the Sabbath (*Rashi*). The laws in our Mishnah are not as complex as the laws of the next Mishnah, and that is why they are discussed first, before the Mishnah proceeds to dwell at length on the laws of the Sabbath (*Rav*).

2. *Minchah,* the afternoon prayer, may be prayed at any time that is after one half-hour past midday and before nightfall. This time frame is called מִנְחָה גְדוֹלָה [*Minchah Gedolah*], *the greater Minchah,* i.e., the longer time frame in which the prayer may be recited. [There is a shorter time frame known as מִנְחָה קְטַנָּה (*Minchah Ketannah*), *the lesser Minchah,* that consists of the last two and one-half halachic hours of daytime before nightfall. According to many authorities, this shorter time frame is the preferred time for praying *Minchah.*] Many authorities understand that when the Mishnah here speaks of *the time to pray Minchah,* it refers to the onset of *Minchah Gedolah.*

3. *Near* is defined as within one half-hour before the onset of *Minchah Gedolah* (*Rashi*). Thus, a person may not begin to have his hair cut (or begin any of the other activities listed in the Mishnah) from midday until he prays *Minchah.*

4. This law applies even if a person enters a bathhouse in order to simply sit in the steambath and not to bathe, since he may possibly become faint and not recover until after nightfall (Gemara 9b).

5. This law applies even if a person enters a tannery only to inspect it, since he might detect a flaw in the process and occupy himself the whole afternoon rectifying the flaw (*Rav; Rambam*).

6. This law applies even if a person enters with the intention to eat only a small meal, since he might become preoccupied with the meal and extend it through the entire afternoon (*Rav; Rambam*).

7. This law applies even if the court convened only to announce a verdict, since evidence to overturn the verdict might be presented. The case would then have to be reopened, and might extend through the entire afternoon (*Rav; Rambam*).

Other authorities maintain that the expression *near the time to pray Minchah* people) already **began** any of these activities,[8] אֵין מַפְסִיקִין — **they need not interrupt** to pray; rather, they may finish their activity and then pray afterward.[9] מַפְסִיקִין לִקְרוֹת קְרִיאַת שְׁמַע — **We do,** however, **interrupt** such activities **to recite the Shema** when the time to recite it arrives,[10] וְאֵין מַפְסִיקִין לִתְפִלָּה — **but we do not interrupt for Prayer.** [11]

—————— NOTES ——————

discussed in this Mishnah refers to one half-hour before the onset of *Minchah Ketan-nah* (see *Shulchan Aruch* and *Rama, Orach Chaim* 232:2). Moreover, some authorities maintain that even during this shorter time frame, it is only actual *bathing,* the *entire* tanning process, a *large* feast, or a *complete* court case that are forbidden (see *Tur* loc. cit.).

8. I.e., they acted improperly (see next note).

9. Although they were forbidden to begin, we do not require them to interrupt their activities after the fact, even if they began the activities after the time of *Minchah* actually arrived (*Tosafos* to 9b, as explained by *Maharsha*).

This law applies only if, after completing the activity, the person will still have time to pray *Minchah* before nightfall (*Rashi*).

10. The recitation of the *Shema* is a Torah obligation (*Rashi*). It must be recited twice daily: in the morning, between dawn and the end of third halachic hour of the day, and at night, between nightfall and dawn. Since the recitation of the *Shema* is a Torah obligation, the Rabbis ruled that a person must even interrupt an activity he has already begun in order to fulfill that obligation — even if there is enough time left to finish the activity and fulfill the obligation before the end of the relevant time frame (*Ran;* see, however, *Gems from the Gemara*).

11. The obligation to pray the three daily prayers is a Rabbinic decree. Since the prayers are of Rabbinic origin, a person need not interrupt an activity he has already begun in order to fulfill that obligation — as long as there is enough time left to finish the activity and fulfill the obligation before the end of the relevant time frame (*Ritva*). [This final statement of the Mishnah would seem to be a repeat of the Mishnah's earlier ruling concerning *Minchah.* For discussion of this point, see *Gems from the Gemara.*]

GEMS FROM THE GEMARA

In our explanation of the Mishnah, we explained the Mishnah's last statement — *We do interrupt to recite the Shema, but we do not interrupt for Prayer* — as referring to the interrupting for the activities listed earlier in the Mishnah (such as a haircut or a feast). Thus, the Mishnah is teaching that while one must interrupt even activities already begun to fulfill the Biblical obligation of reciting the *Shema,* he need not do so to pray.

פָּרָשַׁת בְּרֵאשִׁית

TUESDAY

PARASHAS BEREISHIS

The Gemara questions this interpretation however, noting that the second part of this ruling is redundant; for the Mishnah stated earlier, *but if they began, they need not interrupt*!

To resolve this difficulty, the Gemara explains the final ruling of the Mishnah as dealing with a different case. The Mishnah does not speak here of interrupting activities such as haircuts and feasts; rather, it speaks of interrupting one's Torah study. Thus, the final ruling of the Mishnah is teaching that while one must interrupt his Torah study to recite the *Shema,* he is not required to do so in order to satisfy the Rabbinic obligation of Prayer.

The Gemara qualifies this ruling by stating that this exemption from Prayer to continue one's Torah learning applies only to great Sages of the caliber of R' Shimon ben Yochai and his colleagues, whose only occupation was their study of Torah. Such scholars need not interrupt their studies for prayer. The overwhelming majority of people, on the other hand — who do interrupt their Torah studies for their work — must interrupt their studies for prayer as well. And even scholars of the highest caliber must interrupt their studies to recite the *Shema,* since this is a Biblical obligation.

According to this interpretation, it emerges that the phrase אֵין מַפְסִיקִין, *we need not interrupt,* which appears twice in the Mishnah, has a different meaning each time. In the beginning of the Mishnah, it means that one who has started his haircut or his feast is not required to interrupt his activity to pray, *provided that he will have time to pray after he finishes the activity* (see above, note 9). But in the end of the Mishnah, which discussed exceptional Torah scholars, it means that they are not required to interrupt for prayer *at all,* even if the time for prayer will pass, and they will not pray as a result (*Baal HaMaor; Meiri;* see also *Maharam*).

A MUSSAR THOUGHT FOR THE DAY

R' *Eliyahu E. Dessler,* in his classic work *Michtav MeiEliyahu,* discusses the love that exists between husband and wife:

"This love [between man and wife] is an amazing power of the soul . . . At first glance, it would seem that there is no explanation for it, but rather that it is a natural instinct instilled in man by the Creator to insure the survival of mankind, just as He created hunger within man to ensure that he would eat. However, this answer does not suffice; for the physical desires of man, in combination with the natural longing for children,

already suffice to ensure the continuance of the species.
Why, then, did love between man and wife have to be
added?

"I have heard some say that this love is born of
hakaras hatov, gratitude. Because a husband and wife
assist each other in the fulfillment of their natural urges,
they come to love one another. But this explanation,
too, is mistaken; for there is no lack of people who do not possess the
trait of *hakaras hatov,* and yet we see that they are not lacking in love
for their spouses!

"Thus, we must explain that a husband and wife love one another
because they complete each other. It is part of the very nature of man
that he is incomplete without a wife; as the Midrash states (*Bereishis
Rabbah* §17), *One who has no wife . . . is not a whole man.* One who is
single and alone cannot complete his mission in life. It is for this reason
that man and wife love each other. As we have explained before, a
person who is a 'giver' naturally loves the recipient of his gifts. And since
enabling one to complete his mission in life is the greatest gift of all,
man and wife are naturally inclined to love each other, and to want to
make each other happy . . .

"This is what I always tell couples on the joyous occasion of their
wedding: 'Always strive to please each other, and to give each other
pleasure and happiness, as you wish to do at this moment. For as soon
as you cease to wish to please each other, and instead begin to demand
things of each other, your happiness will flee . . .' If a husband and wife
work to always be giving to each other, their lives will be filled with good
fortune and happiness."

HALACHAH OF THE DAY

We learned earlier that activities that protect the growth of plants
are included in the prohibition of *planting.* Some examples of
activities forbidden for this reason would be covering a plant to protect
it from the cold, or closing a curtain so that sunlight will not damage a
plant. [It is, however, permitted to open the curtain before the sun rises,
since the plant is not yet being affected by the rays of the sun.] Additionally, applying pesticides to plants or trees on the Sabbath would be
forbidden, since they protect the vitality of the plant or tree.

We will conclude our discussion of this *melachah* with two common
practical applications of this prohibition, both of which pertain to the
Yom Tov of Succos:

פרשת בראשית

TUESDAY

PARASHAS BEREISHIS

It has become a common practice to place a waterproof covering on top of a *succah* when it is not in use, in order to prevent rain from falling into the *succah.* Depending on the specific situation, removing the covering from the *succah* often results in water that is on the covering falling onto grass or vegetation that is surrounding the *succah.* In a situation where this is an inevitable result of removing the covering, there are those *poskim* who prohibit it as a violation of the *melachah* of *planting.* There are, however, several ways to avoid this problem. A principle of the laws of the Sabbath is that it is permitted to perform a *melachah* through a *grama,* that is, *indirectly,* when this is done for the sake of a mitzvah. Thus, if the *succah* is placed on a porch or paved area, so that the water will first fall on the floor of the porch or the pavement, and only then flow to a grassy area, there would be no violation of *planting,* since the watering is only an indirect effect of the removing of the covering, which is being done for a mitzvah. If no such location is available for the *succah,* one may cover the vegetation surrounding the *succah* with plastic. This will serve to render any eventual watering that results from the removal of the covering an indirect, and thus permitted, action. It is also permitted to ask a non-Jew to open the covering. [It is permissible to ask a non-Jew to perform any inherently permissible act, even though it will inevitably result in the violation of a prohibited *melachah.*]

We previously discussed the prohibition against watering plants on the Sabbath. It is common practice for people to place their *lulavim, hadassim,* and *aravos* into water on Succos, in order to prevent them from drying out. In accordance with the guidelines previously discussed, one should place them into water prior to the onset of Yom Tov, so that he will be permitted to remove and replace them on Yom Tov. In the event that one forgot to do so before Yom Tov, he may rely on the *poskim* who permit placing fully opened flowers into a vase that was filled with water before Yom Tov.

QUESTION OF THE DAY:

Where in the Torah do we find a situation where a man was saved from sin (or punishment) because his wife protected him?

For the answer, see page 53.

In the *berachah* of *Hashkiveinu*, which we say after *Krias Shema* of *Maariv*, we request of Hashem, וְהָסֵר שָׂטָן מִלְּפָנֵינוּ וּמֵאַחֲרֵינוּ, *and remove the Satan from in front of us and from behind us.* This request requires explanation. While we certainly do not wish the Satan to impede our path, why must he be removed from behind us?

R' *Shamshon Raphael Hirsch* understands this *tefillah* in a non-literal manner. He translates "Satan" as a reference to impediments to our spiritual growth, and "in front of us" and "behind us" as referring to the passage of time. Thus, the sense of the prayer is: Protect us from spiritual harm in the future (*before us*), as well as from the consequences of what has already occurred (*behind us*).

R' *Yechezkel Abramsky*, however, explains the verse literally. He notes that the Satan can entice a person to sin in one of two ways — by persuading him to do things that are forbidden, or by dissuading him from positive acts, such as studying Torah and performing mitzvos. In fulfilling each of these roles, the Satan takes up a different position. When a person wishes to act correctly, the Satan stands in front of him, attempting to bar his way. But when a person is tempted to sin, the Satan is behind him, pushing him toward the forbidden path. For this reason, we ask Hashem to remove the Satan from both of these positions, allowing him neither to push us to do wrong nor to prevent us from doing right.

By looking elsewhere in the *siddur,* we can discover how to achieve this level. In the introduction to the *Korbanos* section of *Shacharis* (which is taken from *Tanna D'Vei Eliyahu*), we say, לְעוֹלָם יְהֵא אָדָם יְרֵא שָׁמַיִם בְּסֵתֶר וּבַגָּלוּי, *A person should always be God-fearing, both privately and publicly.* R' *Yechezkel Sarna* explains that some people always act correctly when others can see them, but they are tempted to sin when their misdeeds will remain undiscovered. To them, the Baraisa exclaims: Fear God in private, for He sees all! Other people have the opposite problem; while they behave correctly in private, they are ashamed to do mitzvos in public, for fear of being labeled old-fashioned or nonconformist. To such people, the Baraisa says: Fear God in public as well, for He is the Creator and Master of the world and all its creatures.

One who succeeds in embodying both of these ideals, and keeps the fear of Heaven before him always, will indeed be empowered to remove the Satan from both in front of him and behind him.

וַתֹּאמֶר הָאִשָּׁה אֶל־הַנָּחָשׁ מִפְּרִי עֵץ־הַגָּן נֹאכֵל.
וּמִפְּרִי הָעֵץ אֲשֶׁר בְּתוֹךְ־הַגָּן אָמַר אֱלֹהִים
לֹא תֹאכְלוּ מִמֶּנּוּ וְלֹא תִגְּעוּ בּוֹ פֶּן תְּמֻתוּן.
וַיֹּאמֶר הַנָּחָשׁ אֶל־הָאִשָּׁה לֹא־מוֹת תְּמֻתוּן.

The woman said to the serpent,
"Of the fruit of any tree of the garden we may eat.
But of the fruit of the tree that is in the center of the garden
HASHEM *has said: 'You shall not eat of it and you shall not touch it,*
lest you die.' " And the serpent replied to the woman:
"You will not surely die . . ." (Bereishis 3:2-4).

*R*ashi explains that Chavah came to grief because she added to the words of Hashem. While Hashem had forbidden Adam and Chavah to *eat* from the tree on pain of death, Chavah told the snake that they had been forbidden to *touch* the tree as well. The snake, knowing that this was not the case, took advantage of Chavah's mistake by pushing her until she touched the tree. He then told her, "See that you did not die from touching the tree; you will not die even if you eat from its fruits!"

The Gemara in *Sanhedrin* (29a) cites this episode as proof of the principle that כָּל הַמּוֹסִיף גּוֹרֵעַ, *Whoever adds, detracts.* For by adding to Hashem's restriction against eating from the tree by forbidding touching it as well, Adam and Chavah created a situation that allowed the snake to trick Chavah into eating from the tree.

However, there remains a difficulty that must be addressed. The concept of adding restrictions to distance oneself from sin is actually encouraged by the Torah; indeed, the first Mishnah in *Pirkei Avos* enjoins us: עֲשׂוּ סְיָג לַתּוֹרָה, *Make a fence around the Torah.* Moreover, in *Avos D'Rabbi Nassan*(1:5) we find that Adam himself is lauded for creating a fence around the Torah by issuing *this very* restriction, against touching the forbidden tree! How can this be reconciled with the Gemara in *Sanhedrin,* which states that one who adds to the Torah is to be criticized for detracting therefrom?

Hagahos Yaavetz (to *Avos D'Rabbi Nassan* ibid.) and *Chasam Sofer* explain that while it is indeed admirable to create restrictions that will distance one from sin, care must be taken to emphasize that these restrictions are not part of the Torah itself, but additional fences erected by man; for adding fences without making clear what is Torah and what is not can indeed lead to detraction. It was in this that Adam erred; while he was correct in warning Chavah against even touching the tree, he should have made it clear to her that this restriction was one that he had added, and not part of Hashem's injunction. Had he done so, the snake would not have been able to trick Chavah by pushing her into the tree, as she would have known that touching the tree did not carry the penalty of death.

R' Irving Bunim (author of *Ethics from Sinai* on *Pirkei Avos*) noted that this concept can be gleaned from the Mishnah's characterization of such preventive restrictions as *fences* around the Torah. A fence, said R' Bunim, performs two functions: It prevents one from trampling that which it protects, and it also provides a clear demarcation between what is inside the fence and what is not. This is the rule that must be followed whenever such restrictions are issued; they must prevent transgression, and at the same time they must be clearly identified as man-made, and not part of the Torah.

MISHNAH OF THE DAY: SHABBOS 1:3

This Mishnah begins by citing a pair of laws that were enacted by the Sages as precautionary measures, so that one would not forget and come to transfer things from one domain to another on Shabbos. לֹא יֵצֵא הַחַיָּט בְּמַחְטוֹ סָמוּךְ לַחֲשֵׁכָה — *A tailor may not go out with his needle close to nightfall*[1] on Erev Shabbos, שֶׁמָּא יִשְׁכַּח וְיֵצֵא — *for he may forget* that he is carrying it, *and go out* into the street on Shabbos while carrying it.[2] וְלֹא הַלַּבְלָר בְּקֻלְמוֹסוֹ — *Similarly, a scribe may not go out with his pen* close to nightfall, lest he forget and carry it on Shabbos.[3]

The Mishnah now lists other precautionary laws enacted by the Sages for the purpose of preventing violation of the Shabbos laws:

──────────────── NOTES ────────────────

1. "Close to nightfall" in this context means within a half-hour of the twilight period (see *Beur Halachah* to 252:6).

[For a discussion of how the needle (or the pen in the Mishnah's next case) is being carried, as well as a discussion of whether this law applies specifically to tailors (or scribes), see *Gems from the Gemara* below.]

2. The Sages were afraid that at some point, the tailor, while still holding the needle, will forget that it is Shabbos, and carry the needle into the street (*Tosafos* to 11a); alternatively, he might carry the needle 4 *amos* in the public domain (*Mishnah Berurah* 252:53). They thus required him to divest himself of the needle well in advance of Shabbos.

3. The reasoning behind this decree is essentially the same as that of the previous one. The Mishnah adds this case to teach us that there is no difference between a small item such as a needle, and a larger item such as a pen (see *Tos. R' Akiva Eiger*).

וְלֹא יְפַלֶּה אֶת כֵּלָיו — *And [a person] may not remove lice from his clothing,* וְלֹא יִקְרָא — *nor may he read* from a text לְאוֹר הַנֵּר — *by the light of an* oil *lamp* on Shabbos.[4]   בֶּאֱמֶת אָמְרוּ — *In truth, they said:*[5] הַחַזָּן רוֹאֶה הֵיכָן הַתִּינוֹקוֹת קוֹרְאִין — *The chazzan may see where the children are reading* by lamplight,[6] אֲבָל הוּא לֹא יִקְרָא — *but he* himself *may not read* by the lamp's light.[7]

The Mishnah concludes with a precautionary decree unrelated to the laws of Shabbos:

לֹא יֹאכַל הַזָּב עִם הַזָּבָה — *a zav may not eat* alone *with* his wife who is *a zavah,* כַּיּוֹצֵא בוֹ — *Similarly,* מִפְּנֵי הֶרְגֵּל עֲבֵרָה — *since this might lead to sin.*[8]

---------------------------------- NOTES ----------------------------------

4. It frequently occurs that the oil in a lamp draws away from the wick, causing the lamp to grow dim. One rectifies this by tilting the lamp so that the oil flows back toward the wick. This act, however, is forbidden on Shabbos, as it constitutes *kindling,* one of the principal labors forbidden on Shabbos. The Sages thus prohibited one from performing certain tasks by lamplight, lest he forget and adjust the lamp should it dim while he is absorbed in his task (*Rashi*).

The Gemara (12a) concludes that both prohibitions mentioned here (delousing clothing and reading) are prohibited only by lamplight. It is permitted, however, for one to delouse his clothing on Shabbos during the day, and we are not concerned that he might kill a louse (see Gemara there).

5. This expression is often used to introduce a הֲלָכָה לְמשֶׁה מִסִינַי, *an oral law taught to Moses at Sinai.* Here, this cannot be the case, as the law being discussed is Rabbinic in nature. However, this term is also used to introduce a statement that is universally accepted as law (see *Rav* to *Terumos* 2:1), for in this way it is *similar* to an oral law received by Moses.

6. The *chazzan* referred to here is the sexton (*shamash*) of the synagogue. Occasionally, he would be unsure which portion of the Torah was to be read the following day, and he would identify it by seeing which section the children (who would learn in the synagogue on Friday night) were studying. Since he needs only a brief glance at the text to achieve this, we are not concerned that he will become engrossed and adjust the lamp absentmindedly (*Rashi,* first explanation). [The students were allowed to study by lamplight, since they would not dare to touch the lamp in the presence of their teacher (*Rav,* from Gemara 12b).]

7. If the sexton would actually read the text instead of merely glancing at it, he might come to adjust the lamp. Therefore, this is forbidden.

8. This decree is explained as follows: A *zav* is a man who has become *tamei* (ritually impure) through a certain type of gonorrheal emission (see *Vayikra* 15:1-15); a *zavah* is a woman who is *tamei* due to her experiencing a flow of blood that is between the times for her usual menstrual flow (ibid. vs. 25-28). Now, when a woman is a *zavah,* relations with her husband are forbidden under pain of *kares* (Divinely imposed pre-

The Mishnah taught that a tailor may not go out with his needle, and a scribe may not go out with his pen, close to nightfall on Erev Shabbos. The Gemara (11b) cites a dispute between Tannaim concerning the proper understanding of this decree:

According to R' Yehudah, the Mishnah is speaking of a needle that is pinned to one's clothes, and a pen that is carried behind one's ear. For an ordinary person, carrying these items in such a manner would not be forbidden Biblically even on Shabbos, because one is liable for a *melachah* only if he performs it in the conventional manner (see Mishnah 10:6). Since carrying them this way on Shabbos would be only a Rabbinic violation, the Sages would not forbid him from carrying them in this manner on Friday (in accordance with the rule that אֵין גּוֹזְרִין גְּזֵירָה לִגְזֵירָה, *the Rabbis do not issue a decree to prevent one from violating another [Rabbinic] preventive decree*). However, tailors or scribes, who *do* usually carry their implements in this manner, *would* be liable Biblically for carrying them out on Shabbos, and thus the Sages forbade *specifically those craftsmen* from carrying these items in this manner even shortly before nightfall.

R' Meir understands the Mishnah differently. In his view, even tailors and scribes who carry their implements in this way on Shabbos are not liable Biblically, and therefore the decree outlined in the Mishnah cannot refer to such cases, as explained above. Rather, the Mishnah speaks of needles and pens that are being carried out *in one's hand,* in a normal manner. The Sages decreed that *any person* is forbidden to carry needles or pens outside close to nightfall, lest he forget and carry them outside on Shabbos. [Indeed, *Shulchan Aruch, Orach Chaim* 252:6 states: A person may not go out on Erev Shabbos shortly before dark with his needle in his hand (see also *Mishnah Berurah* ibid. §52).] According to R' Meir, the Mishnah speaks specifically of tailors and scribes only because they are the ones most likely to be carrying such objects; the decree applies equally to everyone.

───────────── NOTES ─────────────

mature death). The Sages enacted the safeguard taught in the Mishnah to prevent the intimate atmosphere of a private meal from leading to forbidden relations. This applies even when her husband is a *zav* (for whom relations are painful), and certainly if he is healthy (*Rashi; Rav*).

However, if an item that does not belong on the table is placed between them to serve as a reminder of the wife's forbidden state, or if separate tablecloths are used, they may eat together at the table (see *Shulchan Aruch, Yoreh Deah* 195:3).

We learned earlier (see *A Torah Thought for the Day*) that the Gemara in Sanhedrin (29a) states the principle: כָּל הַמּוֹסִיף גּוֹרֵעַ, *Whoever adds, detracts.* In his classic work *Sichos Mussar,* R' Chaim Shmulevitz addresses the question: Why is one who adds to the Torah equated with one who detracts from it? He has done no wrong! Why is he at fault?

R' Chaim explains that every person is under constant attack by the *yetzer hara,* his evil inclination, whose only purpose and goal is to cause the person to sin. The main protection that a person has against the wiles of the *yetzer hara* is his strict adherence to the rules and boundaries established by the Torah. For Hashem erected the 613 mitzvos as a barrier against the *yetzer hara;* as long as the barrier remains intact, the person is safe.

The *yetzer hara,* however, leaves no stone unturned in its efforts to breach that barrier. He urges the person to commit even the slightest sin, for this creates a breach in the fence. And it is well known that a field that is protected by a breached fence is not protected at all . . .

The *yetzer hara* will even attempt to breach this fence by encouraging one to *add* to the Torah's commandments. For once the person can be persuaded that he is in charge of deciding what may be done and what may not be done, he is no longer performing the mitzvos as a servant of Hashem. Rather, he is doing that which he deems correct! Such a person can easily be persuaded that there are mitzvos that do not apply to him, or that he is above certain prohibitions. Thus, although his error began with adding to the Torah, it is certain to end in transgression.

It is for this reason, adds *R' Chaim,* that the confession of *Rabbeinu Nissim Gaon* contains both the statement "that which You prohibited, I permitted," and its opposite, "that which You permitted, I prohibited." It is just as much of a sin to prohibit that which Hashem permits as it is to transgress His prohibitions, for both misdeeds come from a single root — one's belief that he may decide what is permitted and what is forbidden (adapted from *Sichos Mussar,* 5731:25 and 5732:34).

QUESTION OF THE DAY:

Hashem cursed the snake, saying: I will place hatred between you and the woman, and between your offspring and her offspring (Bereishis 3:15). Where else in Scripture does the verse speak of snakes attacking man?

For the answer, see page 53.

The second of the ל"ט מְלָאכוֹת, the *thirty-nine categories of labor* forbidden on the Sabbath, is the *melachah* of *choreish*, plowing. The act of plowing was a necessary part of the production of the herbs used for dyes in the Mishkan, as well as the wheat that was ground into the flour used for the *lechem hapanim* and the meal-offerings (see Sunday, where this was explained with regard to the *melachah* of *planting*).

The purpose of plowing is to prepare land for planting. We may therefore define the *melachah* of *plowing* as any action that helps to prepare land for planting. In addition to the specific act of plowing (making furrows in the ground), acts that improve the land and make it more suitable for planting will also be forbidden. This includes any form of loosening the ground, leveling the surface of the ground, removing obstacles or debris attached to the ground, or making holes in the ground. Since all of these acts improve the land's suitability for planting, they are forbidden as *plowing*.

We learned earlier that one is liable for the *melachah* of *planting* even if he plants only a single seed. With respect to *plowing*, a similar law applies; if one improves enough soil to facilitate the planting of even a single seed, he has violated the *melachah* of *plowing*. Since only a tiny amount of earth is necessary for the planting of a seed, one transgresses the *melachah* of *plowing* by digging or preparing even a minute amount of soil.

Since the *melachah* of *plowing* applies only where the act improves the suitability of the soil for planting, the soil in question must be arable land that is fit for planting. Thus, plowing in desert sand would not be prohibited, since nothing can grow in such sand.

[*Tosafos* (to *Chullin* 88b) note that the Jews were in the Wilderness when the Mishkan was constructed. Where, ask *Tosafos*, did the Jews find arable land to plant the herbs and dyes that they needed? They answer that perhaps the sands of the desert became miraculously productive wherever the Jews had need of growing things.]

Another example of an act that would not be forbidden as *plowing* because of this rule would be the pouring of caustic chemicals upon the ground. Although the pouring of other liquids onto hard ground is forbidden if this causes the soil to be loosened and thereby prepared for planting, such chemicals will impair the ability of the soil to nourish plants, rather than enhance it. For this reason, it would be permitted.

The principle of כָּל הַמוֹסִיף גוֹרֵעַ, *Whoever adds, detracts,* has an application, albeit a limited one, to *tefillah* as well as mitzvos. The Gemara in *Berachos* (33b) relates that a certain man once served as *shliach tzibbur* (prayer leader) before R' Chanina, and the man added to the standard text of the first blessing of the *Shemoneh Esrei*. Instead of saying *"the great, mighty, and awesome God,"* as we do, he added, "the glorious, the potent, the feared, the strong, the powerful, the definite and the esteemed God." R' Chanina waited until he finished praying, and then asked him: "Have you then finished all the praises with which your Master can be praised? [Obviously not, for no man can praise God adequately.] Why, then, have you added all these praises? Even the fact that we recite three praises (*great, mighty,* and *awesome*) in *Shemoneh Esrei* stems from the fact that Moshe Rabbeinu stated them in the Torah (*Devarim* 10:17), the prophet Ezra used them in prayer (*Nechemiah* 9:32), and the *Anshei Knesses HaGedolah* established them as part of the *Shemoneh Esrei* (see *Rashi* to *Berachos* ibid., and *Turei Even* to *Megillah* 25a). By adding your own praises, you are in fact denigrating God; for your feeble attempts at praise can be likened to praising a king who possesses millions of gold *dinars* by saying that he has some silver. Is this "praise" not in truth a disgrace?"

Rambam, in his *Moreh Nevuchim* (1:59, cited in *Ritva* to *Berachos* ibid.), makes this point even more starkly. He notes that the Gemara does not compare one who offers additional praise to a person who praises the king for possessing a smaller amount of gold; rather, it compares him to one who praises the king for possession of a different item altogether. This, says *Rambam*, is because any praises that we ourselves can offer to Hashem cannot help but fail to miss the mark completely, for the true extent of His glory and majesty is far beyond our comprehension.

There is, however, a difficulty that we must address. It is evident from our prayers that we are *not* restricted to uttering those praises of Hashem that were stated in the Torah. The vast majority of our prayers, in fact, speak of Hashem's kindness to His creations, and His vast powers. What is the difference between this and the praises mentioned in the Gemara, of which R' Chanina disapproved?

Ritva (ibid.) provides us with the answer. He explains that *describing* Hashem Himself, or His attributes, is a task that is beyond us, so we are bidden to be silent rather than fall so very short. However, speaking of the wonders that He does, or the kindnesses that He performs for us, is certainly correct; and the more one does so, the more he is deserving of praise. This, writes the *Ritva*, was the intent of King David when he wrote *Tehillim,* as well as the praises composed by righteous men throughout history.

A TASTE OF LOMDUS

In *A Torah Thought for the Day,* we introduced the concept of כָּל הַמּוֹסִיף גּוֹרֵעַ, *Whoever adds, detracts.* This concept is, of course, closely linked to the Torah prohibition of *bal tosif,* which forbids us to add to any of the mitzvos of the Torah (such as by adding a fifth string to *tzitzis,* or sitting for an extra day in the *succah*).

Tosafos (to *Rosh Hashanah* 16b ד"ה ותוקעים and to 28b ד"ה ומנא תימרא) raise an interesting question: We know that although the Torah commands us simply to blow a set of *tekios* and *teruos* on Rosh Hashanah, we actually blow many sets of *shofar* blasts — one hundred blasts in all. Why, ask *Tosafos,* is this not a violation of *bal tosif?*

Tosafos answer that since a person is allowed to blow the *shofar* many times lawfully (for example, if there are many groups in different places for whom he must blow), a second performance of the mitzvah is not considered *bal tosif.* Moreover, add *Tosafos,* even if he has fulfilled his obligation, and there is no one present who has not yet heard the *shofar,* merely repeating the mitzvah performance is not *bal tosif. Tosafos* add that this is true of many mitzvos — for example, one may eat more than one *kezayis* of matzah at the Pesach Seder, or wave the Four Species on Succos as many times as he likes.

Kehillos Yaakov (*Rosh Hashanah* §15) explains *Tosafos'* distinction, and thereby gives us a clearer understanding of the nature of the *bal tosif* prohibition. *Bal tosif* forbids the performance of a mitzvah in a manner that Hashem did not command — whether at the wrong time, or with additional parts. Only Hashem can determine how and when to do a mitzvah, and he who adds in truth is only subtracting. However, Rosh Hashanah is the *correct* time to blow the *shofar,* and Pesach is the *correct* time to eat matzah. As long as the mitzvah is being performed correctly, and at the proper time, Hashem considers this an appropriate act, even if it is performed many times. Thus, even a person who has discharged his obligation may perform the mitzvah again. While *bal tosif* forbids a person to invent his own system for serving Hashem, it does not proscribe multiple performances of a single mitzvah.

בְּזֵעַת אַפֶּיךָ תֹאכַל לֶחֶם

By the sweat of your brow shall you eat bread . . .
(Bereishis 3:19).

*R*ashi explains that "the sweat of your brow" is an expression signifying toil. Thus, Adam was told that as a result of his sin, he would no longer come by his food effortlessly, as had previously been the case; rather, it would be obtained only through great effort. *Ibn Ezra* notes that as a result of this, man actually was placed at a disadvantage with respect to all other creatures; for while other animals find their food ready to eat, man must plant and reap, and knead and bake, before he can eat bread. This thought is also echoed by the Tanna R' Shimon ben Elazar in *Maseches Kiddushin* (82b): "In all my life I have never seen a deer that produced dried figs, a lion that was a porter, or a fox that was a storekeeper. Yet, they sustain themselves without difficulty. Now, they were created to serve me, while I was created to serve my Master (Hashem). If they can sustain themselves without difficulty, should I not certainly be able to do so? Rather, it is only because I have corrupted my deeds by sinning, and thus forfeited my sustenance."

According to the Gemara in *Pesachim* (118a), however, this verse actually represents an *easing* of Hashem's original curse. The Gemara explains that Adam was first told, "*Thorns and thistles shall [the land] sprout forth for you, and you shall eat the grasses of the field* (Bereishis 3:18). Adam was to be treated exactly like any other domestic livestock, eating herbs and grasses. The Gemara relates that when Adam heard this pronouncement, he began to weep, saying: "Master of the Universe! Must I and my donkey eat from the same manger?" Hearing his distress, Hashem had mercy upon Adam, and stated, *by the sweat of your brow you shall eat bread.* [*Maharsha* (*Pesachim* ibid.) explains that Adam's distress was based upon his fear that eating the same food as the animals would cause him to regress to the nature and intelligence level of the animals. Hashem therefore assured him that he would have bread to eat; and the Gemara indeed states in several places (see *Berachos* 40a and *Succah* 42b) that grain foods help intelligence to develop.]

The Midrash cites a variation of this incident, in which Adam broke into an anxious sweat when he heard that he would have to eat the same diet as the animals. According to the Midrash, this sweat is referred to in our verse. Hashem reassured Adam, telling him: *By the sweat of your brow* — that is, due to your anxious sweating upon hearing the punishment that has been pronounced upon you — *shall you* be given the ability to *eat bread.*

MISHNAH OF THE DAY: SHABBOS 1:4

שֶׁאָמְרוּ בַּעֲלִיַּית — *And these*[1] *are* some *of the laws* וְאֵלּוּ מִן הַהֲלָכוֹת — *that* the Sages *stated in the upper chamber of Chananyah ben Chizkiyah ben Gurion*[2] חֲנַנְיָה בֶּן חִזְקִיָּה בֶּן גֻּרְיוֹן — *when they went up to visit him.*[3] כְּשֶׁעָלוּ לְבַקְּרוֹ — On that occasion, they voted, *were counted,* נִמְנוּ — *and* those supporting the view of *Beis Shammai outnumbered* those who supported the view of *Beis Hillel.*[4] וְרַבּוּ בֵּית שַׁמַּאי עַל בֵּית הִלֵּל — *And that day they issued decrees* concerning *eighteen matters.*[5] וּשְׁמוֹנָה עָשָׂר דְּבָרִים גָּזְרוּ בּוֹ בַיּוֹם

―――――――― NOTES ――――――――

1. I.e., the laws cited in the previous Mishnah — viz., the prohibitions on removing lice from one's clothing and on reading by the light of an oil lamp on the Sabbath (*Rav, Rashi*).

2. At one time, the Rabbis considered removing the Book of *Ezekiel* from the Bible because some of its statements seem contrary to the Torah. The Tanna mentioned in our Mishnah, Chananyah ben Chizkiyah, took upon himself the task of resolving the apparent contradictions. In order to focus on this task, he secluded himself in a chamber in the upper story of his house.

3. The Rabbis often came to visit Chananyah ben Chizkiyah in order to critique his commentary. On this particular occasion, many great scholars of the time were present, and they decided to utilize the opportunity to enact new decrees regarding various matters (*Rambam; Rav*). [*Rambam* actually translates כְּדֵי לְבַקְּרוֹ as *to test him,* and explains that on this occasion many of the Sages gathered for the purpose of passing judgment on Chananyah's commentary.]

4. They voted on the eighteen decrees that they wished to enact, and those supporting the view of Beis Shammai were found to be in the majority that day. Consequently, these eighteen laws were enacted in accordance with the opinions of Beis Shammai, rather than in accord with those of Beis Hillel (although generally the halachah accords with Beis Hillel).

5. The two laws cited in the previous Mishnah (see note 1), together with sixteen other laws listed in the Gemara, are known collectively as the שְׁמוֹנָה עָשָׂר דָּבָר, *the Eighteen Matters.*

The Gemara (13b) discusses another accomplishment of Chananyah ben Chizkiyah, in whose upper chamber the Eighteen Matters were enacted: He was the primary author of *Megillas Taanis.*

Megillas Taanis (which literally translates as *Scroll of the Fasts*) was compiled toward the end of the Second Temple era. It lists the calendar dates on which fasting is prohibited because those dates were declared minor festivals, on account of miraculous salvations that occurred on them.

[Sometime later, after the Destruction of the Temple, these minor festivals were abolished amid the trials and tribulations that beset the Jews. Consequently, the prohibitions against fasting on these dates were lifted (*Rosh Hashanah* 18b). According to many Rishonim, however, only personal fasts are permitted on these dates, but public fasts are still forbidden (see *Tur* and *Beis Yosef, Orach Chaim* 573).]

Our extant version of *Megillas Taanis* contains thirty-five dates, but it is obvious that some of them are later additions, added even as late as after the Destruction of the Temple. Hence, Chananyah ben Chizkiyah, who lived approximately 100 years before the Temple was destroyed, was the primary author of the original version. The Baraisa cited in the Gemara attributes the authorship to "Chananyah ben Chizkiyah and his colleagues" — this is possibly a reference to the later Tannaim who made the subsequent additions (see the preface of *R' Yaakov Emden* to his glosses on *Megillas Taanis*).

The Gemara states that Chananyah and his colleagues composed *Megillas Taanis* because "they cherished the troubles" — that is, they realized that their suffering was the result of their shortcomings, and they therefore appreciated Hashem's salvation even more, as they knew that they were unworthy. [Had they attributed the troubles to happenstance, the deliverance would not be cause for celebration, as it, too, could be due to happenstance (see *Maharshal* ibid.).]

Five generations later, the situation of the Jews had deteriorated, and troubles abounded. Yet, time after time, the Jews were miraculously saved. However, the leader of the nation, Rabban Shimon ben Gamliel, did not record the dates of these miracles. Rabban Gamliel offered three reasons for this decision: (1) There were so many miracles, that every date would have had to be declared a holiday — not a practical proposition. (2) "An imbecile is not harmed" — that is, the Jews were so overwhelmed with hardships that they were numb to the troubles, and did not fully appreciate the miracles. (3) And, in a similar vein, "Dead flesh (such as that of a scab or scar) cannot feel the knife" — i.e., the multitude of tribulations had rendered the Jews as insensitive as dead, nerveless skin. Thus, the only dates recorded remained those in *Megillas Taanis.*

A MUSSAR THOUGHT FOR THE DAY

R' *Shlomo Wolbe,* in his epic *mussar sefer Alei Shur,* explains the effect that the curse of *by the sweat of your brow shall you eat bread* had upon the world and man's role in it:

Before the sin of Adam HaRishon, everything that was to be found in Gan Eden was completely good. However, once Adam sinned, evil and good were intermixed, and it became the task of man to separate the good from the evil. If a person wishes to, he can grow wheat; but he must weed his field, for thorns and thistles will grow there as well. He is capable of mining the earth for silver and gold, but these precious elements are not to be found in their pure state. Rather, he must smelt and refine the ore before he can obtain unadulterated metal.

When it comes to food and drink as well, a person is given the choice to choose, for there are permitted foods and forbidden ones; and even the permitted foods are permitted only if one thanks Hashem for them by making *berachos* before and after he eats. When a person is successful in this task, and eats permitted foods while making the correct *berachos,* the food fuses with his body, providing him with renewed energy to serve Hashem by studying Torah and fulfilling mitzvos . . .

In fact, in regard to all of man's toil, this concept of separating good from evil also exists. For man has been given the task of providing for his livelihood; and, as the Gemara states (*Bava Metzia* 38a), a person enjoys the fruits of his own labor more than fruits given to him by another. Yet, it is incumbent upon every person to always remember that all he has is a gift from Hashem, and not to fall into the trap of believing that any of his accomplishments are the result of his own strengths and abilities. This, too, is a task of separating good from evil; one must always strive to strengthen his belief in Hashem, so that he can attribute his successes to Hashem, rather than having faith in his own powers.

THURSDAY

Let us continue our discussion of the *melachah* of *plowing,* and examine some everyday situations where an act might be forbidden as *plowing.*

The most basic type of plowing is the creating of a furrow in the ground, as one does with a plow. When one prepares a field for plowing, he typically begins by plowing a furrow, and then sows seeds into the furrow and covers them with earth. This assures that the seeds will not be blown away, but will rather remain in firm contact with the soil so that they can germinate, take root and grow. [Above, on Sunday, we discussed why *planting* is listed before *plowing* in the ל"ט מְלָאכוֹת even though one usually plows before he plants.]

Even if one has no intention of planting anything, digging a furrow in the ground, or performing an act that will result in a furrow being made in the ground, is nevertheless forbidden (as long as the ground is fit for planting). Moreover, it is not necessary to use a plow or an implement intended for digging to do this. Indeed, one can violate the *melachah* of *plowing* with a heavy chair, a stick, or even the heel of one's shoe, as we shall see.

There are two different ways to create a furrow in the ground. One can break the ground and move some soil away, thereby creating a hole into which seed may be placed; or one may compress the soil without moving any of it, creating an indentation in the ground. Although both of these actions create a furrow in the ground, they are *not* equivalent from a halachic point of view, as will be explained.

One may not drag a heavy object along the ground, if this will *definitely* cause the item to break the earth's surface and move soil, creating a furrow. Although the creation of the furrow may be unintentional, it is nevertheless forbidden as *an inevitable consequence* (פְּסִיק רֵישֵׁיהּ) — see *Halachah of the Day* above, Monday). One is permitted, however, to drag a light object across the ground, despite the *possibility* that it might create a furrow. Since the person has no intent to create the furrow, and it is not definite that one will be created as a result of his action, his creating the furrow is classified as a דָּבָר שֶׁאֵינוֹ מִתְכַּוֵּון, *an unintended action,* and is permitted.

In the case just cited, one is forbidden to create the furrow by breaking the soil. It is permitted, however, to push a baby carriage or a wheelchair over the ground, although the wheels will compress the ground and create grooves that are similar to furrows. The reason for this distinction is that the compressed ground has not been made more suitable for planting. Since no soil has been broken up, the seeds will not be placed *into* the ground; and there is no loose soil available with which to cover the seeds. If the seeds are placed into the depressions they will simply be blown away. Therefore, such a furrow is not considered fit for planting, and one who creates it has not violated the *melachah* of *plowing*.

A CLOSER LOOK AT THE SIDDUR

פּוֹתֵחַ אֶת יָדֶךָ וּמַשְׂבִּיעַ לְכָל חַי רָצוֹן

*You open Your hand, and satisfy the desire
of every living thing (Psalms 145:16).*

This verse is found in the prayer of *Ashrei*, which we say three times daily in our prayers. The Gemara in *Berachos* (4b) makes the remarkable statement that one who recites this prayer three times daily can trust that he is worthy of the World to Come, and explains that this particular prayer is distinguished in two aspects: Its verses follow the order of the *aleph-beis* (so that one who recites it has used the entire alphabet to praise the Creator — see *Ritva* ibid.), and it contains this essential verse, which is an unsurpassed declaration of Hashem's generosity and goodness toward His creatures. Although there are other verses that speak of Hashem's provision of sustenance (for example, *Psalms* 111:5, *He gives food to those who fear Him*), this verse is unparalleled, for it states that Hashem satisfies the need of *every living thing*. Indeed, the Gemara in *Avodah Zarah* (3b) states that Hashem personally provides every day for each of His creatures, from the majestic *re'eim* to the lowliest louse. *Rabbeinu Bachya* (in *Kad HaKemach, Pesach* §3) states that the Sages attached so much importance to this prayer to underscore the basic truth that everything comes from Hashem.

If we examine the verse more closely, we will see that it reveals even greater depths of Hashem's kindness to us. The end of the verse teaches us that Hashem satisfies not only the *needs* of every creature, but the *desire* of every living thing. The commentators offer several interpretations of this. Some (*Sforno, Roke'ach*) explain that while Hashem provides us with all our needs, He does not automatically grant us everything *we* desire — for a person does not always know what is best for him. Rather, He considers the situation of each creature individually, and grants that creature what is best for it, in accordance with *His* will.

However, the Midrash (*Shemos Rabbah* 25:3) explains the verse as simply stating that Hashem indeed satisfies the desire of each and every creature. The verse thus teaches that Hashem's powers have no limitations, as He is able to give all creatures exactly what they desire. As an example of this, the Midrash cites the gift of the manna, which miraculously took on whatever taste the one who was eating it desired.

A third explanation, advanced by *Gra* and *Chasam Sofer* (among others), is that Hashem provides us not only with our sustenance, but with the ability to be satisfied and happy with what we possess. This, too, is a great gift; for one who is unsatisfied with his lot, no matter how great his material wealth, can never be considered rich (see *Avos* 4:1).

When a person truly accepts the fact that everything he has comes from Hashem, this enables him to observe the mitzvos of the Torah without worrying that doing so will negatively impact upon his financial status. This point is illustrated by the story told of a man who came to the Chazon Ish with a complaint. "Rabbi," he said, "I have no choice but to keep my business open seven days a week. I cannot afford to lose the customers that come to me on the Sabbath!"

The Chazon Ish asked: "What is the nature of your business?"

"I am a plumber," was the reply.

"In that case," the Chazon Ish said, "I have a job for you. My home keeps running out of hot water. I would like you to enlarge the pipe that brings the water from the *dud shemesh* (a hot-water tank located on the roof of the building and heated by the sun) into my home."

The plumber looked at the *tzaddik* incredulously. "But surely you realize, Rabbi, that making the pipe larger isn't going to get you more water! All you will accomplish is that that water will come out faster — but once it's gone, it's gone!"

"Listen to the words of your own mouth!" chided the Chazon Ish. "Do you think that it is you who determines the success of your business? Hashem decrees every Rosh Hashanah how successful you will be and what money you will receive. By keeping your shop open on the Sabbath, all you are doing is opening a larger pipe. You may receive your allotment faster — but once it's gone, it's gone!"

QUESTION OF THE DAY:

When is the curse of "by the sweat of your brow you shall eat bread" not in force, even today?

For the answer, see page 53.

A TORAH THOUGHT FOR THE DAY

פרשת
בראשית

FRIDAY

PARASHAS
BEREISHIS

וַיָּבֵא קַיִן מִפְּרִי הָאֲדָמָה מִנְחָה לַה'.
וְהֶבֶל הֵבִיא גַם־הוּא מִבְּכֹרוֹת צֹאנוֹ וּמֵחֶלְבֵהֶן. . .

And Kayin brought an offering of the fruit of the ground to HASHEM. And Hevel brought as well, from the firstborn of his flock and from their choicest . . . (Bereishis 4:3-4).

The Torah relates that first Kayin and then Hevel brought offerings before Hashem; Hevel's was accepted, while Kayin's was not. Kayin was angered by this, whereupon Hashem rebuked him. Afterward, Kayin, jealous of his brother's success, quarreled with Hevel, and killed him.

Why was Kayin's sacrifice rejected and Hevel's accepted? The commentators (*Ibn Ezra, Radak,* et al.) explain that while Hevel was careful to offer only the *firstborn* and the *choicest* of his flocks to Hashem, Kayin offered only a meager tribute (according to the *Midrash Tanchuma,* it was flaxseed).

R' Shamshon Raphael Hirsch explains that the sacrifice offered by each brother was indicative of his attitude toward the service of Hashem. Kayin was willing to bring *something* as a tribute to Hashem, but could not be bothered to bring the best; he was content with the minimum. Such a person will devote only spare time to serving Hashem, and will devote only expendable resources to Him. This attitude is worthy of rejection and rebuke, both of which Kayin suffered.

Hevel, on the other hand, gave his relationship with Hashem the highest priority. For him, only the best was good enough to offer — the sacrifice had to be the choicest. Such a person views his primary purpose in life to be the service of Hashem, and it is to this, first and foremost, that he dedicates his energies, talents and resources. Hashem was pleased with Hevel's attitude, and his sacrifice was accepted.

R' Moshe Feinstein, in his *Darash Moshe,* struggles to understand Kayin's rationale for offering inferior produce. Surely, he asks, Kayin, who was the first of the two brothers (according to most commentators) to actually realize that it was proper to offer a sacrifice to Hashem, should have realized that it was proper to offer only the best to Him! How did he come to make such a basic error?

R' Moshe suggests that perhaps Kayin reasoned that Hashem, Who is the Creator of all, does not need the actual tribute that is offered; what is more important is the thought *behind* the offering, of subservience to Hashem and His will. [In this, Kayin was correct; as the prophet Shmuel said to King Shaul: *Behold! To obey is better than a choice offering, to listen carefully [is better] than the fats of rams (I Shmuel 15:22).]* Thus, thought Kayin, it makes no difference what type of sacrifice I offer, as long as the thought behind it is pure.

The problem was, though, that the thought behind Kayin's offering was *not* pure. Hashem saw that Kayin's love for Him was weak — had it been strong enough, he would have felt *compelled* to offer only the best to Hashem, in gratitude for the bounty with which Hashem had graced him. His ability to rationalize an inferior offering revealed this potentially dangerous shortcoming that was within him, and so Hashem rejected his tribute.

MISHNAH OF THE DAY: SHABBOS 1:5

The next seven Mishnahs deal with the question of whether it is permitted to begin, before the Sabbath, various types of work that will continue automatically on the Sabbath:[1]

בֵּית שַׁמַּאי אוֹמְרִים — *Beis Shammai say:* אֵין שׁוֹרִין דְּיוֹ וְסַמָּנִים וְכַרְשִׁינִין — *We may not soak* the ingredients that combine to form *ink or dyes* before the Sabbath,[2] *and,* likewise, we may not soak *vetch* [3] in water before the Sabbath, אֶלָּא כְּדֵי שֶׁיִּשׁוֹרוּ מִבְּעוֹד יוֹם — *unless* there is *enough* time *for them to become* completely *soaked while it is yet day.* [4]

——————————— NOTES ———————————

1. These laws were also discussed in the upper chamber of Chananyah ben Chizkiyah ben Gurion at the meeting mentioned in the previous Mishnah; however, they were not voted upon (and the halachah does not follow Beis Shammai).

2. Were one to soak the ingredients necessary to make ink or dye on the Sabbath, he would be liable for violating the Sabbath prohibition of לִישָׁה, *kneading.* [In the course of the soaking process, these ingredients fuse in the same way as do the ingredients of a dough (see *Tosafos* to 18a; cf. *Rambam, Hil. Shabbos* 9:14, who maintains that the *melachah* violated would be צְבִיעָה, *dyeing*).]

3. Vetch is a type of bean that is soaked in water and then used for animal fodder (*Rav*). The soaked beans form a mass that resembles dough. Thus, here too the prohibition involved is *kneading* (*Meiri*).

4. According to Beis Shammai, the Torah's prohibitions on Sabbath labor apply not only to a person himself and to his animals, but even to his vessels, and even when the labor that occurs within those vessels will occur automatically (this prohibition is known as *shevisas keilim*). By combining the ink or dye ingredients or the vetch with water in a vessel before the Sabbath, he is allowing the labor of *kneading* to take place in his vessel on the Sabbath. It is, therefore, prohibited to do so (*Gemara* 18a).

וּבֵית הַלֵּל מַתִּירִין — *But Beis Hillel permit* starting the soaking before the Sabbath even if there is not enough time remaining for the process to be completed before the onset of the Sabbath.[5]

——————————————— NOTES ———————————————

5. According to Beis Hillel, the Torah's prohibitions on Sabbath labor apply only to a person himself and to his animals, but not to his vessels. Hence, he is permitted to combine the ink or dye ingredients or the vetch with water in a vessel before the Sabbath, even though the labor of *kneading* will continue in his vessel on the Sabbath (Gemara 18a).

GEMS FROM THE GEMARA

We learned in the Mishnah that according to Beis Shammai, the prohibitions on Sabbath labor apply not only to a person and his animals, but even to the vessels that he owns. Moreover, he may not allow *melachah* to take place within his vessels, even if that *melachah* occurs automatically, and is completely passive. Beis Hillel, on the other hand, maintain that a person is not required to ensure that his vessels desist from working on the Sabbath, even if that work is performed actively by the vessel on the Sabbath (as in the case of traps and snares — see Mishnah 6).

The Gemara notes that there are several common practices that seem to involves having one's vessels perform work on the Sabbath that were *not* challenged by Beis Shammai. For instance, Beis Shammai would permit the lighting of incense and spices before the Sabbath, even though the spices would continue burning on the Sabbath. Why were they not concerned for the vessel that held the incense? The Gemara deflects this challenge by answering that perhaps Beis Shammai indeed require that such spices be placed on the ground rather than in a vessel. [The prohibition of *shevisas keilim* applies only to one's vessels; even Beis Shammai concur that *melachah* may occur within one's *property* (see *Rashba* to 17b-18a).]

However, the Gemara (18b) notes that other permits of Beis Shammai still pose difficulty. For example: It is impossible to make beer without soaking barley for longer than eight days, and this process requires that the barley be kept in a vessel of some sort. Now, soaking of barley for long periods can result in violation of the *melachah* of *planting* (see *Orach Chaim* 336:11 with *Magen Avraham*), and yet Beis Shammai allow the beer to be brewed on the Sabbath! Also, Beis Shammai certainly allow lamps to burn on the Sabbath even though the fuel is being

FRIDAY

PARASHAS BEREISHIS

consumed within the lamp, and they allow pots of cooked food to simmer on the stove on the Sabbath even though the food is being improved. Similarly, Beis Shammai concur with the ruling of the Mishnah (1:11) that we may lower the spit holding a *korban pesach* into the oven on Friday and allow it to roast on the Sabbath (see *Rashi* to 18b). Why is the labor performed by these vessels not a violation of the prohibition of *shevisas keilim?*

The Gemara concludes that Beis Shammai will permit these activities only when the vessels involved are declared ownerless prior to the Sabbath. One is responsible only for the "resting" of *keilim* that he owns on the Sabbath. [Although people do not actually go through the formal procedure of declaring their vessels ownerless, *beis din* legally removes everyone's ownership from their candlesticks and pots before the Sabbath (see *Rashba;* see *Tosafos* to 18b for another explanation).]

A MUSSAR THOUGHT FOR THE DAY

*R*av Elazar Menachem Man Shach, the late Rosh Yeshivah of Ponevezh, once used the lesson of the story of Kayin and Hevel to settle a dispute that arose in the yeshivah.

The problem began when there was a sudden surge in the number of students attending the yeshivah, and there was no room in the *beis midrash* to accommodate them. A suggestion was made that some new benches be added to the *beis midrash* for the newcomers; however, many of the veteran students objected, noting that the additional benches would further crowd the already barely-navigable aisles.

Rav Shach, in his weekly address to the students, cited the *Midrash Rabbah,* which relates several opinions as to the matter that was at the root of the dispute between Kayin and Hevel. According to one opinion, the two brothers had decided, as Adam HaRishon's heirs, to divide ownership of the earth. They decided that Hevel would own all the movable property, while Kayin would own all of the land. Suddenly, an argument ensued. Hevel said, "The clothes you are wearing belong to me — take them off!" Kayin countered, "The ground you are standing on is mine! Start flying!" The quarrel became heated, until Kayin rose up against Hevel and killed him.

According to another opinion, the brothers each took a share of both land and movables, but disagreed over another matter altogether; Kayin

42 / A DAILY DOSE OF TORAH

wanted the Temple to be constructed on *his* land, while Hevel insisted that it be constructed in his portion.

Now, there is a known rule that Midrashic explanations are not exclusive. Thus, it is possible that the brothers argued over *two* issues, the division of property, and the location of the Temple.

Rav Shach looked at his *talmidim* and said: "Dear students! You are presently involved in an argument over the right to use the *beis midrash.* Each group wishes to assert its right to a piece of holy ground upon which to study Torah. But the sad truth is that such an argument can easily degenerate to the point where one group will totally reject the other, saying: 'You are on my ground. Start flying!' Now, who among you is willing to play the role of a Kayin?"

After that address, the conflict suddenly eased, and an amicable solution was found.

(from *Rav Shach on Chumash*)

HALACHAH OF THE DAY

As we learned above, leveling the surface of the ground is also prohibited as *plowing.* Since an uneven section of ground is difficult to plant, leveling it by removing a mound or filling in a hole improves its suitability for planting, and is therefore forbidden.

In earlier times, it was common for homes to have earthen floors. The floors would become rough and uneven over time, and would need occasional leveling and smoothing out. Now, since the earth inside a house is unsuitable for cultivation, leveling it cannot be forbidden as *plowing.* It is, however, a violation of the *melachah* of *building,* since it improves the utility of the floor as a part of the house. For this reason, the Sages prohibited sweeping an earthen floor on the Sabbath, since this will inevitably result in the leveling of some part of the floor. They even prohibited the sweeping of *non-earthen* floors, to prevent one from sweeping an earthen floor. However, the Sages permitted the sweeping of non-earthen interior floors in cities where most homes have non-earthen flooring. For this reason, nowadays, when most homes do not have earthen floors, sweeping the floor on the Sabbath is permitted. [One must take care, however, to use a soft broom, whose bristles will not break off (see *Mishnah Berurah* 337:14).]

Washing an earthen floor is also prohibited due to the possibility that one will come to level the floor. Here, too, the Sages extended the

prohibition even to non-earthen flooring. Although we explained above that in a city where most of the flooring is non-earthen, the prohibition against sweeping does not apply, some authorities maintain that this is not true of washing, and they prohibit washing of even the non-earthen flooring found in today's homes. The rationale for this distinction is that sweeping is a daily necessity, and prohibiting it on the Sabbath would be considered a hardship. Washing the floor, however, is not a daily necessity, and thus the Sages did not deem it necessary to permit it on the Sabbath.

A CLOSER LOOK AT THE SIDDUR

תפילות השבת

Once each week, we will use this section
to focus on the *tefillos* of the Sabbath.

In basic structure, the *Shacharis, Minchah,* and *Maariv* prayers of the Sabbath are similar, if not identical, to those of the weekdays. The *Shemoneh Esrei* Prayers, however, are very different. The central section of the weekday *Shemoneh Esrei,* which consists of thirteen blessings that contain supplications for personal and communal needs, is omitted on the Sabbath, for the Sages wished to make the Sabbath prayers shorter and simpler (see *Berachos* 21a); moreover, on the Sabbath, when we are enjoined to turn away from pursuit of our livelihood, personal requests are less appropriate (*Midrash Tanchuma, Vayeira*). Instead, the Sages inserted a single blessing called קְדוּשַׁת הַיּוֹם, which speaks of the holiness of the day. Furthermore, unlike the weekday *Shemoneh Esrei* Prayers, which are identical for the three daily prayers, the Sabbath *Shemoneh Esrei* changes with each prayer, as the central blessing for each prayer deals with a different thought. The Friday night blessing (אַתָּה קִדַּשְׁתָּ) speaks of the world's creation and the first Sabbath; the Sabbath morning blessing (יִשְׂמַח מֹשֶׁה) speaks of the Sabbath on which the Torah was given; and the *Minchah* blessing represents the future Sabbath of the times of the Mashiach.

R' *Munk* (*World of Prayer*) notes that all three blessings contain a single expression — וְיָנוּחוּ בָהּ יִשְׂרָאֵל מְקַדְּשֵׁי שְׁמֶךָ, *and may Israel, the sanctifiers of Your Name, rest upon it.* However, according to *Magen*

Avraham (Orach Chaim 268:3), there are minor varia-
tions in the phrase. On Friday evening, we say וְיָנוּחוּ בָהּ,
using the feminine form; on Sabbath morning we say
וְיָנוּחוּ בּוֹ, using the masculine form; and at *Minchah* we
say וְיָנוּחוּ בָם, in the plural. *R' Munk* explains that this
change reflects the subject of each blessing. The Friday
night blessing deals with the Sabbath of Creation, which
was similar to a lonely woman without a husband — for a nation to
observe the Sabbath and realize its potential was not yet in existence.
Thus, the feminine form is used. The morning blessing speaks of the
Sabbath when the Torah was given, and at that time, the Jewish nation
was regarded as the *kallah,* and the Torah (and the Sabbath) as the
chassan — thus, we speak of the Sabbath as masculine. And the Sabbath discussed in the *Minchah* prayer speaks of the future, when *all* of
the days will have the serenity and holiness of the Sabbath. Therefore,
we use the plural form.

These three themes — Creation, the Giving of the Torah, and the time
of the ultimate redemption — must all be personified in our observance
of the Sabbath. We are obligated to sanctify the Sabbath with the recital
of *Kiddush,* which relates that Hashem created the world in six days and
rested upon the seventh. It is during the Sabbath, when we rest from our
weekday endeavors, that we can reflect upon the fact that it is Hashem
Who grants us all that we possess.

The restful atmosphere of the Sabbath is also conducive to Torah
study and contemplation. During the week, one is often distracted by his
pursuit of a livelihood from pursuing his spiritual goals. Indeed, *R' Simcha Zissel Ziv* noted that man's constant striving is the source of all his
woes, for when he rushes from goal to goal, he cannot evaluate his
actions and change his direction, if he must. On the Sabbath, however,
we are given the gift of holy, blessed *menuchah* — the opportunity to
take stock, assess the spiritual content of our lives, and adjust our
priorities and orientation as necessary.

Finally, the Sabbath is מֵעֵין עוֹלָם הַבָּא, *a semblance of the World to
Come.* The curse of בְּזֵעַת אַפֶּיךָ תֹּאכַל לֶחֶם, which requires us to toil to earn
our daily bread, is suspended (see *Pri Tzaddik, Bo* §10), and we are free to
enjoy our closeness to Hashem, just as we will in the World to Come.

QUESTION OF THE DAY:

*What Torah prohibition (other than murder) can be
connected to the episode of Kayin and Hevel?*

For the answer, see page 53.

וַיְהִי־נֹחַ בֶּן־חֲמֵשׁ מֵאוֹת שָׁנָה וַיּוֹלֶד נֹחַ אֶת־שֵׁם אֶת־חָם וְאֶת־יָפֶת

When Noach was five hundred years old, he begat Shem,
Cham and Yefes (Bereishis 5:32).

*R*ashi cites the question of *Midrash Rabbah* (26:2): Why is it that all of the generations before Noach fathered children at the much younger age of approximately 100 years, while Noach had no children until the age of 500? The Midrash answers that this occurred because Hashem had mercy on Noach. Hashem reasoned: A flood is soon to come. If I give children to Noach in his youth, and they are wicked, they will be destroyed in the Flood, and this will cause him grief. And even if they are righteous, his descendants will be great in number by the time the Flood will occur, and he will have to construct a multitude of Arks to save them all! Accordingly, he made Noach infertile during the beginning of his life, until he was 500 years old. This ensured that the oldest of his children would be less than 100 years old at the time the Flood commenced; and in the times before the Torah was given, a person was not liable to Divine punishment until the age of 100 (see *Yeshayah* 65:20). Thus, even if his children were to be wicked, Noach's merit would be able to save them.

Tanchuma, however, cites an opinion that Noach was not infertile; rather, he intentionally abstained from fathering children because he foresaw that the world would be corrupt, and he did not wish to bring children who would anger Hashem into the world. However, when he reached the age of 500, he realized that he might well die childless, and Hashem had commanded man to be fruitful and multiply. Thus, he relented, and fathered children (who, in the end, were the only ones to survive the Flood and repopulate the earth). [In *Bamidbar Rabbah* 14:12, these two approaches are interwoven. Noach voluntarily abstained from having children until Hashem revealed to him that the Ark would be built to save him from the Flood. At that point, 100 years before the Flood, he married and fathered Shem, Cham and Yefes.]

QUESTION OF THE DAY:
What other person mentioned in the Torah
held back from having children
because he was afraid they would not survive?

For the answer, see page 53.

The following Mishnah discusses other cases that are similar to the previous Mishnah's case, in that, before the Sabbath, work is begun that will continue unaided on the Sabbath:

אֵין נוֹתְנִין אוּנִין שֶׁל פִּשְׁתָּן לְתוֹךְ — *Beis Shammai say:* בֵּית שַׁמַּאי אוֹמְרִים הַתַּנּוּר — *We may not place bundles of flax into the oven*[1] אֶלָּא כְּדֵי שֶׁיַּהֲבִילוּ מִבְּעוֹד יוֹם — *unless* there is *enough* time *for them to become heated while it is yet day;*[2] וְלֹא אֶת הַצֶּמֶר לַיּוֹרָה — *nor* may we place *wool into a* dyer's *vat* אֶלָּא כְּדֵי שֶׁיִּקְלוֹט הָעַיִן — *unless* there is *enough* time *for it to absorb the color* while it is yet day.[3] וּבֵית הִלֵּל מַתִּירִין — *But Beis Hillel permit* starting these processes before the Sabbath, even if there is not enough remaining time for the bleaching or dyeing processes to be completed before the onset of the Sabbath.[4]

A similar dispute:

אֵין פּוֹרְסִין מְצוּדוֹת חַיָּה וְעוֹפוֹת — *Beis Shammai say:* בֵּית שַׁמַּאי אוֹמְרִים וְדָגִים — *We do not spread traps for beasts, birds or fish* before the Sabbath, אֶלָּא כְּדֵי שֶׁיִּצּוֹדוּ מִבְּעוֹד יוֹם — *unless* there is *enough* time *for them to have trapped* their prey *while it is yet day.*[5] וּבֵית הִלֵּל

--- NOTES ---

1. Were one to place bundles of combed flax in an oven to be bleached by the heat of the oven on the Sabbath, he would be liable for violating the *melachah* of מְלַבֵּן, *whitening.*

2. When the flax is sufficiently heated, the bleaching process is complete, and the flax may be left in the oven over the Sabbath.

However, as we saw in the previous Mishnah, according to Beis Shammai the Torah's prohibitions on Sabbath labor apply even to a person's vessels, and even when the labor that occurs within those vessels occurs automatically. Hence, according to Beis Shammai, if the bleaching is not completed by the onset of the Sabbath, he may not leave the flax in the oven, as he would be allowing the labor of kneading to take place in his vessel on the Sabbath (Gemara 18a).

3. צְבִיעָה, *dyeing,* is prohibited on the Sabbath. Hence, according to Beis Shammai, if the dyeing is not completed by the onset of the Sabbath, the wool may not be left in the vat, as he would be allowing the labor of dyeing to take place in his vessel on the Sabbath (Gemara 18a). However, once the wool has absorbed the dye, it may be left in the dyer's vat over the Sabbath.

4. As we saw in the previous Mishnah, according to Beis Hillel, the Torah's prohibitions on labor apply only to a person and his animals, but not to his vessels. Hence, he is permitted to leave flax in his oven, or wool in his vat, and to allow the labors of *bleaching* and *dyeing* to take place automatically in his vessel on the Sabbath (Gemara 18a).

5. צֵידָה, *trapping,* is prohibited on the Sabbath. Hence, Beis Shammai forbid a

מַתִּירִין — *But Beis Hillel permit* the spreading of such traps even if there is not enough time remaining before the onset of the Sabbath for the beasts, birds or fish to be trapped.[6]

───────────── NOTES ─────────────

person to spread his traps at a time which makes it inevitable that they will capture their prey on the Sabbath, as he would be allowing the labor of trapping to take place in his vessel on the Sabbath. If, however, it is clear that the trapping will take place before the onset of the Sabbath, spreading the traps is permitted. [For the details of this permit, see *Gems from the Gemara.*]

6. As above, since the Torah's prohibitions on Sabbath labor apply only to a person and to his animals, but not to his vessels, he is permitted to set traps and to allow the labor of *trapping* to take place automatically in his vessel on the Sabbath (Gemara 18a). [Not only do Beis Hillel allow vessels to perform labor on the Sabbath when they occur passively (such as *bleaching* and *dyeing*), but even when the vessels perform the labor actively, as in the case of *trapping* (*Tos. Yom Tov*).

GEMS FROM THE GEMARA

We learned in the last two Mishnahs that according to Beis Hillel, the prohibition against Sabbath labor does not extend to one's vessels. Thus, Beis Hillel are not concerned if a person owns vessels that perform *melachah* on the Sabbath (and it is thus never necessary, according to Beis Hillel, for a person to declare his vessels ownerless before the Sabbath, as it would be according to Beis Shammai [see *Gems from the Gemara,* Friday]).

However, the Gemara (18b) notes that there is one type of case where even Beis Hillel do not allow cooking to take place in one's vessels on the Sabbath — where a concern exists that the person will see the pot in the oven and stir up the coals that are in the oven, so that the cooking will be accelerated (thus violating the *melachah* of *kindling*). [This is not a concern with regard to ordinary pots of cooked food that are left on the fire, for Beis Hillel certainly allows this; there is no concern that a person would stir up the coals beneath a pot of food that is already cooked. The Gemara refers to foods that require many hours of cooking, which a person does not plan to use until after the Sabbath. In such a case, we are concerned that he will stir up the coals so that the food will be cooked by the end of the Sabbath.]

The Gemara seeks to reconcile this ruling with several of the permits mentioned in the Mishnah we just studied. For example: We learned (see above) that Beis Hillel allows the placing of bundles of flax into an oven before the Sabbath, even though the flax will continue to be heated during the Sabbath. Why, asks the Gemara, are we not concerned that the person will stir the coals under the flax, to spur the heating process?

The Gemara answers that an oven containing flax must be sealed, and opening it would ruin the flax. Since the coals are inside the sealed oven, he will not come to stir them up.

The Gemara then questions Beis Hillel's ruling permitting placing wool into a boiling vat containing dye. Wool need not be sealed into the oven — why, then, are we not concerned that a person might come to stoke the coals?

The Gemara answers that this is indeed a concern, and Beis Hillel do *not* permit leaving wool boiling in a vat over a fire on the Sabbath. Although the Mishnah states that leaving the wool in the vat over the Sabbath is permitted, this speaks only of a vat that was removed from the fire, and has merely been left to steep.

A MUSSAR THOUGHT FOR THE DAY

R' Chaim Shmulevitz, in his *Sichos Mussar* (5732:6), cites the Midrash discussed above (see *A Torah Thought for the Day*) and finds it puzzling. Can it be, he asks, that Hashem made Noach infertile for hundreds of years because of the worry that Noach would have many descendants, and this would cause him the bother of constructing many Arks? Surely the anguish that Noach must have suffered from experiencing centuries of childlessness must have been an even greater trial for him! Even the righteous Avraham Avinu exclaimed before Hashem: *What can you give me, if I am childless? (Bereishis* 15:2). Furthermore, if Noach's children were to be righteous, surely they would assist him in the construction of the necessary Arks; and since Noach built the one Ark without any assistance, how would having children to help him make the task harder?

R' Chaim answers that the salvation of Noach and his family was not provided by the Ark; it was provided by Noach himself. We find throughout history that ordinary, inanimate objects are given the power to behave in miraculous ways, when they are fueled by the dedication and *mesiras nefesh* of the righteous people who use them. Thus, the prophet Elisha told his attendant Geichazi to take his staff and use it to revive the son of the Shunamite woman who had died — and, if Geichazi had

believed in its ability, this would indeed have occurred (see *II Kings* 4:23 and *Radak* there). Similarly, when Nikanor was willing to sacrifice his life rather than allow the remaining door he had fashioned for the Temple to be tossed overboard, the storm that had threatened him vanished — and the first door miraculously followed the ship into port (see *Yoma* 38a).

The Ark would not have survived the Flood due to its seaworthiness; it was only the *mesiras nefesh* of Noach, who had been chosen by Hashem as the one human being worthy of saving mankind, that was capable of imbuing the Ark with its lifesaving qualities. Thus, if ten Arks would have been needed, Noach would have had to build them all himself — and this would have been an impossible task. In the end, then, Noach would have had to watch some of his children die — and Hashem chose to spare him that grief.

HALACHAH OF THE DAY

We will conclude our discussion of the *melachah* of *plowing* by noting other instances where common actions may be forbidden as *plowing*. As noted previously, filling in a hole in uneven ground can be a violation of this *melachah,* and this is so even if it is not done with specialized tools. Thus, some authorities forbid scraping mud from one's shoes onto an earthen surface. This is because a convenient way to scrape mud from one's shoes is to scrape the shoe against the lip of a depression in the ground. This will result in the filling of the hole and a leveling of the ground — a violation of *plowing.* To ensure that one will not come to violate the *melachah* of *plowing* in this manner, these authorities forbid scraping mud from one's shoes onto *any* earthen surface. Scraping one's shoes onto a paved or otherwise non-plantable surface, however, is permitted.

One is permitted to walk with a cane even if the tip of the cane makes holes in the ground. Similarly, one may walk on soft ground with high-heeled shoes even though they will form holes in the ground. Since these holes are depressions rather than true furrows, creating them does not violate the *melachah* of *plowing,* as explained above.

Playing with sand on the Sabbath can involve up to three possible prohibitions. First, sand and pebbles are ordinarily considered *muktzeh.* Second, there is the possible transgression of the *melachah* of *plowing.* And third, there is the possibility of transgressing the *melachah* of *building.*

Now, if the sand is in a sandbox, *muktzeh* is not an issue, since it has been designated for this use prior to the onset of the Sabbath. If the sand is dry and powdery, so that any depression formed in it will immediately collapse, then *plowing* or *building* are not concerns either. [In addition, most playground sand is not arable soil, and is not subject to the prohibition of *plowing*.] Accordingly, children may play in a sandbox that contains dry, powdery sand. If, however, the soil is moist and will hold sculpted shapes, children (who have reached the age where such *chinuch* is appropriate) should not play with it on the Sabbath, because their sculptures will not collapse immediately, and they will violate the *melachah* of *building*.

פרשת בראשית

SHABBOS

PARASHAS BEREISHIS

A CLOSER LOOK AT THE SIDDUR

Most editions of the *siddur* contain, after the weekday morning *Shacharis* prayers, a listing of the עִיקָרִים ג׳׳י, the Thirteen Principles of Faith as codified by *Rambam* in his *Commentary to the Mishnah* (*Sanhedrin,* Chapter 10). Many people follow the practice of reciting them daily; indeed, *Rambam* himself writes that one will not become imbued with them unless he constantly reviews and studies them. We will present one of the principles each week, and discuss it briefly.

The First Principle states:

אֲנִי מַאֲמִין בֶּאֱמוּנָה שְׁלֵמָה,
שֶׁהַבּוֹרֵא יִתְבָּרַךְ שְׁמוֹ הוּא בּוֹרֵא וּמַנְהִיג לְכָל הַבְּרוּאִים,
וְהוּא לְבַדּוֹ עָשָׂה וְעוֹשֶׂה וְיַעֲשֶׂה לְכָל הַמַּעֲשִׂים.
I believe with perfect faith that the Creator, Blessed is He,
creates and guides all creatures,
and that He alone made, makes, and will make everything.

Rambam explains that this principle requires that one must believe:
❑ That there is a Being, perfect in every possible way, Who is the ultimate Cause of all existence.
❑ That all existence is dependent on, and derived from, only Him.
❑ That it is inconceivable that He not exist; even if all else would cease to exist, He would remain, undiminished in any way.
❑ That only He is self-sufficient, and Unity and Mastery belong only to Him. He has everything He needs, and has no need of anyone or anything else at all.
❑ That everything else that exists, be it an angel, a star, or any other being or entity, depends on Him for its very existence.

פרשת
בראשית

SHABBOS

PARASHAS BEREISHIS

Rambam notes that we are commanded to believe everything embodied in this principle by the first of the *Aseres HaDibros* (Ten Commandments), which states (*Shemos* 20:2): *I am Hashem, your God.* He adds (in *Hil. Teshuvah* 3:7) that one who denies these truths is classified as a *min* (heretic). It is important to note that it is not sufficient simply for one to "believe," in the abstract, in these essential truths; his belief must permeate his being and affect his actions and the choices he makes in his life. Furthermore, one must strive to deepen his understanding of Hashem, and to strengthen his *emunah* at every opportunity, so that his faith is an integral part of his very being. This level of belief is illustrated in a famous story:

A great *talmid chacham* was sitting with his *talmidim*, when he suddenly asked them, "Do you believe in Hashem?" At first they were taken aback by the question, but after a moment a resounding "Yes!" issued from every mouth. "That's very interesting," said the rebbi, "because I don't believe in Hashem."

The students were dumbstruck by their rebbi's comment. How could he say that he did not believe in Hashem, God forbid? But the rebbi explained himself. "Do you all *believe* that you are sitting here with me now at my table? No, you do not! You all *know* that you are sitting here with me — it is not just a mere *belief*. By the same token, when I look at the wonderful world that Hashem has created with all its wonders, I don't just *believe* in Hashem — I *know* that He is the Creator. That is what true *emunah* requires."

ANSWERS TO QUESTIONS OF THE DAY

Sunday:

The Gemara in *Rosh Hashanah* (10b) records a dispute whether the world was created in Tishrei or in Nissan. However, *Tosafos* (ibid. 8a) and other Rishonim explain that this refers to the sixth day of Creation, when man was created; Creation *began* six days earlier. Thus, the anniversary of the world's creation is either the 25th of Elul, or the 25th of Adar.

Monday:

The prayer for rain that is added to the ninth blessing of *Shemoneh Esrei*, וְתֵן טַל וּמָטָר, is inserted (outside Eretz Yisrael) into the blessing starting from ninety days after the autumnal equinox.

Tuesday:

We find that the wife of Moshe Rabbeinu saved him from death by circumcising their son (see *Shemos* 4:24-25). Additionally, the Gemara in *Sanhedrin* (109b) tells us that On the son of Peles, who was originally one of those who wished to join Korach in rebellion against Moshe Rabbeinu (see *Bamidbar* 16:1), was persuaded by his wife to withdraw.

Wednesday:

The angel that attacked Moshe for failing to circumcise his son in a timely manner (see answer to Tuesday) was in the guise of a snake (see *Rashi* to *Shemos* 4:24); the Torah also mentions a plague of snakes that attacked the Jews when they complained about the manna (*Bamidbar* 21:6).

Thursday:

On the Sabbath. We find that the manna was gathered by the Jews on Friday in the same manner that it was gathered on the preceding five days; yet, when they returned home, they found that there was twice as much, although they did not attempt to collect more manna (see *Shemos* 16:22 with *Rashi*). This is one of the reasons that the Sabbath is referred to as מֵעֵין עוֹלָם הַבָּא, *a semblance of the World to Come.*

Friday:

Midrash Tanchuma (*Bereishis* §9) connects this episode to the prohibition against wearing *shaatnez* (a mixture of linen and wool). According to one opinion in the Midrash, Kayin's offering consisted of inferior flaxseed, while Hevel offered the finest wool of his flocks. Thus, Hashem said: It is not proper to mingle the offering of a sinner with the offering of the righteous.

Shabbos:

The Gemara in *Sotah* (12a) states that Amram, the father of Moshe, separated from his wife Yocheved when Pharaoh decreed that all male children would be killed. [However, when his daughter Miriam noted that his decree was worse than Pharaoh's, for it targeted even female children, he took his wife back — see Gemara there.]

פרשת נח

Parashas Noach

SUNDAY

אֵלֶּה תּוֹלְדֹת נֹחַ נֹחַ אִישׁ צַדִּיק תָּמִים הָיָה בְּדֹרֹתָיו אֶת הָאֱלֹהִים
הִתְהַלֶּךְ נֹחַ. וַיּוֹלֶד נֹחַ שְׁלֹשָׁה בָנִים אֶת שֵׁם אֶת חָם וְאֶת יָפֶת

These are the children of Noach; Noach was a righteous man, he was perfect in his generations — Noach walked with HASHEM. And Noach had sired three sons — Shem, Cham, and Yefes (Bereishis 6:9-10).

There are two separate questions that must be addressed with respect to these verses. First, why does the Torah list the sons of Noach here for a second time, after having done so earlier, in *Parashas Bereishis*? (see above, 5:32). Second, why does the Torah interrupt with the listing of Noach's praises before actually naming the three sons?

The commentators offer several answers to these questions. *Akeidas Yitzchak* and *Abarbanel* state that since Noach and his children were destined to be the sole survivors of the Flood, Noach was, like Adam, the father of mankind. For this purpose, the Torah lists him and his children again upon beginning the narrative of the Flood. *Radak* states that the Torah praises Noach for "walking with Hashem" before mentioning his children to indicate that Noach had trained his sons to do the same.

Rashi offers two explanations for the insertion of Noach's praises between the verse's opening statement (*These are the children of Noach*) and the actual naming of the sons. In his first interpretation, he states that having mentioned Noach, the Torah [accorded him honor and] praised him. In his second interpretation, however, *Rashi* understands the verse as teaching a lesson: that the real progeny of the righteous is not their physical offspring, but their good works. *Kli Yakar* expands upon this theme, citing a Midrash which states that Noach lived to see the world repopulated by seventy nations that descended from him alone; and yet, the Torah describes his primary offspring as his good deeds!

Ibn Ezra takes a different approach to the passage. He understands the words אֵלֶּה תּוֹלְדֹת נֹחַ to mean: *This is the history of Noach;* thus, there is no interruption in the verse at all, for it is perfectly natural to begin the story of Noach's life with a statement of his greatness. According to this interpretation, various solutions may be offered as to why his children are mentioned here for a second time (in addition to the approach of *Radak* cited above). *Sforno* states that Noach was given children as a reward for rebuking the members of his generation and attempting to persuade them to repent (even though he was ultimately unsuccessful). In addition, according to those authorities who maintain that Noach had children relatively late in life because of the coming Flood (see above, *A Torah Thought for the Day, Bereishis, Shabbos*), it can be understood why they are mentioned again here.

Another perspective on the mention of Noach's sons here can be found in *R' Shamshon Raphael Hirsch,* who notes that the name of each of the sons offers a clue to his nature. *Shem* (whose name means literally *name*) was the thinker, as man's wisdom lies in his ability to comprehend the nature of a thing and to define and "name" it. *Cham* (from חוֹם, *heat*) was the passionate brother; while *Yefes* (from פֶּתַח, *open*) was the seeker of beauty, open to influence from external impressions. The Torah lists the sons here to show that all these characteristics were deserving of being saved from the Flood, as all of them are valuable and can be used in the service of Hashem, when they are guided by the spiritual greatness of a Noach.

MISHNAH OF THE DAY: SHABBOS 1:7

The following Mishnah considers the prohibition of אֲמִירָה לְנָכְרִי, *telling a non-Jew,* to do work for a Jew on the Sabbath. [Although this prohibition is a Rabbinic decree, the Rabbis found an allusion to this law in the verse (*Exodus* 12:16): כָּל־מְלָאכָה לֹא יֵעָשֶׂה בָהֶם, *no labor shall be done in them.* The Torah does not state: "Do not do any labor," but, rather, "No labor shall be done," suggesting that a Jew should not be the cause of prohibited labor, even when if it is done by a non-Jew (*Mishnah Berurah* 243:5).

בֵּית שַׁמַאי אוֹמְרִים – *Beis Shammai say:* אֵין מוֹכְרִין לְנָכְרִי – *We may not sell* objects *to a non-Jew,*[1] וְאֵין טוֹעֲנִין עִמּוֹ – *nor help him load* his animal,[2] אֶלָּא כְּדֵי – *nor lift a load onto him,*[3] וְאֵין מַגְבִּיהִין עָלָיו – *unless* there is *enough* time *for him to reach a*

── NOTES ──

1. According to Beis Shammai, it is forbidden to sell an object to a non-Jew late on the eve of the Sabbath, because people who observe the non-Jew leaving the Jew's home or shop carrying his purchases may think that he is acting as an agent for the Jew, and will be carrying the objects on the Sabbath as an errand for the Jew (*Rav*).

2. It is also forbidden, for the same reason, to help the non-Jew load his donkey late on Friday afternoon, as people may think that the Jew is helping him because he will be transporting the load on the Sabbath as an errand for the Jew (*Rav*).

3. For the same reason, it is forbidden to help the non-Jew by lifting a load onto his shoulders late on Friday afternoon, as people may think that the Jew is helping him because he will be carrying the load on the Sabbath as an errand for the Jew (*Rav*).

nearby place before the onset of the Sabbath.[4]   **וּבֵית**
הַלֵּל מַתִּירִין — **But Beis Hillel permit** these activities.[5]

——————————— NOTES ———————————

4. Since the prohibitions that Beis Shammai promulgated here are based on the fact that it may appear that a non-Jew is performing labor on the Sabbath on behalf of a Jew, this concern does not apply if the non-Jew completes the labor before the onset of the Sabbath by arriving at his destination (*Rav*).

[According to *Rashi* (17b), the term כְּדֵי שֶׁיַּגִּיעַ לְמָקוֹם קָרוֹב means *unless his place is near enough to reach* before the Sabbath begins. For another understanding, see *Rashash.*]

5. Beis Hillel do not share Beis Shammai's concern that the non-Jew might appear to be performing a labor on the Sabbath on behalf of a Jew. Hence, all these activities are permitted (*Ran*). [However, even according to Beis Hillel, the non-Jew must leave the Jew's home before the onset of the Sabbath. Otherwise, it will appear that a transaction took place between a Jew and a non-Jew on the Sabbath (*Tos. Yom Tov*).]

GEMS FROM THE GEMARA

The Gemara (18b-19a) cites a Baraisa that enumerates three other disputes between Beis Shammai and Beis Hillel that parallel the dispute in our Mishnah:

(1) In a three-way dispute, Beis Shammai maintain that it is not permitted to sell, lend or give a gift to a non-Jew before the Sabbath unless the non-Jew has sufficient time to reach his home before the onset of the Sabbath. Beis Hillel maintain that it is necessary only that the non-Jew be able to reach the first house within the city in which the non-Jew resides before the Sabbath; and R' Akiva maintains that it is sufficient that the non-Jew leave the Jew's home before the Sabbath begins. [The prohibition against lending refers to both loans that will be consumed (such as loans of food or money) and lending of objects that must be returned.]

(2) Beis Shammai maintain that it is forbidden to sell one's *chametz* to a non-Jew before Pesach unless he knows that the non-Jew will have consumed all of it before Pesach arrives. Beis Hillel, however, maintain that it is permitted for the *chametz* to be in the non-Jew's possession on Pesach. Thus, up until the time that it is no longer permitted to eat *chametz,* it can still be sold to a non-Jew, although he will definitely not consume it before Pesach.

(3) Beis Shammai maintain that a Jew may send a letter with a non-

Jewish letter carrier before the Sabbath only if (a) a fee has been fixed, and (b) the letter will reach its destination before the Sabbath. Beis Hillel disagree, and maintain that if there is a fixed fee, the letter carrier need reach only the first house of the city that is the letter's destination before the onset of the Sabbath. [Where a fee has not been fixed, the non-Jew is considered to be working for the Jew, and even Beis Hillel agree that the letter may not be delivered on the Sabbath. If the fee has been fixed, however, the non-Jew is deemed to be acting in his own interest by delivering the letter on the Sabbath, and Beis Hillel therefore permit it.]

A MUSSAR THOUGHT FOR THE DAY

The *Alter of Slabodka,* R' Nosson Tzvi Finkel, would use Noach as an example of the far-reaching extent of Heavenly judgment. Consider, he would say, how righteous a man Noach was. The Torah itself testifies: *Noach was a righteous man; he was perfect in his generations; Noach walked with Hashem.* Could there be a more glowing description? Moreover, Noach was chosen from all mankind as worthy of being saved. It can even be said that, in a sense, during his year in the Ark he took on the task of emulating Hashem, in becoming the sustainer of all living creatures. He fed branches to the elephants and grass to the ostriches, all the while not sleeping at all (see *Tanchuma* §9).

Finally, as that long year drew to a close, Noach, who had become ill from the grueling physical labor (see *Tanchuma* ibid.), was once late when coming to feed the lion. Surely, Noach cannot be overly faulted for this slight lapse. Yet, what was the result? The lion attacked Noach, wounding him and rendering him blemished (see *Rashi* to *Bereishis* 7:23). [For this reason, the Midrash (*Bereishis Rabbah* 30:6) states that it was actually Shem, not Noach, who offered the sacrifices brought after the Flood.]

And what does the Midrash (*Tanchuma* ibid.) say about this punishment? "Of him (Noach) it is said in the verse (*Mishlei* 11:31): *Behold! The righteous man shall be paid* (i.e., punished for his sins) *while he is on the earth.*" Thus, we see that Noach is considered *fortunate* that he received his punishment in this world, rather than in the World to Come. This shows us, the *Alter* would say, the awesome extent of Hashem's judgment.

HALACHAH OF THE DAY

The *melachah* of קוֹצֵר, *reaping,* is the third of the thirty-nine *melachos* Biblically forbidden on the Sabbath. *Reaping* was required to harvest the herbs used to make the dyes needed in the Mishkan, and the wheat necessary for the *lechem hapanim* had to be reaped as well.

The definition of *reaping* is the uprooting or detaching of a living plant (or part of a living plant) from its source of growth. [The law regarding trees or fruits that have dried up but are still attached will be discussed below.] It is not necessary to uproot an entire plant to transgress the *melachah* of *reaping* – even removing a single fruit from a tree is *reaping,* though the tree remains attached to the ground.

Some examples of actions forbidden under the prohibition against *reaping* are: harvesting grain; breaking off a branch or tearing off a leaf from a tree; picking flowers, vegetables or fruits; and uprooting grass or weeds. The *melachah* applies equally whether the fruit is ripe or unripe, whether it is still growing, or it is fully mature and no longer has need of nutrition from the soil. Likewise, it makes no difference whether the plant is being detached for human consumption, animal fodder, fuel, seed, or any other use.

The *melachah* of *reaping* does not require the use of any specialized tools; one transgresses this prohibition even by plucking a plant from the ground with his hands.

The amount that must be detached for one to have violated the prohibition varies according to the purpose for which the reaping was performed. For instance, if one picked fruit for human consumption, the amount necessary for liability is the equivalent of a dried fig.

As a rule, one is Biblically liable for transgressing a *melachah* only if his act is a constructive one. Therefore, *reaping* is Biblically forbidden only when it is done for a constructive purpose, e.g., picking a fruit in order to eat it, or uprooting wood with the intent to use it as fuel. The Sages, however, forbade *reaping* on the Rabbinic level even when it is done for no purpose at all (as in the case of one who plucks from a tree a leaf of which he has no need).

The Biblical prohibition of *reaping* applies only if one detaches from the ground a plant that is already rooted in the ground. If, however, a seed or plant has recently been planted and had not yet taken root, nothing has been truly "detached," and a Biblical violation has thus not occurred. [It must be assumed that a seed has taken root if three days have passed since it was planted.] Even if a plant or seed has not yet taken root, the Sages forbade its removal from the ground, provided that it was placed there in order to take root and grow.

A CLOSER LOOK AT THE SIDDUR

Above (see *A Mussar Thought for the Day*), we noted that Noach's travails in the Ark are an eye-opening example of the extent of Hashem's judgment. The Chofetz Chaim notes in his *Toras HaBayis* (Ch. 8) that Dovid HaMelech himself stated that he feared the judgment of Hashem (*Tehillim* 119:120). Yet, three times each day we state in *Shemoneh Esrei* that Hashem is the King of Judgment! While it is true that we characterize Hashem not simply as the God of Justice, but as the God Who loves charity and justice, which implies that He will be charitable in His justice rather than strict, who can say that he is able to withstand even a small measure of Hashem's justice? Seemingly, this realization should cause every person to tremble in anticipation of the Day of Judgment; yet we find that even righteous and upright people are not affected in this manner.

The Gemara (*Megillah* 17b; see also *Tur, Orach Chaim* §118) notes that this blessing of the *Shemoneh Esrei* serves as a bridge to those that follow it — the blessings in which we request that the wicked be destroyed and the righteous exalted. This can be understood in light of our earlier discussion as well. In this world, the positions of the righteous and the wicked often seem reversed, with the wicked wielding power while the righteous are weak. However, this is often a result of Hashem's wish to reward the wicked for their few good deeds in this world, while punishing the righteous for their few misdeeds. When the ultimate redemption arrives, however, order will be restored; the wicked will be judged, and the righteous will be exalted.

QUESTION OF THE DAY:

By what other name was Shem, the son of Noach, known?

For the answer, see page 100.

MONDAY

PARASHAS NOACH

וַתִּשָּׁחֵת הָאָרֶץ לִפְנֵי הָאֱלֹהִים וַתִּמָּלֵא הָאָרֶץ חָמָס

And the earth had become corrupt before HASHEM,
and the earth became filled with robbery
(Bereishis 6:11).

*R*ashi, following the Gemara in *Sanhedrin* (57a), explains that the "corruption" mentioned in this verse is a reference to the sins of idolatry and immorality. We may ask two questions: Why does the verse characterize only the sins of idolatry and immorality as being committed "before Hashem," while making no mention of this concerning the sin of robbery? Furthermore, although it would seem that the sins of idolatry and immorality are more grievous than that of robbery, the Torah states (see v. 13 with *Rashi*) that the decree of the Flood was sealed due to robbery. Why was this so?

R' Dovid Feinstein explains that in human terms, it is easy for people to fool themselves into thinking that immorality and idolatry are not crimes at all, for they are apparently victimless crimes. After all, who is hurt when someone worships an idol? Who is affected by the "private" lives of consenting adults, even if they are relatives whose union is forbidden by the Torah? These sins are thus described as having occurred only "before Hashem," for the people thought of them as "individual" matters, which would not lead to "real" sin.

Hashem, however, knows otherwise. Thus, the verse continues: *and the earth became filled with robbery.* In the end, violence and banditry erupted into the public's attention in a way that no one could deny — not only "before Hashem." Finally, and tragically, it became clear that what had seemed to be only private acts of impropriety had broken down human decency so that civilization could no longer endure. The signs were present all along, but only Hashem knew what was happening.

If the sins of the generation had remained only in the private realm, sins between man and Hashem, then the world would have remained a viable place, and it would not have been deserving of such total destruction (as we find that the world was not destroyed in the time of Achav, despite the prevalence of idolatry). However, once the sin of robbery had become universal, there was no hope left for the generation, as they had conclusively proven that they could not coexist with one another. [See also *Ramban,* who adds that robbery is a sin against both Hashem and man, as it demonstrates not only a lack of regard for another's rights, but a lack of belief that Hashem provides each person with whatever he should rightfully possess.]

his Mishnah continues the theme of the previous one, citing other cases where Beis Shammai and Beis Hillel dispute what may be done on Friday afternoon:

אֵין נוֹתְנִין עוֹרוֹת לְעַבְּדָן — Beis Shammai say: בֵּית שַׁמַּאי אוֹמְרִים — We may not give hides to a non-Jewish **tanner** for tanning, **וְלֹא כֵלִים לְכוֹבֵס נָכְרִי — nor** may we give **clothing to a non-Jewish launderer** to be washed,[1] **אֶלָּא כְּדֵי שֶׁיֵּעָשׂוּ מִבְּעוֹד יוֹם — unless** there is **enough** time **for them to be done while it is yet day.** [2] **וּבְכוּלָן בֵּית הִלֵּל מַתִּירִין עִם הַשֶּׁמֶשׁ — But in all these** cases, **Beis Hillel permit** giving the items to a non-Jewish tradesman **while the sun** is still up, although the non-Jew will do the work on the Sabbath.[3]

――――――――――― NOTES ―――――――――――

1. According to Beis Shammai, it is forbidden for a Jew to contract with a non-Jewish tanner or launderer late on the eve of the Sabbath to work on his [the Jew's] hides or clothing, because people who observe the transaction may think that the Jew is commissioning the non-Jew to perform forbidden labor (*tanning* is one of the thirty-nine *melachos,* and laundering clothes is forbidden under the *melachah* of *whitening*) for him on the Sabbath (*Tosafos* 18b).

2. If there is still enough time for the non-Jew to *potentially* complete the work before the onset of the Sabbath, it does not appear that the Jew is commissioning the non-Jew to do the work for him on the Sabbath. Accordingly, even Beis Shammai permit contracting with him to do the work in such a case — even if, in practice, the non-Jew will perform the task on the Sabbath. That the non-Jew will actually *perform* the work on the Sabbath does not concern Beis Shammai, since it is understood that he is not doing so at the Jew's direction, but for personal convenience. [Moreover, the work performed by the non-Jew upon the Jew's hides or clothing on the Sabbath does not in any way violate their ruling concerning *shevisas keilim,* since that forbids only labor performed *by* the vessels of a Jew, not labor performed *upon* them (*Tosafos* 18b, *Ran*).]

3. Beis Hillel permit the Jew to contract with the non-Jewish tanner or launderer any time right up to the onset of the Sabbath (even if there is not enough time remaining for the non-Jew to complete the work). [The term *all of these* used in the Mishnah here refers not only to the cases of tanning and laundering, but to all the cases in Mishnayos 5-8 (*Tos. Yom Tov*).]

QUESTION OF THE DAY:

Why, when describing the sins of the generation of the Flood, does the verse state that the earth became corrupt, rather than stating that the people were corrupt?

For the answer, see page 100.

Our Mishnah, as well as the other Mishnahs in this series, discuss cases where a person may be forbidden to contract with a non-Jew to work for him shortly before the Sabbath. The Gemara (19a) cites several cases where this prohibition applies for a longer period of time:

(1) A person may not rent his vessels to a non-Jew at any time on Friday. The rental must begin no later than Thursday, since if the rental takes place on Friday it appears as if the Jew is renting the vessels to the non-Jew for use on the Sabbath (*Rashi*).

In general, *any* rental of vessels to a non-Jew for use on the Sabbath is forbidden (even according to Beis Hillel, who does not subscribe to the decree of *shevisas keilim* — see *Tosafos*), because taking money for a service provided on the Sabbath has the semblance of conducting business on the Sabbath. However, this prohibition applies only if the Sabbath rental payment is distinct (e.g., the article is rented by the day). But if the Sabbath rent is "swallowed up" in a longer period (this is known as *havlaah*), such rental is permitted, even though the rental fee for the Sabbath is included in the payment. Here, the Gemara teaches us that the permit of *havlaah* is not effective if the rental is begun on Friday, because it appears that the rental is being contracted for Sabbath use (even if the rental fee is calculated on a weekly or monthly basis).

(2) Similarly, a non-Jewish letter carrier or courier who is being paid for his time (e.g., by the hour) may not be hired on Friday to deliver a letter if he cannot do so before the Sabbath begins, for it appears as if he is carrying the letter as the agent of the Jew, which is forbidden. Hence, the letter must be given to him no later than Thursday. [For the law in a case where the letter carrier is *not* being paid for his time, see the previous Mishnah.]

(3) A person may not embark upon a journey by ship less than three days before the Sabbath (unless he is traveling for the purpose of a mitzvah). [The authorities differ as to how the three-day period is reckoned; some include the Sabbath, and permit setting out even on Thursday, others require that the voyage must have begun on Wednesday (three days before the Sabbath), while others forbid setting out later than Tuesday (see *Beis Yosef, Orach Chaim* §248).

The *Rishonim* cite several reasons for this prohibition. *Rif* explains that the Rabbis prohibited sea travel three days before the Sabbath because people are prone to seasickness during the first three days of a voyage, and one cannot enjoy the Sabbath properly while seasick. *Tosafos*

explain that sea travel falls under the Rabbinic decree
against swimming on the Sabbath or Yom Tov (see
Beitzah 36b). And *Baal HaMaor* explains that the Rabbis
were concerned that a seafarer would likely have to
perform *melachah* to preserve his life while at sea. Although this is permitted (and even required) in a situation where one's life is threatened, it is nevertheless

better to avoid placing oneself into such a situation (and three days
before a Sabbath is already considered close enough to the Sabbath to
have to worry about this possibility [see *Pesachim* 106a]).

A MUSSAR THOUGHT FOR THE DAY

Robbery and thievery are sins that the average person does not usually feel he has transgressed. Yet, we find that the most righteous of
men feared transgressing these prohibitions. As the Gemara states in
Chullin (91a; see *Rashi* to *Bereishis* 32:25): The righteous treat all of their
property with care, so that they should not send forth their hands in theft.
For this reason, Yaakov crossed back over the river to retrieve some
small jars he had left behind, although he thereby exposed himself to
danger (and was ultimately attacked). Why are righteous men so concerned, while most of us are not?

One answer lies in the fact that we are not careful enough in determining what is ours and what is not. People will often assume that they have
a right to help themselves to items that they have been given for a
certain purpose, even though they are not using them for that purpose.
But this, too, is thievery! Witness the behavior of a *gadol* in this regard:
The electricity in the home of R' Eliyahu Dushnitzer, the renowned
mashgiach of the Lomza Yeshivah, was paid for by the yeshivah. Due to
this, he was always extremely careful to use as little electricity as possible. Whenever he would learn Torah late into the night, he would shut off
the electric lamp and light a kerosene lamp in its stead. When asked why
he did this, he would reply: "Who knows? Perhaps I will fall asleep while
learning, and the electricity will continue running at the yeshivah's ex-
pense for no reason!"

Another point: *R' Moshe Feinstein* would often note that thievery has
its roots in a lack of *emunah*. One who truly believes that Hashem
provides for him and will gives him what he requires will never resort to
thievery, for it can accomplish nothing; all things, whether acquired

legally or illegally ultimately come from Hashem. Thus, while the average person will not be guilty of openly stealing, the very belief that a person is in control of determining what possessions he will have is connected to the sin of thievery.

HALACHAH OF THE DAY

We will now discuss some common situations that would involve the *melachah* of *reaping.*

When a person walks upon vegetation, it is possible that in the course of his walking he may uproot some of the growth beneath his feet. As mentioned previously, one is liable for transgressing a *melachah* only if he had intent to do so, or if the forbidden act is an *inevitable* consequence of his action. Thus, walking upon grass or the like, which *may* result in uprooting, but may not, is permitted, since the person does not intend to uproot anything, and the uprooting is not inevitable. However, walking upon delicate or brittle plants that will *certainly* become detached as a result would be forbidden, as their uprooting is an *inevitable consequence* of his action. [Still, the violation would not be a Biblical one unless he needed the detached plants for a constructive purpose.]

The *melachah* of *reaping* applies even to growth that does not actually come from the ground. For example, it is prohibited to detach mushrooms from where they are growing even though they do not draw sustenance from the ground. Similarly, it is forbidden to scrape algae from the walls of a fishtank on the Sabbath, since one thereby separates the algae from its place of growth.

Flowerpots present a special category with regard to these laws, and the following introduction is necessary: The halachah recognizes two distinct types of flowerpots — an עָצִיץ נָקוּב, *perforated flowerpot,* and an עָצִיץ שֶׁאֵינוֹ נָקוּב, *non-perforated flowerpot.* A plant in a perforated flowerpot is considered to be attached to the ground, because the hole in the pot allows the plant to draw nutrition from the ground beneath it. It does not matter whether the hole is in the bottom of the pot or on its side; as long as it is at least the size of a small root, the pot is considered perforated, and therefore it is viewed as attached to the ground. Moreover, the pot need not even be resting upon the ground to attain this status; as long as it is suspended above the ground, at any height, it is deemed as attached if there is no obstruction between the pot and the ground. In addition, a plant whose leaves extend beyond the walls of the pot, so that *they* are directly above the ground, is also considered to be attached to the ground even if the pot is *not* perforated, for the plant can draw nutrition from the ground through its leaves.

A plant in a non-perforated pot, whose leaves do not extend beyond its confines, is unable to draw nutrition from the ground. Therefore, it is not considered attached to the ground with respect to the Sabbath laws. [It should be noted that there is extensive debate in the *Rishonim* with respect to the exact parameters of these laws, which are beyond the scope of this discussion.]

Tomorrow, we will learn how these distinctions relate to the *melachah* of *reaping*.

A CLOSER LOOK AT THE SIDDUR

Although the severity of the sin of robbery and theft is underscored by the fact that it is mentioned not once, but twice, in the *Shemoneh Esrei* of *Neilah* which we recite on Yom Kippur (לְמַעַן נֶחְדַל מֵעֹשֶׁק יָדֵינוּ, *in order that we be spared [the punishment due us for] the oppression of our hands,* which is a reference to illegally withheld money belonging to others), we do not ask Hashem directly, during the daily prayers, to protect us from the sin of theft. We do find, however, a prayer in which we beseech Hashem to protect us from *all* sin. This prayer is contained in the last of the morning blessings, and contains the request, וְאַל תְּבִיאֵנוּ לֹא לִידֵי חֵטְא וְלֹא לִידֵי עֲבֵרָה וְעָוֹן, which translates literally as: *and do not bring us to the hands of sin, nor into the hands of transgression and iniquity.*

R' Shimon Schwab makes two important points concerning this prayer: First, he writes that we do *not* mean to pray that Hashem should not *lead* us into sin, for such a request smacks of heresy; Hashem *never* leads people to sin. Rather, our request is that when we find ourselves faced with temptation, Hashem assist us in fighting our *yetzer hara,* so that we can overcome it and escape wrongdoing. Second, he writes that the three types of sins mentioned here — חֵטְא, עֲבֵרָה and עָוֹן — constitute a progression toward greater evil. חֵטְא is an unintentional sin; עֲבֵרָה refers to sins done as a result of habit, which one comes to consider permissible; and עָוֹן is deliberate, brazen sin. We pray that Hashem protect us from even the least of the three, as we know that one sin leads to another, and one who sins unintentionally will come to sin habitually, and ultimately to sin even willfully.

TUESDAY

PARASHAS NOACH

וַיַּעַשׂ נֹחַ כְּכֹל אֲשֶׁר צִוָּה אֹתוֹ אֱלֹהִים כֵּן עָשָׂה

*And Noach did so; in accordance with
all that HASHEM commanded him, so he did
(Bereishis 6:22).*

The verse ends with a repetitive phrase, *so he did,* to emphasize that Noach followed every specification of Hashem's commands scrupulously; he omitted nothing, and did exactly as Hashem told him to do (*Ramban, Radak*).

R' Mordechai Gifter (in his *Pirkei Torah*) notes that when Noach entered the Ark, the verse (7:5) simply states, *And Noach did so, in accordance with all that Hashem commanded him,* without the additional phrase, *so he did,* that is found in our verse. Why, he asks, is the extra phrase omitted there?

He explains that the term *so he did* denotes an act performed precisely as commanded, with the only motivation being the fulfillment of the command itself. When Noach built the Ark, he did so exactly as commanded, with his only stimulus being his desire to fulfill the will of Hashem. When he entered the Ark, however, he was not motivated purely by his wish to perform the Divine Will; the Torah states that he entered the Ark *because of the waters of the Flood* (7:7). Noach entered the Ark only when the rising waters compelled him to do so; indeed, the Midrash (*Bereishis Rabbah* 32:7) therefore notes that Noach's faith was less than perfect.

This, however, still requires explanation. Why was Noach's faith deemed less than perfect simply because he entered the Ark only when the waters began to rise? There was no reason for him to enter earlier!

R' Gifter explains that the verse does not state that Noach entered the Ark *when* the waters forced him to do so; rather, it states that he entered *because* of the floodwaters. One who possesses an absolute belief in Hashem, he states, cannot be affected by external stimuli; his motivation to fulfill Hashem's will is such that no other reason can strengthen it. From the fact that the waters could move Noach to greater urgency, it was clear that his faith, while great, was not absolute; if it had been, the sight of the rising water would have had no effect upon him at all. For this reason, the verse does not repeat the supreme praise, *so he did,* that is stated in the earlier verse, in connection with the construction of the Ark.

The Mishnah cites an instance where the view of Beis Shammai was followed:

אָמַר רַבָּן שִׁמְעוֹן בֶּן גַּמְלִיאֵל — *Rabban Shimon ben Gamliel said:* נוֹהֲגִין הָיוּ בֵּית אַבָּא — *They were accustomed in my father's household* שֶׁהָיוּ נוֹתְנִין כְּלֵי לָבָן לְכוֹבֵס נָכְרִי — *that they would give white clothes to a non-Jewish launderer* שְׁלֹשָׁה יָמִים קוֹדֶם לַשַּׁבָּת — *three days before the Sabbath.* [1]

The Mishnah identifies an instance where Beis Shammai and Beis Hillel are in agreement:

וְשָׁוִין אֵלוּ וָאֵלוּ — *And both these and those* [Beis Shammai and Beis Hillel] *concur,* שֶׁטּוֹעֲנִין קוֹרַת בֵּית הַבַּד וְעִגּוּלֵי הַגַּת — *that we may place the beam of the olive-press* on crushed olives *and the circular planks of the wine-press* on crushed grapes[2] on the eve of the Sabbath, even though they will continue to press oil and juice from the fruits on the Sabbath itself.[3]

--------------------------------------- NOTES ---------------------------------------

1. Although the halachah is in accordance with Beis Hillel that clothing may be given to a non-Jewish launderer until right before the onset of the Sabbath (see the previous Mishnah), Rabban Gamliel's family conducted themselves in accordance with the more stringent opinion of Beis Shammai, and gave clothing out to the non-Jewish launderers to be cleaned only when they could be finished before the Sabbath. Moreover, white clothes are more difficult to clean than colored clothes, and require three days of cleaning. Thus, they were accustomed to give the clothes to the launderer three full days before the Sabbath (*Rav*).

2. The first step in the production of olive oil and wine is the crushing or grinding of the fruit. The pulp is then placed in a large vat, and a heavy beam (or planks) is lowered onto the crushed mass of pulp, to press out the oil or juice.

3. The primary extraction of the juice from the fruit is deemed as having already been accomplished by the initial crushing or grinding, as from that time onward the juice will inexorably flow from the fruit even without further processing; the weight of the beam or the planks only hastens and expedites the flow. Since the forbidden labor of מְפָרֵק, *extracting* (a derivative of the primary category of דִּישָׁה, *threshing*, which consists of detaching the kernel of the grain from its husk), applies only to the initial detaching of the juice from the fruit, only the crushing or grinding is forbidden by Torah law. Subsequent application of pressure to expedite the flow is prohibited only by Rabbinic decree.

In the case of the Mishnah, the initial crushing of the fruit took place before the Sabbath. Thus, placing the beam or the planks upon the pulp will only expedite the flow, something that is forbidden only by Rabbinic decree even on the Sabbath itself. For this reason, even Beis Shammai agree that one may allow the process to continue on its own into the Sabbath.

[Moreover, the fact that the pressing is being done by the beam or the planks of a Jew does not violate Beis Shammai's ruling concerning *shevisas keilim,* as that applies only to cases in which vessels perform labor that is a violation of Torah law.]

The Gemara (19a) cites a Baraisa that elaborates upon the practice of Rabban Gamliel's household: "R' Tzadok said: It was the custom of Rabban Gamliel's household that they would give white clothes to the launderer three days before the Sabbath, but colored clothes they would give the launderers even on Friday. And from their words we can derive that white clothes are more difficult to launder [properly] than colored ones."

The Gemara then relates an incident in which Abaye invoked the lesson learned from this Baraisa to avoid being swindled:

Abaye once gave an article of colored clothing to a launderer, and asked what the cost would be to launder it. The launderer responded that the price was the same as would be for a white piece of clothing of similar size. Abaye retorted, "The Rabbis have already anticipated you!" It is clearly seen from the Baraisa cited above that white clothing is more difficult to clean than colored clothing. Accordingly, the price for cleaning colored clothing should be lower, and anyone who charges as much for colored clothing as for white clothing is clearly a swindler.

Ben Yehoyada focuses on the closing words of the Baraisa cited above: "and from their words we can derive that white clothes are more difficult to launder than colored ones." He explains that with this phrase, R' Tzadok (the Baraisa's author) meant to address the following difficulty: The stringency adopted by Rabban Gamliel's family in giving the white clothes to a launderer a full three days before the Sabbath is not the halachah in practice. Why, then, did the Mishnah mention it? The answer is — precisely to teach us that white clothing is more difficult to clean than colored clothing. This is a practical piece of knowledge that *does* impact upon halachah, as it helps determine the proper price for laundering colored clothes.

A MUSSAR THOUGHT FOR THE DAY

The Torah states that Noach entered the Ark *because of the waters of the Flood*. As we learned above (see *A Torah Thought for the Day*), this is seen as an imperfection in Noach's faith, for he waited to enter the Ark until the waters forced him to do so. However, the *Brisker Rav* notes that there would seem to be a contradiction within *Rashi* with regard to this matter; for while *Rashi* in his commentary to *Bereishis* 7:7 does state this, two verses earlier *Rashi* writes that Noach did exactly as he was commanded with respect to his coming to the Ark!

Various commentators explain that there is no contradiction, for the first *Rashi* refers to *coming* to the Ark (which Noach did exactly as commanded) rather than entering it; alternatively, the first *Rashi* refers to the preparations that were necessary, such as the assembling of the animals and the provisions (see *Ohr HaChaim* and *Akeidas Yitzchak*).

The *Brisker Rav,* however, understands that the two statements of *Rashi* do not contradict one another. Indeed, he states, Noach was reluctant to enter the Ark until forced to do so by the floodwaters — still, the fact that he did so when prompted constituted doing exactly as Hashem commanded. With this, he explains, we are taught an important lesson — all people, no matter how great they may be, are affected by their surroundings, and the people with whom they live. Surrounded as he was by a generation of totally wicked people, even a supremely righteous individual such as Noach could not be characterized as *disobedient* for not entering the Ark immediately, for these people could not fail to affect him. True, he was not of *perfect* faith, as *Rashi* states; but it can be said of him nevertheless that he did as Hashem commanded — for his realization that the wicked were about to be punished spurred him to do as he was told. This too was considered "doing as Hashem commanded."

HALACHAH OF THE DAY

We will now continue our discussion of *reaping* as it applies to flowerpots. As was explained yesterday, a plant in a perforated flowerpot that is suspended above the ground is considered to be attached to the ground. Therefore, detaching a plant from such a flowerpot is equivalent to picking a fruit from a tree, and is Biblically forbidden. If, however, the flowerpot is located indoors, above a non-earthen floor, or if non-porous material (such as plastic) separates between it and the ground, then it is *not* considered as attached to the ground, and detaching a plant growing therein is prohibited only Rabbinically.

[One might ask: Why is detaching such a plant any different than detaching a mushroom or algae from its place of growth? Surely by picking it, one has detached it from its place of growth! The answer is that while it is normal for mushrooms or algae to grow while not attached to the ground, it is not normal for other plants to grow in this manner. Thus, *reaping* such plants is not akin to the *reaping* performed in the Mishkan, and as such it is forbidden only Rabbinically.]

Since a plant in a perforated pot suspended above the ground is deemed as attached to the ground, one need not pick a plant from the flowerpot to violate the prohibition — even if he picks up the entire pot and moves it indoors, he has also transgressed, as this effectively detaches the plant from its attachment to the ground. *Raising* the flowerpot is *not* a Biblical violation, because the plant can still draw nourishment from the ground. It is nevertheless prohibited Rabbinically, because one thereby *decreases* the amount of nourishment the plant is able to draw from the ground.

The above laws apply only to a perforated pot, or one whose leaves extend beyond the pot. A non-perforated pot is not considered attached to the ground, as we learned above; thus, picking a plant from such a pot is prohibited only Rabbinically. It is permitted to relocate such a pot from outdoors to indoors, because the plant in the pot was never considered attached to the ground (and since no act of detaching is being performed, the Sages did not prohibit this even Rabbinically).

It should be stressed that it is not necessary for something to be growing in soil for it to be subject to the prohibition of *reaping*. Often, children will come home from school with beans that have been placed in water to sprout, or they will be instructed to place a potato or an avocado pit into water so that it will strike roots. Once any of these items has struck roots, it is forbidden to remove it from the water, as to do so would be removing it from its place of growth. Similarly, if one places an *aravah* branch into water and it sprouts roots, it may not be removed from the water on the Sabbath.

A CLOSER LOOK AT THE SIDDUR

We do not speak of the Flood during our daily prayers (possibly because we concentrate upon praises of Hashem and our requests of Him, rather than episodes of sin and punishment). We do, however, find one mention of the Flood in *Kabbalas Shabbos,* where we recite the verse (*Tehillim* 29:10): ה' לַמַּבּוּל יָשָׁב וַיֵּשֶׁב ה' מֶלֶךְ לְעוֹלָם, *Hashem sat enthroned at the Flood; Hashem sits enthroned as King forever.* The commentators offer several interpretations of this enigmatic statement:

Rambam (*Moreh Nevuchim* I:11; see also *R' Shamshon Raphael Hirsch*)

explains that the first part of the verse comes to emphasize Hashem's absolute power, and His total control over
the world. Even as the cataclysmic forces of the Flood
ravaged the earth and destroyed all of its inhabitants,
Hashem sat on His throne on high, unaffected and un-
changed. The sinners were eradicated, and He continued with his plan, bringing forth the continuation of
mankind from the one man (Noach) whom He had determined to be
worthy. This theme continues into the second part of the verse; when
Hashem will eradicate the sinners upon the coming of the ultimate
redemption, that upheaval will also not affect Him in the least (*Rashi*).
Moreover, just as the Flood firmly established Hashem as the true King
in the eyes of all mankind, Hashem's destruction of the idolaters will
result in similar acknowledgment of His dominion (*Radak*). [It is this
ultimate and total acknowledgment of Hashem's mastery that we pray
for in the *Aleinu* prayer that ends every *Shacharis, Minchah,* and *Maariv*;
we pray that Hashem *remove the detested idolatry from the earth,* and that
He *utterly cut down the false gods*; as a result, *all humanity will call upon
Your Name, and all the earth's wicked will turn to You.*]

These interpretations translate the word יָשַׁב as meaning *sat,* in reference to Hashem "sitting" (as it were) on His throne. *Vayikra Rabbah*
(23:3), however, understands the word to mean *return* (as in *teshuvah*),
and explains that the verse refers to a period where Hashem actually
contemplated returning to destruction of the world, as had previously
occurred during the time of the Flood. This, says the Midrash, was the
situation as the Jews were asked to accept the Torah. Had they refused,
the world would have ceased to exist (see *Rashi* to *Bereishis* 1:31; see also
Rashi to *Tehillim* ibid., who cites a Midrash attributing these words to the
fearful nations of the world, who, upon witnessing the thunder and
lightning of the Revelation at Sinai, wonder whether God was *returning*
to destroy the world with another Flood). However, Hashem saw that the
Jews willingly accepted the Torah and His Kingship forever — thus, the
world was spared in their merit.

פרשת
נח

TUESDAY

PARASHAS
NOACH

QUESTION OF THE DAY:

*With regard to one mitzvah, we request of Hashem every
day that we merit to fulfill it lishmah (for the sake of the
mitzvah itself, without any ulterior motives).
Which mitzvah is this?*

For the answer, see page 100.

TUESDAY — PARASHAS NOACH / 73

וַיִּגְוַע כָּל בָּשָׂר הָרֹמֵשׂ עַל הָאָרֶץ בָּעוֹף וּבַבְּהֵמָה וּבַחַיָּה
וּבְכָל הַשֶּׁרֶץ הַשֹּׁרֵץ עַל הָאָרֶץ וְכֹל הָאָדָם

*And all flesh that moves upon the earth died — among
the birds, and the cattle, and the wild beasts,
and all the things that creep upon the earth,
and all mankind (Bereishis 7:21).*

The progression of this verse is difficult to understand. Seemingly, the most important aspect of the Flood was the destruction of mankind — yet man is listed last! [Indeed, we find that in verse 23 man is listed *first.*] What is the meaning of this seemingly inverted order?

Malbim explains (see also *Haamek Davar*) that the verse lists the creatures in the order in which they were overcome by the Flood. The birds were overcome first, because they were frail, and perished in the initial downpour of the waters. They were followed by the domestic animals, who were situated on the low-lying plains that were inundated first by the floodwaters. The wild beasts survived a bit longer, for many of them dwelled in caves that were high in the mountains, which could provide them with shelter from both the lower and the upper waters. However, they, too, ultimately perished when the waters reached the mountain peaks. Man, who possessed the greatest intelligence, survived longest, because he used every means available to him to try and survive, including scaling the highest mountains, climbing the tallest trees, and building rafts and the like. Indeed, there were individuals who survived longer than others. But by the time the waters reached their highest point of 30 cubits above the mountain peaks, the last man (other than those in the Ark) succumbed.

[Although the floodwaters did not enter Eretz Yisrael, the people and animals living there died as well. The Gemara in *Zevachim* (113b) explains that the intense heat generated by the floodwaters made the entire world as hot as a furnace, and all air-breathing creatures perished (see also *Rashi* there). However, the fish were not affected by the heat of the waters, either because they were able to escape to the depths of the sea, which remained cool (*Ramban*), or because they had received a special blessing from Hashem that enabled them to survive (*Rabbeinu Bachya*).]

Me'am Loez suggests that Hashem engineered the events of the Flood so that man would expire last, to give mankind one final opportunity to repent.

MISHNAH OF THE DAY: SHABBOS 1:10

The Mishnah discusses whether one may begin to cook items on Friday afternoon that will continue to cook on the Sabbath:

אֵין צוֹלִין בָּשָׂר בָּצָל וּבֵיצָה — *We may not roast meat, onions or eggs* on the eve of the Sabbath אֶלָּא כְּדֵי שֶׁיִּצוֹלוּ מִבְּעוֹד יוֹם — *unless* there is *enough* time *for them to become roasted while it is yet day.* [1] אֵין נוֹתְנִין פַּת לַתַּנּוּר עִם חֲשֵׁכָה — *We may not place bread in the oven close to nightfall,* i.e., the onset of the Sabbath, וְלֹא חֲרָרָה עַל גַּבֵּי גֶחָלִים — nor may we place *a biscuit upon coals* to bake, אֶלָּא כְּדֵי שֶׁיִּקְרְמוּ פָּנֶיהָ מִבְּעוֹד יוֹם — *unless* there is *enough* time *for its "face" to form a crust while it is yet day.* [2] רַבִּי אֱלִיעֶזֶר אוֹמֵר — *R' Eliezer says:* כְּדֵי שֶׁיִּקְרוֹם הַתַּחְתּוֹן שֶׁלָּהּ — There must be *enough* time *for its bottom* surface *to form a crust* while it is yet day.[3]

————— NOTES —————

1. It is forbidden to begin roasting meat, onions or eggs late Friday afternoon if there is not enough time before the onset of the Sabbath for them to become sufficiently roasted (see *Gems from the Gemara* for a discussion of what is considered sufficiently roasted in this context), because of a concern that a person may come come to stir the coals (thus violating the prohibited *melachah* of kindling) after the onset of the Sabbath. On the other hand, if these foods were sufficiently roasted before the onset of the Sabbath, the person may leave them roasting over the fire into the Sabbath, since there is no concern that a person will stir coals under food that is already roasted. [Although we learned in the previous Mishnah that Beis Hillel permit a person to begin an activity that involves forbidden labor on Friday even if it will continue into the Sabbath, there is no dispute between Beis Shammai and Beis Hillel regarding the prohibitions in our Mishnah. This is because even Beis Hillel agree that where there is a concern that one might come to stir coals on the Sabbath in order to hasten roasting, cooking, etc., the Rabbis decreed that such activities may not continue into the Sabbath (Gemara 18b).

2. Ovens in Mishnaic times were made of clay and were cone-shaped, with the wide end at the bottom (this design caused the heat to intensify as it rose toward the narrow opening at the top of the oven, and aided in the baking process). Loaves of dough would be stuck onto the oven's inside walls, and left there until they were baked. According to the opinion of the Tanna Kamma, once the "face" of the bread (i.e., the surface of the loaf that is not stuck to the oven wall, and is thus the side of the bread that is visible) or the biscuit has formed a crust, the baking is complete, and there is no concern that the baker may come to stir the coals, since, were he to do so, the bread or biscuit would burn (*Rav*).

3. According to R' Eliezer, once the bottom surface of the bread or biscuit — i.e., the surface that adheres to the wall of the oven or the coals — forms a crust, the baking is complete. Since the inner crust forms first (because it is in contact with the hot oven wall or the coals), R' Eliezer's opinion is the more lenient, for it allows the bread to be put into the oven closer to the onset of the Sabbath (*Rav*).

The Mishnah states that we may roast meat, onions or eggs on Friday unless there is sufficient time for them to "become roasted" before the onset of the Sabbath. The Gemara asks: What level of roasting is required for something to be considered "roasted" in this context?

The Gemara cites R' Eliezer in the name of Rav, who explains that once the food is roasted as much as the food of the robber Ben Derusai (who would often eat his food before it was fully cooked, due to the fact that he was constantly on the move, as a result of the uncertainties of his chosen profession) while it is still day, it may be left to roast further on the Sabbath. The *Rishonim* dispute the level of cooking required for "Ben Derusai's food": *Rashi* maintains that it must be half-cooked, while *Rambam* (*Hil. Shabbos* 9:5) maintains that one-third cooked is sufficient. [Once the food has reached this stage, we are no longer concerned that one will come to stir the coals to hasten its cooking, for he is confident that it will finish cooking on its own, without any help.]

The Gemara then cites other instances where food cooked to the Ben Derusai stage is considered "cooked":

(1) Any food that has been cooked by a Jew to the point of "Ben Derusai's food" is no longer subject to the prohibition of food cooked by an idolater (*bishul akum*), even if the idolater subsequently cooks it further. [Since the food is already considered cooked, any further cooking is deemed inconsequential.]

(2) Any food that has already been cooked to the Ben Derusai stage may be kept on top of a *kirah* on the Sabbath (an oven of a type that was common in Mishnaic times, which consisted of a cylinder filled with coals with room for a single pot on top of it) even if the coals of the *kirah* have not been swept out or banked. It is Rabbinically forbidden to keep a pot of food that is not considered cooked on a *kirah* on the Sabbath unless the *kirah's* coals have been swept away or covered with ashes to diminish their heat, lest one come to stir the coals (see Gemara 36b-37a). However, once food has been cooked to the Ben Derusai stage this is not a concern, for one will be confident that such stirring is not necessary, as explained above. Hence, it is permitted to keep such food even on a *kirah* whose coals have not been swept out or banked. [This reflects the view of the Tanna Chananyah. Other Tannaim disagree, and require that the food be *fully* cooked before it can be kept on such a *kirah*.]

A MUSSAR THOUGHT FOR THE DAY

We learned above (see *A Torah Thought for the Day*) that even as the floodwaters climbed above the mountaintops and all the birds and animals had perished, Hashem stood ready to accept the *teshuvah* of any desperate surviving man, should he repent. *Rambam,* in his *Hilchos Teshuvah* (7:6-7), discusses the amazing transformation in a person's very existence that *teshuvah* can bring about. To paraphrase his words:

"*Teshuvah* has the power to bring close those who were previously far away from Hashem. Yesterday, this sinner was viewed as a hated one before Hashem — repulsive, distanced and disgusting. Today, however, once he has done *teshuvah,* he is beloved and precious, a close and valued friend . . . How wonderful are the changes that are brought about by *teshuvah*! Yesterday, while this man was still an unrepentant sinner, he was separated from Hashem, the God of Israel. When he would cry out in prayer, his prayers were not answered, as the verse states (*Isaiah* 1:15): *even when you increase your prayers, I will not listen.* Even his mitzvos did not find favor before God, as it is stated there: *Who sought this from your hand, to trample upon My Courtyard?* Today, however, once the sinner has repented, he is closely connected to the *Shechinah* . . . When he cries out in prayer, he is answered immediately, and his mitzvos are accepted with pride and joy. Not only this, but Hashem eagerly awaits his good deeds, as it is stated (*Malachi* 3:4): *Then, the offerings of Judah and Jerusalem will be [once again] pleasing to Hashem, as they were in the days of old and in former years."*

[Of course, while Hashem accepts *teshuvah* from any person at any time, even in the most dire of circumstances, repentance is most valued when it is not the result of extreme duress or fear of retaliation. For a discussion of how one can begin to prepare oneself for *teshuvah,* see *A Closer Look at the Siddur.*]

QUESTION OF THE DAY:

What practical halachah may be derived from the fact that birds are much frailer physically than animals?

For the answer, see page 100.

As a safeguard against the possibility of a person inadvertently transgressing the prohibition against *reaping* on the Sabbath, the Sages prohibited various activities that may lead to reaping. One group of these activities is known as מִשְׁתַּמֵּשׁ בְּאִילָן, *"using a tree."* The Sages feared that by engaging in an activity that in some way involved the use of a tree, a person would often come dangerously close to transgressing the *melachah* of *reaping,* and might actually come to perform the *melachah.* Some of the activities that the Sages prohibited are: climbing a tree, leaning on a tree, placing an object on a tree, removing an object from a tree, shaking a tree, or even moving fruit that fell from a tree on Shabbos. Likewise, to distance people from the prohibition against *reaping* on the Sabbath, the Sages forbade touching certain types of plants, as well as riding animals on the Sabbath (lest one come to cut a branch with which to prod the animal).

It is forbidden to climb a tree on the Sabbath because this is categorized as using a tree. Swinging from a tree is similarly forbidden. If one climbed a tree on the Sabbath while unaware of the prohibition against doing so, he must get off the tree as soon as possible. He may not remain sitting upon the tree, for that, too, is deemed using the tree. [While climbing down is also a forbidden use of the tree, it is only a momentary use of the tree, while remaining in the tree would be a continuous act of violation. It is preferable, in such a scenario, to opt for the lesser transgression, which is climbing down from the tree.]

The law is different, though, for one who *intentionally* transgressed the prohibition against tree climbing on the Sabbath. If a person intentionally climbed a tree on the Sabbath knowing full well that such activity is forbidden, he must remain on the tree until the conclusion of the Sabbath. This is a penalty that was enacted by the Sages in order to prevent a person from transgressing the prohibition again at some future time. In such a case, it is permitted for others to give the person on the tree food, clothing, or other things he requires. However, these items must be given directly into the hands of the person on the tree, and not placed on the tree itself — for placing the items on the tree is itself a forbidden use of the tree.

Although the penalty requires the person to remain on the tree until the Sabbath is concluded, if the person on the tree must attend to his bodily needs, or if he feels that he will become ill if he remains on the tree until the Sabbath ends, the Sages are lenient, and allow him to descend prior to the end of the Sabbath.

In the fifth *berachah* of the *Shemoneh Esrei*, we ask Hashem to enable us to return to Him in repentance. The *berachah* opens with the words: הֲשִׁיבֵנוּ אָבִינוּ לְתוֹרָתֶךְ וְקָרְבֵנוּ מַלְכֵּנוּ לַעֲבוֹדָתֶךְ וְהַחֲזִירֵנוּ בִּתְשׁוּבָה שְׁלֵמָה לְפָנֶיךָ, *Return us, our Father, to Your Torah; and bring us close, our King, to Your service; and bring us back, in complete repentance, before You.*

It seems strange that we do not actually ask Hashem to help us to repent until the end of the *berachah*, first requesting assistance with respect to Torah and the service of Hashem. However, the sequence of these requests actually teaches an important truth about repentance — it cannot exist in a vacuum. Simply asking Hashem to stiffen our resolve to repent is insufficient, for simply making up one's mind to be better, while an admirable idea, is not likely to result in lasting repentance. The same situations, weaknesses and desires that caused one to fall short in the first place will all too often triumph once again. [Indeed, one of the three key components of *teshuvah* is עֲזִיבַת הַחֵטְא, *leaving the sin behind.* To do this properly, one must analyze his actions and determine what the underlying causes of his sins are — whether they are triggered by certain friends, circumstances, or locations. Only then he can avoid temptation and pitfalls.]

What, then, should one do to attain *teshuvah*?

The Gemara in *Kiddushin* (30b) teaches that Hashem provided us with a powerful tool to drive away the *yetzer hara* (evil inclination) — the study of Torah. Drag the *yetzer hara* into the study hall, advises the Gemara, and this formidable foe will crumble. The Gemara there also cautions that the *yetzer hara* is a wily adversary that man alone cannot overcome even by putting forth his finest effort. Only with Hashem's help is it possible to prevail over its attempts to entice us to sin.

In light of the lessons taught in this Gemara, the reason for the structure of our *berachah* becomes clear. We begin by asking Hashem to return us to His Torah, so that we may engage in its study and thereby combat the *yetzer hara*. Then, we request that He cause us to always remember and realize that He is our King, so that we will have the fortitude to act as His devoted servants, who are deserving of His aid. Only then, when we are possessed of the tools we require to vanquish the *yetzer hara* (Torah study and Divine assistance), do we ask that He assist us in reaching complete and lasting repentance.

וְלֹא מָצְאָה הַיּוֹנָה מָנוֹחַ לְכַף רַגְלָהּ
*But the dove did not find a resting place
for the sole of its foot . . . (Bereishis 8:9).*

*R*amban explains that although the mountaintops were no longer covered with water at this point (according to the chronology of the Flood in the opinion of *Rashi* and *Ramban,* the dove was sent out forty-seven days *after* the mountaintops first became visible), the dove still could not find a place to rest. For birds do not perch upon land that is bare of trees; rather, it is their nature to seek a branch upon which to alight. Since the dove could not find any trees, it returned to the Ark. [Later, when it was sent a second time, it returned with a freshly plucked olive leaf (see verse 11); this told Noach that even the relatively short olive trees were at least partially uncovered. And when the dove did not return at all, he realized that it has found trees in which it felt it could safely nest; this proved that the waters had receded.]

Sforno explains that although the mountaintops were no longer covered with water, they were still very wet and muddy, and the dove could not land upon them; it was for this reason that it returned to the Ark.

In many instances, we find that the Jews are likened to the dove. *Midrash Aggadah* notes that in our verse, the dove was sent away, but could not find a resting place, so it returned to the Ark. This, says the Midrash, will be the fate of the Jewish nation in exile as well. Although the Jews dwell among the nations in exile, they will find no rest there (compare *Eichah* 1:3); that is, they will not make the land of their exile into their true homes. Ultimately, just as the dove returned to the Ark because of the waters, the Jews will return to their land, driven by the pressures of the nations; and they will be welcomed back by Hashem, just as the dove was welcomed by Noach.

MISHNAH OF THE DAY: SHABBOS 1:11

*T*he Mishnah discusses cases where the decree taught in the previous Mishnah does not apply:

מְשַׁלְשְׁלִין אֶת הַפֶּסַח בַּתַּנּוּר עִם חֲשֵׁכָה — *We may lower the pesach* offering *into the oven close to nightfall* on Pesach Eve and allow it to roast on the Sabbath.[1] **וּמְאַחִיזִין אֶת הָאוּר בִּמְדוּרַת בֵּית הַמּוֹקֵד —** *And* similarly, ***we may ignite the fire of the bonfire of the*** Temple's ***Chamber of the Pyre*** on the eve of Sabbath even close to nightfall.[2] **וּבַגְּבוּלִין —** *But outside* ***the confines of the Temple,*** [3] **כְּדֵי שֶׁתֶּאֱחוֹז הָאוּר בְּרוּבּוֹ** — a pyre may be ignited only if there is ***enough*** time *for* ***the fire to take hold of most of it*** before the onset of the Sabbath.[4] **בְּפֶחָמִין כָּל שֶׁהוּא — רַבִּי יְהוּדָה אוֹמֵר —** *R' Yehudah says:* ***With charcoal,*** it is permitted to ignite the fire just before the onset of the Sabbath, as long as the charcoal ignites ***even slightly.*** [5]

------------------------------ NOTES ------------------------------

1. The *pesach* sacrifice is slaughtered during the afternoon of the 14th of Nissan. Its sacrificial parts (*emurin*) are offered atop the Altar, and the remaining meat is roasted and eaten in the evening (*Exodus* 28:8-9). The Mishnah teaches that if the first night of Passover coincides with the Sabbath, it is permitted to place the *pesach* into an oven immediately before nightfall, even though it will continue to roast on the Sabbath.

Although the previous Mishnah rules that, generally, meat may not be put up to roast late on the eve of the Sabbath unless enough time remains for it to become roasted while it is yet day, the Rabbis made an exception in this case. This is because all the people who are engaged in roasting the *pesach* sacrifice are extremely careful. Hence, should one person forget about the Sabbath and move to stir the coals, one of the other people will immediately remind him to stop. [Although this will not prevent a person from *willfully* violating the Sabbath laws, the intent of the Rabbinic decree was only to prevent a person from stirring the coals *inadvertently,* and in this case the extra care that is taken by those involved in the *pesach* will prevent this from occurring] (*Rav*).

2. The Chamber of the Pyre was a large chamber in the Temple, where a bonfire was always kept burning. The Kohanim, who walked barefoot on the marble floor of the Temple, would warm themselves in this chamber (*Rav*). [Here, too, no precautionary decree was necessary, because the Kohanim in the Temple were extraordinarily alert, and would always remind themselves not to stir the coals (*Rav*).]

3. In any place in Eretz Yisrael other than in the Temple [in the case of the *pesach*], a person may not ignite a fire on the eve of the Sabbath unless there is enough time for it to start to take sufficient hold before the onset of the Sabbath (*Rav*). [The term גְּבוּלִין, which literally means *in the boundaries,* is used to mean the rest of Eretz Yisrael other than the Temple precincts.]

4. If there was enough time before the Sabbath for a person to fully start the fire, it may be ignited and allowed to burn through the Sabbath. [In the case of a large fire, "fully started" means that the fire has taken hold of the wood to the extent that no more tinder is necessary, and the flame rises spontaneously (*Rav*); in the case of a fire that consists of only one log, most of its thickness and most of its circumference must be ignited before nightfall (*Tiferes Yisrael* from Gemara 20a).] However, if this requirement is not fulfilled, then a person is not permitted to warm himself by the fire, lest he forget and stir the coals, or move some sticks to make the fire burn better (*Ramban, Hil. Shabbos* 3:19).

5. Just as Kohanim are permitted to ignite a fire in the Temple shortly before the onset of the Sabbath, so too, anyone may ignite a charcoal fire shortly before the Sabbath. This is because fire that takes hold of even a small part of [the highly flammable] charcoal will usually continue to burn and spread without need to resort to the stirring of coals or the adding of more tinder (*Rav*).

GEMS FROM THE GEMARA

The Mishnah stated that the bonfire in the Chamber of the Pyre in the Temple may be ignited even close to nightfall on the Sabbath. The Gemara (20a) inquires: From where do we know this?

At first glance, the Gemara's question seems puzzling. The prohibition to kindle fires *before* the Sabbath begins is Rabbinic in nature, as we have learned. How, then, can there be a Scriptural source permitting this in the Temple? On the Biblical level, lighting a fire close to the Sabbath is permitted anywhere!

Pnei Yehoshua (ibid.) explains that the Gemara assumes that if the Rabbis did not forbid lighting the fire in the Temple before the Sabbath, it can only be because on the Torah level, even lighting the fire *on the Sabbath* would be permitted (and thus there was no reason for the Rabbis to issue a decree lest someone stir the coals, as this would be permitted). According to *Pnei Yehoshua,* it is for *this* rule that the Gemara seeks a source.

Rav Huna provides a source — the verse that states (*Shemos* 35:3): *You shall not kindle fire in any of your dwellings on the Sabbath day.* Rav Huna explains that the verse emphasizes *your dwellings* to teach that it is only in your dwellings that kindling a fire is forbidden; in the Temple it is permitted. Thus, the Rabbis did not forbid lighting a fire before the Sabbath in the Temple, for even if the fire were to die down and a person would come and stir the coals on the Sabbath, he would not be violating the Torah's prohibition.

Rav Chisda, however, takes issue with Rav Huna's explanation of the verse. If the Torah permits kindling a fire in the Temple, argues Rav Chisda, why did the Mishnah state only that the fire in the Chamber of the Pyre was kindled *close* to the Sabbath? It should be permitted to kindle it even on the Sabbath itself!

Rather, Rav Chisda says, although there is an indication from the verse that kindling a fire in the Temple is permitted, this refers specifically to the burning of the sacrificial parts and fats on the Temple Altar. This was indeed permitted even on the Sabbath. But the kindling of the fire in the Chamber of the Pyre, which existed solely for the comfort of the Kohanim, would not be permitted on the Sabbath.

According to Rav Chisda, the original difficulty returns: Why did the Rabbis permit the lighting of the bonfire close to the Sabbath, if it is indeed forbidden to stir the coals on the Sabbath? Why were they not concerned that this would come to pass? Rav Chisda explains that the Kohanim in the Temple were diligent and conscientious (*zerizim*), and the

Sages were not concerned that they would forget themselves and stir the coals after the Sabbath had begun (see *Rashi* there).

A MUSSAR THOUGHT FOR THE DAY

E arlier (see *A Torah Thought for the Day*), we mentioned the Midrash that states that just as the dove returned to the Ark because it could not find a resting place when it was initially sent from the Ark, the Jewish people (who are likened to the dove) do not find their resting place in exile, and so they will be privileged to ultimately return to Eretz Yisrael.

Tragically, this has not always been the case. On Tishah B'Av, we recite a *kinnah* concerning the destruction of the Jewish communities of the Rhineland — Worms, Speyer, and Mainz — in the year 1096, during the First Crusade. The *sefer Seder HaDoros* cites the explanation of the author of *Sefer Me'iras Einayim (Sma)* as to why such terrible destruction was visited upon the community of Worms. He writes that the *kehillah* of Worms was founded by Jewish exiles who made their way to Germany following the Destruction of the First Temple. After seventy years passed, many Jews from Babylon returned to Eretz Yisrael, but none returned from Worms. The community in Jerusalem wrote to the *kehillah* in Worms, urging them to join the new settlement in Jerusalem . . . but the complacent Jews of Worms rejected this invitation out of hand. Instead, they responded, "You stay where you are in the great Jerusalem, and we will continue to stay where we are in our little Jerusalem!" This arrogant response was due to the prosperity and prestige the Jews of that time enjoyed in the eyes of the local populace and their rulers.

The very success of Worms was its undoing. Satisfied to remain in exile, they saw no need to return to Eretz Yisrael. The crusaders, meanwhile, were willing to leave everything behind — homes, families, occupations — in their zeal to conquer the Holy Land they called Palestine. This aroused a terrible denunciation in Heaven against those communities, with tragic results.

QUESTION OF THE DAY:

On what day of the week did the dove find a resting place during its final mission?

For the answer, see page 100.

As we learned yesterday, it is Rabbinically forbidden to either sit or lean on a tree on the Sabbath. For the purpose of this prohibition, leaning is defined as using the tree to support one's weight in such a manner that if the tree would be removed, the person would fall. Leaning lightly against a tree is permitted, as long as the tree does not bend or sway as a result of the pressure being placed upon it. This type of leaning is permitted because it is not viewed as making use of the tree, and is therefore not included in the Rabbinic prohibition.

It should be noted that while this prohibition applies even to dead trees that are attached to the ground, one *is* permitted to sit on the dead stump of a fallen tree or one that has been cut down.

One is forbidden to place or lean objects on a tree or its branches on the Sabbath, because this too is considered using the tree on the Sabbath. For example, one may not hang his jacket or hat on the limb of a tree, or lean a chair against the trunk of a tree on the Sabbath.

The Sages prohibited removing an object from upon a tree on the Sabbath for fear that while removing the object, a person would come to lean on the tree for support. This prohibition applies both to objects placed on a tree during the Sabbath as well as to items placed on the tree prior to the Sabbath. Items that came to be on a tree unintentionally, such as a hat that blew onto a tree taller than three *tefachim,* may be removed on the Sabbath.

Included in the prohibition against using trees is using anything that is directly supported by a tree. For example, on the Sabbath one is forbidden to climb a ladder that is leaning against a tree. Since the weight of the ladder is supported by the tree, climbing the ladder is seen as a prohibited use of a tree on the Sabbath.

Something that is only *indirectly* supported by a tree, however, may be used on the Sabbath. For example, it is permitted to use a swing that is suspended from a hook that was screwed into a tree prior to the Sabbath. In this situation, one is not making direct use of the tree, for the swing is supported by the hook, and one is using the swing, not the hook. There are, however, two conditions that must be satisfied for this leniency to apply. First, the hook must have been attached to the tree *before* the swing is attached to the hook, so that it is clear that the swing and the hook are two different entities. If the hook and the swing were attached to the tree together, the swing is viewed as if it is directly attached to the tree, and using it will be forbidden. Second, the tree must be strong enough that it will not shake when the swing is being used.

This concludes our discussion of the *melachah* of reaping.

A CLOSER LOOK AT THE SIDDUR

This week, we will discuss the second of the Thirteen Fundamental Principles (י״ג עיקרים) enumerated by *Rambam.*

The Second Principle states:

אֲנִי מַאֲמִין בֶּאֱמוּנָה שְׁלֵמָה, שֶׁהַבּוֹרֵא יִתְבָּרַךְ שְׁמוֹ הוּא יָחִיד וְאֵין יְחִידוּת כָּמוֹהוּ בְּשׁוּם פָּנִים, וְהוּא לְבַדּוֹ אֱלֹהֵינוּ, הָיָה הֹוֶה וְיִהְיֶה.

I believe with perfect faith that the Creator, Blessed be His Name, He is unique, and there is no uniqueness like Him in any way, and that He alone is our God — He was, He is, and He will always be.

This second principle embodies the eternal truth of the concept expressed in the verse (*Devarim* 6:4): ה' אֱלֹהֵינוּ ה' אֶחָד , *Hashem is our God, Hashem is One.* "One" in this context means many different things. It means that Hashem is unique; there is no other like Him. In addition, it means that He is indivisible; unlike any physical thing, which can be broken down into smaller pieces or component parts, Hashem is One and will always remain complete.

Furthermore, although Hashem manifests Himself to the world in many guises, and one might mistakenly conclude that each of these attributes is representative of a different part of Hashem, as it were, this is not the case. Everything that was created in this world, and everything that occurs in this world, has at its source the One God; He is the sole Master and Guide of the Universe.

Rambam (*Hilchos Yesodei HaTorah* 1:7) links the concept of Hashem's unique Oneness to His qualities of eternity and limitless power. Such attributes, he writes, cannot exist in physical beings, for physical beings by their very nature decay and ultimately cease to exist; by the same token, their power also ceases to exist. As we know that Hashem's power is without end and He exists beyond time, it follows that He cannot be physical. The concept of division is rooted in physicality; thus, as Hashem is not physical, He is indivisible.

If one does not believe in the Oneness of Hashem, he will, God forbid, come to believe that there are many gods, each of which controls a specific part of Creation or time of year. This is a form of idolatry (and indeed was the system of belief in many ancient cultures). Thus, belief in this principle is central to proper belief in Hashem.

אֶת קַשְׁתִּי נָתַתִּי בֶּעָנָן
וְהָיְתָה לְאוֹת בְּרִית בֵּינִי וּבֵין הָאָרֶץ

*I have set My rainbow in the cloud;
and it shall be a sign of the covenant
between Me and the earth (Bereishis 9:13).*

Why did Hashem choose the rainbow as the symbol to recall His promise not to bring another Flood upon the earth?

Ramban explains that the placement of the rainbow in the heavens is a gesture of peace. An enemy goes out to battle his foe with his sword or bow drawn, while one who comes in peace extends his sword hilt-first, and turns his bow so that its curve faces inward, signifying that he does not mean to fight. So too, even when Hashem is angered by the sins of man, He places His bow in the heavens with the curve facing heaven-ward, signifying that He will not rain punishment down upon us, in fulfillment of His covenant.

There is another message inherent in Hashem's choice of the rainbow as His symbol. The Torah teaches that the generation of the Flood was characterized by widespread immorality, and its fate was sealed due to the sin of robbery that was rampant among them (see above, *A Torah Thought for the Day,* Monday). These sins are born both of selfishness, and from a lack of loyalty and unity. The rainbow, with its spectrum of color, symbolizes disunity — for light, when undivided, is white. Only when it is refracted and split through a prism does it separate into the bands of the rainbow.

When humankind acts selfishly, and thereby revisits those character flaws that resulted in the Flood, Hashem places the rainbow in the heavens for a dual purpose. He assures us that He remembers the covenant that He made with Noach and his children, and that He will not destroy the earth with another Flood. At the same time, however, He reminds us of the destructive power of disunity and factionalism, urging us to come together as a unified nation of His servants.

Tos. Rid (to *Chagigah* 16a) notes another lesson that can be learned from Hashem's choice of the rainbow as His sign. A rainbow, he states, is an inherently ambiguous sight; it is impossible to clearly discern precisely where one band of color ends and the next begins. Similarly, it is impossible for a person to attain a clear perception of the Divine Presence; we must be satisfied with the partial understanding of Hashem's ways, which is all we can achieve.

The Rabbis established an obligation to light a lamp or a candle in one's home before the Sabbath, so that the Sabbath meal will take place in a lighted room. They based this decree on the prophet's proclamation (*Isaiah* 58:13): *And if you proclaim the Sabbath "a delight," the holy one of Hashem, "honored one."* Our Mishnah considers which substances may and may not be used as wicks and fuel for the Sabbath lights. The rest of the chapter discusses laws relating to the lighting of the Sabbath lights.

בַּמֶּה מַדְלִיקִין וּבַמָּה אֵין מַדְלִיקִין — *With what may we kindle* the lights for the Sabbath *and with what may we not kindle?*

The Mishnah lists substances that may not be used as wicks:[1]

אֵין מַדְלִיקִין לֹא בְלֶכֶשׁ — *We may not kindle with cedar bast,* [2] וְלֹא בְחוֹסֶן וְלֹא בְכָלָךְ — *nor with uncarded flax,* [3] *nor with floss silk,* [4] וְלֹא בִּפְתִילַת הָאִידָן וְלֹא בִּפְתִילַת הַמִּדְבָּר — *nor with willow bast,* [5] *nor with desert fiber,* [6] וְלֹא בִירוֹקָה שֶׁעַל פְּנֵי הַמַּיִם — *nor with sea-moss.* [7]

The Mishnah next lists substances that may not be used as fuel:[8]

─────────────── NOTES ───────────────

1. The Rabbis were concerned that if the flame of a Sabbath light was to flicker, one might inadvertently tilt the lamp to move more oil to the wick and improve the light, thereby performing the forbidden labor of מַבְעִיר, *kindling,* on the Sabbath (*Rashi* to 21a). Therefore, the wicks must be fashioned from a substance that holds a flame well. The wicks that the Mishnah is about to list do not hold a flame well.

2. "Bast" refers to strong woody fibers that are obtained from the food-conducting tissue of various trees and plants. "Cedar-bast" is the fibrous inner bark of the cedar tree. These fibers do not wick the fuel up to the flame well, and therefore the flame is likely to flicker (Gemara 20b).

3. After the stems of flax have been crushed, they are "carded." [Carding is the disentangling of the fibers with a wire-toothed brush.] Before carding, flax does not wick the fuel up to the flame well (Gemara ibid., *Rashi*).

4. "Floss-silk" is an inferior grade of silk made from the cocoon of the silkworm, which is carded, spun, and woven into cloth. Floss-silk also does not wick the fuel up to the flame well (Gemara ibid., *Rashi*).

5. "Willow-bast" is the fibrous inner bark of the cedar tree (*Rav*).

6. "Desert-fiber" is also known as nettle, a long grass that can be braided and used for wicks, but which does not wick the fuel up to the flame well (*Rashi*).

7. "Sea-moss" is the dark green moss that accumulates on the bottom of ships (Gemara 20b), and it too does not wick the fuel up to the flame well.

8. As we have seen, the Rabbis were concerned that if the flame flickered one might inadvertently tilt the lamp to improve its light (see above, note 1). Therefore, the fuel for the light must be of a type that wicks well (i.e., is easily drawn into the wick). The fuels that the Mishnah is about to list do not wick well.

וְלֹא בְזֶפֶת וְלֹא בְשַׁעֲוָה — *Nor* may we kindle the Sabbath lights *with pitch, nor with wax,* [9] וְלֹא בְשֶׁמֶן קִיק וְלֹא בְשֶׁמֶן שְׂרֵיפָה — *nor with cottonseed oil, nor with oil that must be burned,* [10] וְלֹא בְאַלְיָה וְלֹא בְחֵלֶב — *nor with* fat from *a sheep's tail, nor with tallow.* [11] נַחוּם הַמָּדִי אוֹמֵר מַדְלִיקִין בְּחֵלֶב מְבוּשָׁל — *Nachum the Mede says: We may kindle with boiled tallow.* [12] וַחֲכָמִים אוֹמְרִים — *But the Sages say:* אֶחָד מְבוּשָׁל וְאֶחָד שֶׁאֵינוֹ מְבוּשָׁל — *It is the same* whether it is *boiled and the same if it is not boiled;* אֵין מַדְלִיקִין בּוֹ — *we may not kindle with it* in either case. [13]

─────── NOTES ───────

9. The Rabbis disallow the use of molten pitch or molten wax as fuel for a Sabbath lamp, as they do not wick well (*Rashi, Rav*). [However, when solid pitch or solid wax are made into candles, they burn evenly and may be used (*Mishnah Berurah* 264:24).]

10. Oil which is *terumah* and which has become *tamei* [ritually impure]. [*Terumah* is the part of one's crop (between 1/40 and 1/60) that the owner must set aside and give to a Kohen. A Kohen may not eat *terumah* unless it is *tahor* [ritually pure]. If *terumah* has become *tamei*, it may not be eaten, but must be destroyed by burning. For this reason, *terumah* oil which has become contaminated is called שֶׁמֶן שְׂרֵיפָה, *oil which must be burned*. Unlike the other substances listed here, the *oil which must be burned* is regular olive oil, which does wick well. Its use is disallowed only in the case of a Yom Tov (festival) that fell on a Friday. The candle-lighting for the Sabbath would thus be taking place on Yom Tov (since it must take place before sunset), and the law is that sacrifices that have become disqualified — and must therefore be destroyed — may not be burned on Yom Tov. As we shall see in the next Mishnah, contaminated *terumah* is also governed by this law. Since our Mishnah is dealing with a festival that fell on a Friday, lighting the Sabbath candles with *terumah* oil which has become *tamei* and must be burned would violate this prohibition (Gemara 23b).

11. These are the hard fatty tissues whose consumption the Torah prohibits (*Leviticus* 7:23).

12. Nachum the Mede allows the use of tallow that has been boiled and is still in a molten state, because it wicks well (*Rashi* 24b).

13. The Sages disallow the use of tallow, even if it boiled and is in a molten state, lest people confuse it with tallow that has not been boiled (Gemara 21a).

┌───┐

QUESTION OF THE DAY:
During which generations did the rainbow never appear? Why?

For the answer, see page 100.

└───┘

The Gemara (*Shabbos* 21a-b), after discussing the subject of wicks and oils that may be used for the Sabbath lights, segues into an exhaustive, three-*blatt* presentation of the laws of Chanukah. In the course of this discussion, Rav Huna equates the Chanukah lights with the Sabbath lights, ruling that those oils that may not be kindled for the Sabbath lights also may not be kindled for the Chanukah lights. According to Rava, this law applies even on the weeknights of Chanukah, because Rav Huna holds that the Chanukah lights must burn for the entire length of time prescribed by the Rabbis (approximately half an hour; see Gemara 21b). If they are accidentally extinguished during that time, they must be rekindled. Rav Huna therefore rules that on Chanukah one should not use the inferior wicks and oils which do not produce a steady flame, lest he neglect to rekindle the lights should they flicker and go out.

According to Rav Chisda, however, Rav Huna's ruling applies specifically to the Chanukah lights that are kindled on the eve of the Sabbath, and is based on his position that the Chanukah lights may be used for personal purposes (e.g., for reading or doing work). Therefore, there is the concern that if a flickering flame is produced, one might inadvertently tilt the menorah to improve its light on the Sabbath, thereby performing the forbidden labor of *kindling.* Thus, it is the elimination of that concern that is the function of the prohibition against using inferior wicks and oils on Chanukah.

On the other hand, R' Zeira in the name of Rav is of the opinion that oils that may not be kindled for the Sabbath lights *may* be kindled for the Chanukah lights. R' Yirmiyah explains that this is because Rav holds that the Chanukah lights need not remain lit for the entire length of time prescribed by the Rabbis; if they are accidentally extinguished during that time, they need not be rekindled. Accordingly, Rav is not concerned that the inferior wicks and oils will become extinguished prematurely, since they need not be rekindled in any event.

Moreover, Rav *also* holds that the Chanukah lights may not be used for personal purposes. Accordingly, Rav is not concerned that the use of inferior wicks and oils may cause a person using the lights to adjust them on the Sabbath, as in any event it is forbidden to make use of the Chanukah lights.

As we learned above, the generation of the Flood was lacking in *achdus,* with each person caring only for himself. This leads to an interesting question: How does one cultivate the trait of *achdus?*

R' *Chaim Shmulevitz* explains that the seeds of *achdus* are planted when people care about one another, and are concerned for each other's wishes and needs. He notes that although the Jews reached a high level of *achdus* before receiving the Torah at Mt. Sinai — indeed, the Torah (*Shemos* 19:2) describes their camping there using the singular word וַיִּחַן, and *Rashi* there comments that they camped "as one man, with one heart" — they reached an even higher level during the time of Mordechai and Esther. During the time of Purim, the individual re-accepted the Torah willingly, without Hashem having to remind them that they could not live without the Torah (see *Shabbos* 88b). This, explains R' Chaim, was due to the intense concern generated by the threat of annihilation that hung over every Jew, which caused every individual to worry about the fate of his family, friends and neighbors. The total *achdus* fostered by such a situation created the ideal climate for accepting the Torah anew.

We find also that the Gemara (*Sanhedrin* 20a) singles out the generation of R' Yehudah ben R' Ila'i for special praise, placing them on a level even higher than the generations of Moshe Rabbeinu and Chizkiah. Although the generation of Moshe Rabbeinu merited to receive the Torah, and in the generation of Chizkiah the people were so well-versed in the Torah that every child who lived between Dan and Be'er Sheva was proficient in the laws of ritual impurity, the generation of R' Yehudah ben R' Ila'i was greater still. Why? The Gemara explains that theirs was a poverty-stricken generation, and the children were forced to study while six of them would huddle under a single garment. R' Chaim explains that it is impossible for six children to be sheltered under a single garment unless every one of them is concerned about the others' warmth, and not about his own. It was this merit that gave them such greatness.

We can learn from these sources, concludes R' Chaim, that worrying about the honor and comfort of others is the path to true *achdus,* which will lead in turn to greatness in Torah.

(adapted from *Sichos Mussar,* 5731 §22)

Today we will begin to discuss the *melachah* of מְעַמֵּר, *gathering*, which is the fourth in the list of the thirty-nine *melachos* forbidden on the Sabbath. Gathering was performed in connection with the construction of the Mishkan, when the plants from which the dyes were made were gathered together in one place after they were harvested. These dyes were used to dye the tapestries used in the Mishkan as partitions and roof-coverings.

Gathering is defined as the gathering together of scattered grain, fruits or vegetables into one place (*Chayei Adam* 13:1), to protect the harvested produce from being stepped on or blown away by the wind.

Since the purpose of this *melachah* is to protect the produce, any type of gathering that affords protection is prohibited. This would include piling or bundling the produce, placing it into containers or boxes, or assembling it into units (such as by stringing figs together). Gathering that is done for a purpose other than protection (such as the gathering of items so that people will not stumble upon them) is not a violation of this *melachah*.

Even where the gathering is done to protect the gathered items, one violates this *melachah* on the Biblical level only if the items being gathered are things that grow from the earth. Moreover, most authorities are of the opinion that the Biblical *melachah* applies only if the items are being gathered from their place of growth — for example, gathering apples in an orchard or vegetables in a garden. [Of course, this applies to produce that has already been picked; picking the produce is a violation of the *av melachah* of *reaping*.]

An exception to this rule concerns items that are usually gathered away from their place of growth. For example, figs are usually brought indoors to be strung together. Since the process of stringing them is usually done indoors, one who brings the figs into his house and strings them there has violated the *melachah* of *gathering*.

One is forbidden to gather together any items that grow from the earth even if they are not edible. Thus, gathering twigs for fuel or grass for animal fodder would also be prohibited.

The authorities differ as to whether an animal is considered something that grows from the ground with respect to this *melachah*. According to those who do include it in this category, it would be forbidden to string together pieces of meat or fish to take them to the market for sale [as was often done in Talmudic times — see Mishnah, *Bava Metzia* 21a].

A CLOSER LOOK AT THE SIDDUR

In many *siddurim,* one will find, printed after the daily morning prayers, a list of blessings that are recited upon the occurrence of certain events. One of the blessings that is usually listed there is the *berachah* one makes upon seeing a rainbow. Although the Gemara (*Chagigah* 16a) states that one is forbidden to gaze at a rainbow, this refers to a prolonged viewing; it is, however, permitted to glance at a rainbow (*Abudraham,* citing *Rosh*); indeed, *Iyun Yaakov* (to *Chagigah* ibid.) writes that it is a mitzvah to glance at the rainbow, so that one can make a blessing upon it.

The blessing that one recites upon seeing a rainbow is: בָּרוּךְ אַתָּה ה' אֱלֹהֵינוּ מֶלֶךְ הָעוֹלָם זוֹכֵר הַבְּרִית וְנֶאֱמָן בִּבְרִיתוֹ וְקַיָּם בְּמַאֲמָרוֹ, *Blessed are You, Hashem, our God, King of the Universe, Who remembers the covenant, and is steadfast in His covenant, and fulfills His word.* In this blessing, we thank Hashem for *remembering His covenant* with mankind not to destroy the earth (see *A Torah Thought for the Day*), for *being steadfast* in this commitment even when the wicked and their evil deeds proliferate; and for *fulfilling His words* in the Torah (*Bereishis* 9:15) that the waters shall never again become a Flood to destroy the earth (*Abudraham*).

This blessing is recited each time a person sees a new rainbow, even if he saw the second rainbow on the same day that he saw the first. However, since a rainbow is not a good omen, it is not proper for a person to notify his fellow that there is a rainbow in the sky (*Orach Chaim* 229:1 with *Mishnah Berurah* 1-2; cf. *Iyun Yaakov* cited above).

It is unclear whether one may make the blessing if he sees only a portion of the rainbow and he cannot discern the curve of the bow (*Beur Halachah* ibid.).

[It should be noted that one can recite a blessing only upon a rainbow seen in the clouds, of the sort that appears after a rainstorm. It is only such a rainbow that is a sign of the covenant that Hashem made with mankind, and therefore this is the type of rainbow that necessitates a blessing. A rainbow that is formed over a waterfall, or one that is seen in a body of water, is not a sign of the covenant, and no blessing is recited upon seeing it.]

וַיִּקַּח שֵׁם וָיֶפֶת אֶת הַשִּׂמְלָה וַיָּשִׂימוּ עַל שְׁכֶם שְׁנֵיהֶם
וַיֵּלְכוּ אֲחֹרַנִּית וַיְכַסּוּ אֶת עֶרְוַת אֲבִיהֶם
וּפְנֵיהֶם אֲחֹרַנִּית וְעֶרְוַת אֲבִיהֶם לֹא רָאוּ

And Shem and Yefes took the garment,
and they laid it upon both their shoulders;
and they walked backwards,
and they covered the nakedness of their father.
Their faces were turned away,
and the nakedness of their father they did not see
(Bereishis 9:23).

*R*ashi notes that although both Shem and Yefes participated in this meritorious act, the verse uses the singular form וַיִּקַּח, which literally means *and he took.* This signifies that they did not both perform the mitzvah with equal zeal; rather, says the Midrash, Shem exerted himself to protect his father's honor with more alacrity than Yefes did (that is, he took the initiative, and Yefes went along with him). For this reason, Shem's descendants were privileged to be given the mitzvah of putting *tzitzis* on their garments (see *Bamidbar* 15:37-41), while Yefes earned the right to have his descendants buried in Eretz Yisrael.

Kli Yakar notes that this Midrash, which states that the mitzvah of *tzitzis* was given to the Bnei Yisrael as a reward for this meritorious act of Shem, would seem to contradict the Gemara in *Maseches Sotah* (17a), which states that the Jews received the mitzvah of *tzitzis* in the merit of Avraham Avinu's refusal to take even the slightest portion of the spoils of war offered him by the king of Sodom, even *so much as a string or a shoestrap* (see *Bereishis* 14:23). *Kli Yakar* explains that, in truth, the mitzvah of *tzitzis* was given to the Jews as a result of both of these deeds. *Both* merits were necessary, for the mitzvah of *tzitzis* has two components — a four-cornered garment and the *tzitzis* strings themselves that are tied upon the garment. In the merit of Shem's act of covering his father with a garment, Hashem gave the Bnei Yisrael a mitzvah to perform upon their garments. And in the merit of Avraham's refusal to take so much as a string from the king of Sodom, Hashem gave the Jews the mitzvah of tying the strings of the *tzitzis* upon those garments.

MISHNAH OF THE DAY: SHABBOS 2:2

This Mishnah continues the discussion of which fuels may be used for the Sabbath lights:

אֵין מַדְלִיקִין בְּשֶׁמֶן שְׂרֵיפָה בְּיוֹם טוֹב — *We may not kindle with oil that must be burned, on a* Friday that is a *festival day;* [1] רַבִּי יִשְׁמָעֵאל אוֹמֵר — *R' Yishmael says:* אֵין מַדְלִיקִין בְּעִטְרָן מִפְּנֵי כְּבוֹד הַשַּׁבָּת — *We may not kindle with itran, because of the honor due the Sabbath.* [2] וַחֲכָמִים מַתִּירִין בְּכָל הַשְּׁמָנִים — *But the Sages permit* kindling *with all types of oils:* בְּשֶׁמֶן שׁוּמְשְׁמִין בְּשֶׁמֶן — namely, *with sesame oil,* אֱגוֹזִים בְּשֶׁמֶן צְנוֹנוֹת בְּשֶׁמֶן דָּגִים בְּשֶׁמֶן פַּקּוּעוֹת — *with nut oil, with oil* pressed *from* the seeds of *radishes, with fish oil, with oil* pressed *from* the seeds of *gourds,* [3] בְּעִטְרָן וּבְנֵפְטְ — *with itran or with naphtha.* [4] רַבִּי טַרְפוֹן אוֹמֵר — *R' Tarfon says:* אֵין מַדְלִיקִין אֶלָּא בְּשֶׁמֶן זַיִת בִּלְבָד — *We may not kindle with anything except olive oil.* [5]

---- NOTES ----

1. In the case of a Yom Tov (festival) that fell on a Friday (so the candle-lighting for the Sabbath would thus be taking place on Yom Tov), *terumah* oil that became *tamei* and is therefore subject to burning (see Mishnah 1) may not be used for the Sabbath lights, for *terumah* that is *tamei* may not be burned on Yom Tov, just as sacrifices that have become disqualified — and must therefore be destroyed — may not be burned on Yom Tov (see the previous Mishnah). However, when Friday is a regular weekday, such oil may be used for the Sabbath lamps.

2. עִטְרָן, *itran,* is a clear liquid by-product of the processing of the זֶפֶת, *pitch,* mentioned in the previous Mishnah. However, unlike pitch, *itran* — being of a more liquid consistency — does wick well. Nevertheless, R' Yishmael disallows its use because it gives off a foul odor which may cause one to leave the room in which it is burning and eat his Sabbath meal in a dark room. That would constitute a lack of כְּבוֹד שַׁבָּת, *honor of the Sabbath* (Rav).

3. Unlike olive oil that serves both as food and as fuel, these oils normally serve only as food. Hence, there is a possibility that a person may forget that it is the Sabbath and come to remove some oil from the light, thus violating the prohibition of מְכַבֶּה, *extinguishing.* The Mishnah here teaches that the Sages were not concerned that this might happen, and therefore they permitted the use of these oils in the Sabbath lights (*Tiferes Yisrael*).

4. Unlike R' Yishmael, the Sages do not disallow the use of malodorous fuels, as long as they wick well. They therefore permit the use of tar, and of naphtha — a derivative of pitch that is white and malodorous (*Rashi*).

5. R' Tarfon requires the use of olive oil, because of all oils, olive oil wicks the best, producing the steadiest flame. [Even the Tannaim who disagree with R' Tarfon and allow the use of other oils concede that olive oil is preferred (*Tosafos* 23a).]

We learned in the Mishnah that R' Yishmael said: "We may not kindle with *itran,* because of the honor due the Sabbath." The Gemara asks: How is it that kindling with *itran* diminishes the Sabbath's honor? Rava answers that since tar's odor is foul, the Rabbis issued a decree against kindling with it on the Sabbath, lest one leave the Sabbath lamps and depart from the room.

Abaye then asked Rava: What is the problem in his leaving? What does it matter to us if he vacates the illuminated room?

Rava replied that it indeed matters if he then eats his Sabbath meal in the dark, because the kindling of a light in the place where one eats on the Sabbath is an obligation. [A festive meal has prominence only when it is conducted in an illuminated place. Hence, one honors the Sabbath by dining in a lighted room (*Rashi*). Alternatively, one honors the Sabbath by taking delight in the Sabbath meals, and this cannot be done properly when one eats in the dark (*Tosafos*). Thus, in addition to the basic Sabbath obligation of kindling a light in one's home, one must specifically eat his Sabbath meal in an illuminated place. Hence, one must not kindle with tar, lest he come to eat in the dark (*Tosafos*).]

Another act of preparation that honors the Sabbath is discussed in a statement in the name of Rav — that although there is an obligation to kindle a light in the place where one eats on the Sabbath, the washing of the hands and feet in warm water on the Sabbath eve is optional. Rava disagrees, and maintains that the washing, too, is a mitzvah. The Gemara then inquires as to the source for considering the washing of one's hands and feet in honor of the Sabbath a mitzvah, and finds a source in the practice of R' Yehudah bar Ila'i: "On the Sabbath eve they would bring to him a tub filled with warm water, and he washed his face, hands and feet; he wrapped himself and sat in a fringed linen cloak, and he resembled an angel of the Lord of Hosts." [Since we are obligated to follow the practices of our sages and elders, it follows that we too must wash ourselves in honor of the Sabbath (*Ran*).]

In this vein, *Rambam* writes (*Hil. Shabbos* 30:2): "[One should] wrap himself in a fringed cloak and sit solemnly awaiting the reception of the Sabbath, as if he were going to go out and greet a king. [Indeed] the earlier generations of sages would gather their disciples on the Sabbath eve and wrap themselves [in fringed cloaks] and say, 'Come! We shall go out to greet the Sabbath King!' "

SHABBOS
PARASHAS
NOACH

R' *Shlomo Wolbe* speaks about the *middah* of *zeri-zus,* alacrity: "The Baraisa of R' Pinchas ben Yair (which is the basis of *Sefer Mesillas Yesharim*) begins by stating that 'Torah leads to *zehirus* (watchfulness), and *zehirus* leads to *zerizus.*' This teaches us that *zerizus* is not simply an admirable character trait, for if it were, we would not require the Torah to lead us to its acquisition. Rather, it must be that *zerizus* is itself a level of Torah wisdom that must be attained, and it is as holy and vital as the Torah itself . . .

"The *Mesillas Yesharim* states that *zerizus* is a trait of great importance in attaining complete service of Hashem, and the nature of man pulls him away from it. One who works diligently at the practice of *zerizus* as much as possible will be rewarded in the World to Come by the Creator, Who will repay him for the efforts taken to overcome his natural inclination . . .

"Although the *Mesillas Yesharim* does not identify the root of this *middah,* I have heard from my teachers that attending to all mitzvos with *zerizus* allows them to be completed without giving the *yetzer hara* the chance to dissuade us from performing them. Moreover, performing a mitzvah without *zerizus* is not only creating an opportunity for the *yetzer hara* to intrude; it is the *result* of the *yetzer hara* having *already* involved himself in the person's thoughts, preventing him from prompt fulfillment of the mitzvah. The Divine Presence will not rest (to the same extent) upon such mitzvah performance . . .

"From this we can derive an astounding truth: The trait of *zerizus* is nothing less than the task of ensuring that all of one's deeds are implanted with the Divine Presence! We are enjoined to perform our good deeds with zeal and alacrity, so that the *Shechinah* will always be with us."

(Alei Shur vol. 1, 2:12)

HALACHAH OF THE DAY

Today we will continue our discussion of the *melachah* of *gathering.* We have learned that one violates the Biblical *melachah* of *gathering* only if he gathers the items from their place of growth. The authorities disagree whether the prohibition extends even to produce that was already gathered, but then became scattered once again while still in its place of growth (for example, apples in an orchard were gathered into a basket, and then the basket tipped over, spilling the apples out). In practice, the more stringent view should be followed.

One violates the *melachah* of *gathering* by collecting the scattered items in whatever way this is normally done. For example, if it is customary to gather scattered twigs by pushing them into a pile with one's feet, or to gather fruit by rolling the fruit into a pile, he is liable for doing so. If the gathering is performed in an unusual manner, it is Rabbinically forbidden.

Harvesting produce from the field in which it grew is not necessarily a violation of this *melachah,* which involves only gathering items in their place of growth. If one brings fruits one by one from the field into the house, he has not violated this *melachah,* even though the fruits will then be "gathered" in the house. However, he may not gather together several at a time to bring in, for one is liable for gathering even as few as two items in their place of growth. [Of course, this applies only to fruits that were detached before the Sabbath. Fruits that fall off a tree on the Sabbath are *muktzeh,* and may not be handled.]

Gathering is forbidden only when the produce being gathered is still in its original form. However, if some change has been wrought upon the items (for example, if fallen branches were carved into wooden canes), it would be permitted to gather them together even if they were still in their place of growth.

Moreover, as we learned earlier, one is liable for *gathering* only if the purpose of the gathering is to protect the items being gathered. Therefore, if one gathers flowers together for the purpose of making a flower arrangement, he has not violated this *melachah,* for the gathering in this case is done for beauty rather than protection. [Nevertheless, it is forbidden to make a flower arrangement on the Sabbath in any case, as this violates the *melachah* of *makeh b'patish.*]

Items that come from the ground but do not grow from the ground — such as stones, salt and the like — are not subject to the Biblical prohibition of *gathering* according to most authorities. However, the Sages forbade gathering these items [in the places where they are taken from the ground], lest people see them being gathered, and mistakenly conclude that even items that actually grow from the ground can be gathered.

QUESTION OF THE DAY:

What other reward did Yefes receive for assisting Shem in protecting his father's honor?

For the answer, see page 100.

SHABBOS

תפילות השבת

One of the unique facets of *tefillah* on the Sabbath is the set of prayers that are said as the Sabbath approaches, the section known as קַבָּלַת שַׁבָּת, *Kabbalas Shabbos*. The term *Kabbalas Shabbos* has two meanings. In a literal sense, it means the *acceptance* of the Sabbath — for those praying in shul accept the sanctity of the Sabbath upon themselves as they recite the prayer שִׁיר מִזְמוֹר לְיוֹם הַשַּׁבָּת, *A psalm, a song for the day of the Sabbath* (*Tehillim* Ch. 92), during the *Kabbalas Shabbos* prayers (see *Shulchan Aruch, Orach Chaim* 263:10). However, it also refers to *receiving* the Sabbath, in the sense that one organizes a reception for an honored guest (for a similar usage, see *Rosh Hashanah* 16b).

The section of *Kabbalas Shabbos* as we know it today dates back to the practice of the Kabbalists of Tzefas in the late 16th century. They, in turn, based their actions upon the Gemara in *Maseches Shabbos* (119a) that relates that R' Chanina would wrap himself [in a fine cloak] as the Sabbath approached, and he would say: "Let us go out to greet the Sabbath queen!" ; and R' Yannai would don his fine garments and say, "Come, O bride! Come, O bride!" The Kabbalists of Tzefas, too, would go out into the fields wearing their Sabbath garments, and recite the chapters of *Tehillim* that comprise *Kabbalas Shabbos,* along with the song of *Lechah Dodi* (which was authored by R' Shlomo Alkabetz, and endorsed by the Arizal; it is noteworthy that other versions of *Lechah Dodi,* written by other composers, were said in certain locations, and are extant even today).

Although it is not our practice to actually leave the shul to pray *Kabbalas Shabbos,* it is universally accepted that in remembrance of this custom, we turn to face the door of the shul during the last stanza of *Lechah Dodi.*

[Because the section of *Kabbalas Shabbos* is not part of the standard three daily *tefillos,* and comparatively recent in origin, many congregations have the *minhag* to differentiate between this section and the *Maariv* prayer that follows. They do so by having the *shliach tzibbur* lead the *Kabbalas Shabbos* prayers from the *bimah* at the center of the shul, rather than from the *amud* as is customary. When *Kabbalas Shabbos* is concluded, the *shliach tzibbur* moves up to the *amud* to begin *Maariv.*

A TASTE OF LOMDUS

פרשת
נח

SHABBOS

PARASHAS
NOACH

The Gemara in *Menachos* (41a) cites an argument between Rav and Shmuel concerning when a four-cornered garment requires *tzitzis* strings. Rav maintains that the strings are required only when the garment is being worn, while Shmuel asserts that *tzitzis* must always be attached to every four-cornered garment, even if the garment in question is lying in a drawer, unworn. While Rav understands that the act of *wearing* the garment is what activates the obligation of *tzitzis,* Shmuel understands the Torah's directive (*Devarim* 22:12), *You shall make for yourselves tzitzis on the four corners of your garment with which you cover yourself,* as including any four-cornered garment that is used as clothing, even if it is not being worn.

In the *sefer Oneg Yom Tov* (*Orach Chaim* §1), we find a proof brought against Shmuel's understanding of the mitzvah from a Gemara in *Shabbos* (132b). The Gemara there uses the case of *tzitzis* as an example of the principle that a positive commandment overrides a negative commandment when they are impossible to reconcile (*asei docheh lo saaseh*). Since the Gemara derives from Scripture that one may fulfill the mitzvah of *tzitzis* on a four-cornered linen garment (even though the *techeiles* strings must be wool), we see that the positive mitzvah of *tzitzis* overrides the prohibition of *shaatnez. Oneg Yom Tov* asks: Since one does not violate the prohibition against *shaatnez* unless he actually *wears* the garment, what is the proof that a person may violate the law of *shaatnez* when he has woolen strings and a linen garment? Perhaps he is permitted to fulfill the mitzvah of *tzitzis* by simply placing them upon the garment, but he would not be allowed to wear it! The fact that the Gemara does consider this a proof would seem to support the view of Rav, who maintains that the mitzvah of *tzitzis* can be fulfilled only by wearing the garment.

Oneg Yom Tov deflects the question by explaining that even though, according to Shmuel, the mitzvah of *tzitzis* applies even when the garment is not being worn, it still applies only to garment that *can* be worn. A four-cornered garment that cannot be worn, such as one that contains *shaatnez,* is not considered a garment at all, and would not be subject to the mitzvah of *tzitzis.* Thus, even according to Shmuel, the Gemara's proof still stands, for the fact that a linen garment with four corners is subject to the mitzvah of *tzitzis* proves that it can be worn; and this is true only if the mitzvah of *tzitzis* overrides the prohibition against *shaatnez* and allows the woolen *techeiles* strings to be tied in place.

SHABBOS — PARASHAS NOACH / 99

Sunday:

Shem was also known as Malkitzedek, and is mentioned (*Bereishis* 14:18) as the ruler of Jerusalem who came to greet Avraham after his defeat of the four kings.

Monday:

Midrash Rabbah (28:8) states that the corruption spread even to the earth; man would plant wheat, and weeds would grow instead. Indeed, the Midrash states that the weeds we find among grain stalks stem from that time.

Tuesday:

The mitzvah of Torah study. In the blessings we recite every morning, we ask, *may we and our offspring . . . know Your Name and study Your Torah for its own sake.*

Wednesday:

Toras Chaim (to *Chullin* 27b) notes that animals require the cutting of both pipes (the trachea and the esophagus) during *shechitah*, while birds require the cutting of only a single pipe. He suggests that perhaps this is due to the greater life-force of animals as opposed to the frailty of birds.

Thursday:

On the Sabbath. This is recorded in one of the Sabbath *zemiros*, the song *Yom Shabbason*, authored by R' Yehudah HeLevi.

Friday:

Rashi (*Bereishis* 9:12) cites *Bereishis Rabbah* (35:2), which states that the rainbow was not seen in the generation of Chizkiah, king of Judah, or in the generation of the Tanna R' Shimon bar Yochai. These generations were absolutely righteous, and needed no assurance that the world would not be destroyed in their time (see also *Kesubos* 77b).

Shabbos:

Midrash Zuta to *Shir HaShirim* 1:15 states that Greece, which descended from the family of Yefes, merited to govern Eretz Yisrael as a reward for the good deed that Yefes performed here.

פרשת לך לך

Parashas Lech Lecha

| פָּרָשַׁת לֶךְ לְךָ | # A TORAH THOUGHT FOR THE DAY |

A TORAH THOUGHT FOR THE DAY

פָּרָשַׁת לֶךְ לְךָ

SUNDAY

PARASHAS LECH LECHA

וַיֹּאמֶר יהוה אֶל־אַבְרָם לֶךְ־לְךָ מֵאַרְצְךָ וּמִמּוֹלַדְתְּךָ וּמִבֵּית אָבִיךָ

And HASHEM said to Avram,
"Go for yourself from your land, from your relatives,
and from your father's house . . ." (*Bereishis* 12:1).

Rashi, commenting on the verse's use of the seemingly superfluous word לְךָ, explains that Hashem told Avraham that the journey he was being told to undertake would be for his own benefit. While in Charan, Avraham would not have children, while once in Canaan, he would start the family that would become a great nation, and his fame would spread throughout the world.

This leads us to ask a simple question. The Mishnah in *Avos* (5:3) states that Avraham was tested with ten trials. Although the *Rishonim* differ as to the exact list (see *Rashi* and *Ramban* to *Avos* loc. cit.; see also *Avos D'Rabbi Nassan* §13), all agree that one of the tests was the trial that Avraham faced here — to leave his homeland and travel to parts unknown. But why is this such a trial? Surely if Hashem were to come to any one of us and guarantee blessings, success and family well-being were we to undertake a move, we would do so. Indeed, many people undertake such moves for purely economic reasons, without any guarantee whatsoever that things will turn out well. How could this have been considered a test for a *tzaddik* on the lofty level of Avraham?

R' Moshe Feinstein explains that indeed, there was never a question that Avraham wold obey Hashem's command. The test was to see whether Avraham would wonder why Hashem was requiring him to move in order to grant him success and family. Avraham, being the great *tzaddik* that he was, knew with certainty that Hashem had the power to grant him children and fame anywhere in the world. Thus, he might have asked himself: Why is it necessary for Hashem to uproot me and my family? Can He not do everything for me here in Charan? It is human nature that even the simplest task is difficult to carry out when one does not understand the reason for it; when the demand includes uprooting one's whole life to move to an unknown place, it would have been easy for Avraham to wonder at Hashem's command.

But Avraham did not wonder. Instead, he simply assumed that Hashem had good reason to command as He did, and he obeyed without question. In this, he demonstrated the ability to *walk before Hashem* (see *Bereishis* 17:1), that is, to obey Hashem's commands without needing to comprehend them first (a level that Noach, who walked *with Hashem* [see ibid. 6:9] did not attain).

Alshich adds another dimension to the test. He states that part of the trial was for Avraham to follow Hashem's command not because of the promised rewards, but simply because it was Hashem's will that he do so. Indeed, the verse (12:4) states that even after all that was promised him, *Avram went just as Hashem had told him.* Explains *Alshich:* Avraham did not think of the blessings of children, fame and wealth that Hashem had promised him. Rather, he went simply to fulfill the will of Hashem.

MISHNAH OF THE DAY: SHABBOS 2:3

The Mishnah discusses the laws of the wicks used in the Sabbath lamps:

כָּל הַיּוֹצֵא מִן הָעֵץ אֵין מַדְלִיקִין בּוֹ — *We may not kindle* the Sabbath lights with *any [wick] that comes from a tree,*[1] אֶלָּא פִשְׁתָּן — *except* one made of *flax.* [2]

The Mishnah cites another law regarding tree products, in regard to the laws of *tumah:*

וְכָל הַיּוֹצֵא מִן הָעֵץ אֵינוֹ — *And any [roof] that is derived from a tree* מְטַמֵּא טוּמְאַת אֹהָלִים — *does not become tamei with tent-tumah* when it forms a roof over a corpse,[3] אֶלָּא פִשְׁתָּן — *except* one made of *flax.* [4]

────────── NOTES ──────────

1. A wick made from any derivative of a tree may not be used for the Sabbath lights (*Rashi, Rav*).

2. Both carded flax and linen cloth may be used as wicks, since they produce a steady flame (see above, Mishnah 1).

Although flax does not grow on a tree, we find in *Joshua* 2:6 that flax stalks are referred to as פִּשְׁתֵּי הָעֵץ — literally, *the flax of the tree.* The Tanna therefore found it necessary to teach that, despite the designation of the flax plant as a tree, its products may be used as wicks for Sabbath lights (*Rav*).

3. A roof or awning constructed of wood or any other derivative of a tree, under which there lies a a human corpse, creates a tent that transmits the corpse's *tumah* to any people or vessels that are under the roof. However, the wooden roof itself does not become *tamei* (*Rashi*). [In fact, only three roof materials besides flax (see below) *are* themselves susceptible to this *tumah:* wool, goat's hair and hides. A roof made of any other material — even metal, which is normally highly susceptible to *tumah* — will not become *tamei* from the corpse that lies under it. Our Mishnah teaches this law only in regard to wooden roofs because it comes to compare this law to the earlier ruling regarding Sabbath wicks, which concerned only wood products (*Tos. HaRosh*).]

4. A roof made of flax (i.e., linen) does itself become *tamei* if a corpse lies beneath it. This is because the Torah refers to this *tumah* as טוּמְאַת אֹהֶל, which literally translates as *tent-tumah* (*Bamidbar* 19:14), and the Torah (*Shemos* 40:19) explicitly refers to a

The Mishnah cites a dispute regarding a wick made of folded cloth:

שֶׁקְּפָלָהּ וְלֹא — *A wick* made *of a garment* פְּתִילַת הַבֶּגֶד

רַבִּי הַבְהֲבָהּ — *that one folded,* [5] *but did not singe:* [6]

טְמֵאָה הִיא — *It is* אֱלִיעֶזֶר אוֹמֵר — *R' Eliezer says:*

וְאֵין susceptible to contamination with *tumah,* [7]

מַדְלִיקִין בָּהּ — *and one may not kindle* the Sabbath

טְהוֹרָה רַבִּי עֲקִיבָא אוֹמֵר — *But R' Akiva says:* lights *with it.* [8]

וּמַדְלִיקִין — It is not susceptible to contamination with *tumah,* [9] הִיא

——————— NOTES ———————

structure of linen by the general term הָאֹהֶל, *the tent.* Since the Torah refers to such a linen structure as *the tent* without modifying it by the adjective *linen,* we deduce that elsewhere — such as in regard to the laws of *tent-tumah* — the term *the tent* refers to a *linen tent* unless otherwise specified (*Rav*).

5. A piece of cloth that was three fingerbreadths by three fingerbreadths in area — the minimum size required for a cloth to be considered a significant "garment" and thus susceptible to contamination with *tumah* from a corpse — was folded (i.e., twisted) into a wick, and now (in its twisted state) measures less than three fingers by three fingers (*Rav*).

6. The wick was not charred over a flame, which was generally done to new wicks to make them easier to light (*Rashi, Rav*).

7. The wick remains susceptible to contamination with *tumah* even though it has been folded. Although the cloth that has been twisted into a wick no longer measures three by three fingerbreadths, it nonetheless remains susceptible to *tumah,* because R' Eliezer is of the opinion that a reduction in size effected by folding alone — which is reversible — does not negate the cloth's significance as a garment (*Ritva*). However, had the cloth been charred as well as folded, even R' Eliezer would agree that the cloth's status as a garment has been negated, thereby removing its susceptibility to *tumah.* This is because charring the cloth signals an intention to remove it from its "garment" use to a new use as a wick; the folding therefore takes on greater significance, and is considered a negation of the cloth's status (*Rashi*).

8. R' Eliezer's ruling applies specifically to the case of a Yom Tov that falls on a Friday, when the kindling of the Sabbath lights is being done on Yom Tov. Since, in this case, the folded cloth measured exactly three fingerbreadths square (before being twisted), therefore, the moment it is kindled, it is reduced from the minimum size of a garment, and rendered a mere fragment of a cloth. This is a halachically significant change, since halachah accords a different status to a whole cloth than to a fragment. When such a change in status occurs on Yom Tov, the resulting fragment is deemed *nolad* — i.e., it is in a *legal* sense a newly created object, a form of *muktzeh* — and may not be handled on Yom Tov.

Now, the law is that one must hold the flame to the wick of the Sabbath lights until most of the protruding part of the wick has been ignited. Hence, this wick — which may no longer be handled from the initial moment of its kindling — may not be used on a Yom Tov that falls on a Friday (Gemara 28b).

9. R' Akiva maintains that the folding alone is sufficient to legally reduce the cloth's dimensions so that it is no longer susceptible to *tumah* (*Rav*).

בָּה — *and one may kindle* the Sabbath lights *with it.* [10]

──────────── NOTES ────────────

10. Since the cloth was folded before Yom Tov, it was already no longer considered a garment at that time. Having already lost its status before Yom Tov, no additional change of status takes place when the wick is kindled on Yom Tov. Consequently, *nolad* is not involved, and therefore this wick may be used for the Sabbath lights (*Rav*).

GEMS FROM THE GEMARA

The Gemara (28a) derives the Mishnah's law that a roof made of flax is susceptible to roof-*tumah* from the flax covering that was one of the coverings of the Mishkan: The term *tent* is written regarding roof-*tumah* (*Bamidbar* 19:14), and it is also written regarding the Tabernacle covering (*Shemos* 40:19). Thus, since the flax that was used as the Tabernacle covering is called a "tent," so too in regard to roof-*tumah*, cloth of flax is called a "tent," and can therefore become *tamei* when it forms a roof over a corpse.

Having demonstrated that the Mishnah's inclusion of flax in the law of roof-*tumah* is derived from a comparison to the coverings of the Mishkan, the Gemara goes on to question the Mishnah's exclusion of other wood products from this law, since they too can seemingly be derived through similar expositions. The Gemara asks: Just as in regard to the Mishkan, wooden beams are referred to using the word *tent* (see ibid. 26:15), so too in regard to roof-*tumah*, the word "tent" should include wooden beams! Accordingly, any wood product that forms a roof over a corpse should become *tamei*! Why, then, does the Mishnah rule that wood products other than flax are not susceptible to roof-*tumah*?

The Gemara answers by differentiating between the verse's reference to the Mishkan coverings and its reference to the wooden beams of the Mishkan. The verse regarding the beams states (ibid.): *And you shall make the beams "for" the Mishkan.* The verse says only that the beams are made *for* the Mishkan, not that the beams themselves *are* the Mishkan. On the other hand, the flaxen Tabernacle covering is *itself* called the Mishkan, a term that is interchangeable with "tent." Accordingly, the Tabernacle covering is itself considered a "tent," and its components are subject to roof-*tumah*, while the wooden beams, since they are not themselves called the Mishkan, cannot be categorized as a "tent." Hence, the Mishnah excludes wood products other than flax from the law of tent-*tumah*.

However, persists the Gemara, since with regard to the Mishkan's

cover of animal hides it is stated (ibid. v.14): *And you shall make a Cover for the Tent,* it should be clear that animal hides should *not* acquire roof-*tumah* when they form a roof over a corpse, for they themselves are not called *a tent.* Why, then, does R' Elazar inquire as to the status of nonkosher animal hides with respect to roof-*tumah?* If even the hide of a kosher animal, which is used to cover the Mishkan, does not become *tamei* with roof-*tumah*, hides of nonkosher animals, which are not even used in the Cover of the Mishkan, certainly cannot acquire roof-*tumah!* Since R' Elazar does make this inquiry, he evidently holds that even though kosher animal hides are described only as being *for* the Tent, they still are considered a "tent" with regard to acquiring tent-*tumah;* and therefore he inquires with respect to nonkosher hides. Accordingly, wood products too should be subject to roof *tumah!*

The Gemara answers that since the various coverings of the Mishkan are listed together (*Bamidbar* 4:25), we can therefore derive through analogy that just as the lower, flaxen covering is called "tent," so too the upper coverings are called "tents." Since kosher animal hides, of which one of the covers is composed, are thus referred to as "tent," they *will* acquire tent-*tumah* when used as a roof over a corpse. R' Elazar can therefore rightfully inquire whether it is only the hides of kosher animals that acquire tent-*tumah*, or whether this law applies even to the hides of nonkosher animals.

A MUSSAR THOUGHT FOR THE DAY

Rambam, in his *Hilchos Teshuvah* (10:2), discusses the lofty level of Avraham's Divine service:

"One who serves Hashem out of love (אַהֲבָה) will busy himself with the study of Torah and the performance of mitzvos not due to any external consideration, neither for fear of punishment nor in order to receive reward. Rather, he does what is true simply because it is truth; and the reward will come as a result. This is a very lofty level, and not every wise man is able to achieve it. This is the level attained by Avraham Avinu, whom Hashem called 'My beloved one,' for he served Hashem only out of love. And this is the level that Hashem commanded each of us through Moshe Rabbeinu to try to achieve, as the verse states (*Devarim* 6:2): *And you shall love Hashem, your God.* When one reaches the proper level of love for Hashem, he will immediately perform all of the mitzvos out of love."

We see that *Rambam* defines the basis of service out of love (*avodah mei'ahavah*) as "doing what is true because it is the truth." *R' Shlomo Wolbe*, in his *Alei Shur*, notes that this is also what we call performing a mitzvah *lishmah*, "for its own sake." But the question arises: Why is it necessary for one to perform every mitzvah *solely* because it is the truth? As long as he knows that it is the truth, why does the fact that he has a secondary motive detract from the performance of the mitzvah?

To understand this, *R' Wolbe* directs us to a statement of *Rambam* in *Sefer HaMitzvos* (§3):" . . . we are commanded to love Hashem. This means that we must contemplate and ponder His commandments, His statements and His deeds, until we understand them *and we derive the greatest possible enjoyment from this understanding* — this is the love that we are required to achieve."

From this we see that love of Hashem is based on true understanding of His ways, which can be reached only through delving into His words and deeds. And only when one has reached the level of *the greatest possible enjoyment* from his understanding has he attained the level of loving Hashem. If his understanding does not afford him joy, he has not reached love of Hashem! Thus, one who performs the mitzvos knowing they are the truth, but also has secondary motives, cannot be said to love Hashem, for he has not reached the level of ultimate enjoyment. If he had, there would be no room in his performance for any ulterior motives. One who serves out of true love for Hashem does so for this reason alone, and no other.

We will continue our discussion of *avodah mei'ahavah* tomorrow.

HALACHAH OF THE DAY

Having completed our discussion of the first four of the thirty-nine forbidden *melachos* of the Sabbath, we now turn our attention to *melachah* number five, the *melachah* of דָּשׁ, *threshing*. It is through the process of threshing that wheat kernels are separated from the chaff in which they are enclosed. Threshing took place in the construction and preparation of the Mishkan as part of the agricultural process necessary for the production of dyes, as well as the production of flour from which the *lechem hapanim* were baked.

The literal translation of the Hebrew word דָּשׁ is to *tread*, or step upon, an item. In earlier times, one of the methods through which threshing was accomplished was for people to tread upon the stalks of grain, thereby breaking the kernels away from the stems and chaff.

The basic definition of threshing as it applies to forbidden labor on Shabbos is the extraction of a fruit, vegetable, grain, or other earth-grown object from its naturally occuring shell, peel, or other such attachment.

One of the *tolados*, "derived *melachos*," of the *melachah* of *threshing* that has many common practical applications is סְחִיטָה (*sechitah*; literally, *squeezing*), *extracting liquid* from an item in which it is absorbed. *Sechitah* applies to extracting liquids from foods, as well as to wringing out liquid that is absorbed in fabric. In both of these instances, one extracts a desired commodity — the liquid — from a surrounding object. Since the *toladah* of *sechitah* has so many practical applications, it is upon this *toladah* that we concentrate our discussion of the *melachah* of *threshing.*

In accordance with the restrictions of the *melachah* of *sechitah*, it is generally forbidden to press fruits or vegetables in order to extract their juices. It is also forbidden to squeeze out a liquid that has been absorbed in any food item. There are, however, differences between various groups of fruits and vegetables. In regard to *sechitah*, the halachah recognizes three different categories of fruits and vegetables: olives and grapes, other fruits and vegetables that are commonly pressed for their juice (e.g., oranges), and fruits and vegetables that are not commonly juiced (e.g., potatoes).

The first category includes grapes and olives only. The Biblical prohibition of *sechitah* (as applied to food items) applies only to the squeezing of these two fruits. Olives and grapes are unique in that their ultimate and most valued use is in their liquid forms. The optimal use of grapes lies in the production of wine; similarly, the most important use of olives is the production of olive oil.

A CLOSER LOOK AT THE SIDDUR

Between the opening blessings of the morning *Shacharis* prayers and the section of *Pesukei D'Zimrah*, many people recite the section known as *Korbanos*, which consists mainly of Torah passages that describe the various offerings. Also included in this section is the Torah passage that describes the *ketores* (the special incense that was compounded specifically for use in the *Beis HaMikdash*, and was offered twice daily on the Inner Altar). The prayers include a Baraisa from the Gemara in *Kereisos* (6a) that describes the composition and manufacture of the *ketores*. In this Baraisa, we find the following enigmatic statement:

And Bar Kappara taught further: If one were to put even a kortov (a very small measure, equal to one sixty-fourth part of a *log,* or less than one-quarter of an ounce) *of honey into [the ketores], no person could have resisted its scent. And why did they not mix honey into it? Because* the Torah stated (*Vayikra* 2:11): *"For any leaven or any honey you shall not burn from them a fire-offering to Hashem."*

The commentators note that this Baraisa would seem to be inherently contradictory. First it states that putting honey into the *ketores* would render it irresistible to all, seemingly providing a sound reason for its omission from the *ketores*. Then it states that it was omitted because its addition is forbidden by the Torah — implying that if not for the prohibition, it would indeed have been added!

Radvaz (*Responsa* 4:35) notes that in the beginning of the Baraisa, Bar Kappara speaks of "putting" honey into the *ketores,* while in the end he speaks of "mixing" in the honey. *Radvaz* therefore explains that while adding undiluted honey into the finished *ketores* would indeed produce an irresistible scent that was impossible to use, one might have thought that *adding* a bit of honey while compounding the *ketores,* which would enhance the scent while not making it irresistible, would be desirable. To preclude this, the Torah states that *any* honey cannot be offered (see *Pesachim* 43b, for a similar exposition regarding leaven).

Ginzei Yosef (*Responsa* §14) takes a different approach. He notes that although it is true that the addition of honey would have made the *ketores* irresistible, those who compounded it did not omit it for this reason. Rather, they omitted it solely to fulfill the will of Hashem, who states in His Torah that honey should never be offered in the *Beis HaMikdash.*

QUESTION OF THE DAY:

Hashem told Avraham, לֶךְ לְךָ, *Go for yourself. Where in the Torah do we find that a similar, seemingly extra word* לְךָ *is expounded to mean not for yourself, but rather, if you so desire?*

For the answer, see page 155.

פרשת
לך לך

A TORAH THOUGHT FOR THE DAY

MONDAY

PARASHAS
LECH LECHA

אֶל־הָאָרֶץ אֲשֶׁר אַרְאֶךָּ
. . . to the land that I
will show you (Bereishis 12:1).

W hy did Hashem withhold from Avraham the fact that his destination was Eretz Yisrael (Canaan)? *Rashi* cites the Midrash (*Bereishis Rabbah* 39:9) that states that Hashem purposely did not tell Avraham his destination so that his reward would thereby be increased, and he would "receive reward for each and every step." *Malbim* (see also *Eitz Yosef* ibid.) explains that when one embarking on a journey knows his destination, he can anticipate his arrival, and this makes the journey easier. But one who sets forth without knowing where he is going is beset with uncertainty at every step. Making such a journey without question requires an extraordinary level of unqualified devotion, and carries with it a much greater reward. The Midrash notes that Hashem followed this pattern before the trial of the *Akeidah* as well, where He did not immediately reveal that Yitzchak was the intended sacrifice, nor did He immediately reveal the mountain upon which the sacrifice was to be made (see *Bereishis* 22:2).

Abarbanel maintains that it was Hashem's will that Avraham separate himself at this time from the heathens who resided in Charan. Had Avraham's destination been revealed to him, others might have accompanied him; when it became clear to them that he did not know where he was headed, they decided to remain in Charan. [*Malbim* adds that Hashem did not wish Terach, Avraham's father, to accompany him either, and the lack of a clear destination helped accomplish this. It is noteworthy, however, that in spite of the doubt over their destination, all of Avraham's and Sarah's disciples — the "souls that they made in Charan" (see verse 5) — accompanied them without hesitation.]

Although Hashem did not identify Avraham's destination explicitly, the commentators point out allusions to Eretz Yisrael in the verse. *Midrash HaGadol* notes that the word אַרְאֶךָּ can also be vowelized אֶרְאֶךָ, which means *I will see you*; Hashem thus hinted to Avraham that he would be going to the land that is always watched by Hashem, as the verse (*Devarim* 11:12) states of Eretz Yisrael: *. . . the eyes of Hashem are upon it, from the beginning of the year until the end of the year.*

R' Menachem Yurowitz once pointed out to the *Steipler Gaon* that if the letters of the word אַרְאֶךָ are spelled out (א becoming אלף, ר becoming

ריש, and so on), and the *gematria* of the letters are added together, they will yield the sum of 832, which is precisely the *gematria* of אֶרֶץ יִשְׂרָאֵל. The *Steipler* responded by wishing him "a double *yasher koach!*"

MISHNAH OF THE DAY: SHABBOS 2:4

Extinguishing a fire is one of the 39 categories of *melachah* which one is forbidden to perform on the Sabbath by Torah law. Even removing some oil from a burning lamp renders one liable for extinguishing (*Beitzah* 22a; see *Tosafos* and *Rosh* there). Our Mishnah considers the use of a Sabbath lamp that invites the removal of some of its oil:

לֹא יִקּוֹב אָדָם שְׁפוֹפֶרֶת שֶׁל בֵּיצָה — A person may not perforate an eggshell, [1] וִימַלְאֶנָּה שֶׁמֶן וְיִתְּנֶנָּה עַל פִּי — and fill [the shell] with oil, הַנֵּר בִּשְׁבִיל שֶׁתְּהֵא מְנַטֶּפֶת — and place it over the mouth of a lamp so that [the oil] drips into the lamp;[2] וַאֲפִילוּ הִיא שֶׁל חֶרֶס — and this is so even if [the reservoir] is of earthenware. [3] וְרַבִּי יְהוּדָה מַתִּיר — But R' Yehudah permits this practice.[4] אֲבָל אִם חִבְּרָהּ הַיּוֹצֵר מִתְּחִלָּה מוּתָּר — However, if the potter attached [the reservoir] to the lamp initially, [its use] is permitted even by the Rabbis, מִפְּנֵי שֶׁהוּא כְּלִי אֶחָד — because then [the entire apparatus] is a single vessel.[5]

--- NOTES ---

1. This reading follows most commentaries. *Tos. R' Akiva Eiger* cites *Maharil*, who has the reading שְׁפוֹפֶרֶת שֶׁל בָּצָה, *a tube of swamp reed.*

2. The eggshell (or reed tube) serves as an additional reservoir of oil. A small hole at the bottom of the shell allows the oil to drip into the lamp at a measured rate. Since that oil is designated to be part of the lamp's fuel supply, a person who removes oil from the eggshell violates the prohibition of extinguishing (*Rashi*). The Rabbis therefore prohibited this arrangement on the Sabbath, lest one supply himself with oil from the reservoir. [According to *Rosh* removing oil from the eggshell will cause the lamp to go out earlier than intended. Therefore, the Rabbis prohibited use of the eggshell because of the concern that one may want to take the oil. According to *Tosafos*, the concern is that *all* the oil in the eggshell will be removed at one time, or that the eggshell itself will be detached and taken, and this is actual extinguishing (*Tiferes Shmuel* to *Rosh* ibid. §6).]

3. Even though an earthenware container tends to render any oil inside repugnant, the Rabbis were still concerned that one might come to remove some oil from the earthenware reservoir on the Sabbath. Hence, they prohibited its use as well (*Rashi*).

4. R' Yehudah sees no need for these precautionary decrees, as the sight of the oil dripping onto the wick below will alert one to the prohibition against removing the oil (*Rav*).

5. Since the reservoir and the lamp have been permanently joined to form a single entity, the Rabbis were confident that a person would refrain from removing oil from the reservoir, just as he would refrain from removing oil from an ordinary lamp (*Rashi*).

The Mishnah discusses a similar case:

לֹא יְמַלֵּא אָדָם קְעָרָה שֶׁל שֶׁמֶן — *A person may not fill a bowl with oil,* **וְיִתְּנֶנָּה בְּצַד הַנֵּר** — *and place it beside a lamp,* **וְיִתֵּן רֹאשׁ הַפְּתִילָה בְּתוֹכָה שֶׁתְּהֵא שׁוֹאֶבֶת** — *and put the* unlit *end of the wick into [the bowl] so that it will draw* the oil in the bowl to the other end of the wick.[6] **וְרַבִּי יְהוּדָה מַתִּיר** — *But R' Yehudah permits it.*[7]

NOTES

6. The Mishnah describes another two-piece, makeshift Sabbath lamp. A bowl to be used as an additional reservoir is placed next to the lamp, which holds a long wick. The unlit end of the wick is extended from the lamp to the bowl, thus utilizing the oil in the bowl as an additional fuel supply. The Rabbis disallow such a setup for the same reason they disallow a suspended reservoir — namely, for fear that one will remove some of the oil from the bowl. [However, if the bowl was attached to the lamp with plaster or clay, its use is permitted (*Mishnah Berurah* 265:4).]

7. Here, too, R' Yehudah sees no need for a precautionary decree (*Rashi*).

GEMS FROM THE GEMARA

The Gemara explains why all three (related) rulings of the Mishnah are needed:

If the Mishnah had taught us only about the eggshell (or reed-tube) reservoir, we might have thought that in this case alone the Rabbis rule stringently, since an eggshell (or a reed-tube) is not a repugnant container, and it is reasonable to fear that one might come to draw oil from it for food purposes. However, with regard to an earthenware reservoir, which is repugnant, we might have assumed that the Rabbis concede to R' Yehudah that its use is permitted on the Sabbath, for in this case we need not be concerned that oil will be removed.

Conversely, if the Mishnah had taught us only about the earthenware reservoir, which is repugnant, we might have thought that in this case alone R' Yehudah rules leniently. However, in the case of the eggshell (or reed-tube) reservoir, which is not repugnant, we might have assumed that R' Yehudah concedes to the Rabbis that its use on the Sabbath is forbidden, as one might come to draw oil from it to use for food.

Moreover, if the Mishnah had taught us only about these two cases, we might have thought that it is only in these cases that R' Yehudah rules leniently, because nothing intervenes between the reservoir and the lamp's cup. [Since both these reservoirs are positioned above the lamps, and within the diameter of the lamps' walls, they can be viewed as comprising one unit, and thus resemble an ordinary lamp. For that reason, R' Yehudah maintains that the Sages were not concerned that one would remove oil from the reservoirs (*Rashi*).] However, with regard to a bowl placed *beside* a lamp, where a space intervenes between the two vessels, we might have assumed that R' Yehudah concedes to the Rabbis that this type of arrangement is Rabbinically prohibited. [Since the reservoir and lamp clearly appear as two separate vessels, there is reason to fear that people will perceive no wrong in taking oil from the bowl (*Rashi*).]

Conversely, if the Mishnah had taught us only the case of the bowl, where there is an interval between reservoir and lamp, we might have thought that in that case alone the Rabbis ruled stringently; but in regard to the two cases of the eggshell (or the reed-tube) and the earthenware container, where reservoir and lamp appear as one vessel, we might have assumed that the Rabbis concede to R' Yehudah that their use on the Sabbath is permitted. Thus, it was necessary for the Mishnah to teach the law in each of the three cases (see *Tos. Yom Tov*).

A MUSSAR THOUGHT FOR THE DAY

Yesterday, we introduced the topic of *avodah mei'ahavah,* and discussed the ultimate enjoyment that one will experience when he succeeds in truly comprehending Hashem's will. This subject is discussed further in the first chapter of *Mesillas Yesharim:*

"Our Sages have instructed us that man was not created for any purpose other than to delight in his closeness to Hashem, and to derive pleasure from the radiance of His Presence — for this is the truest of delights, and the greatest of all pleasures that can be found. The place to enjoy this delight most fully is in the World to Come, which was designed by Hashem specifically for this purpose — however, the way to reach this desired destination is through service in this world . . . for the tools that will bring man to this desired result are the mitzvos that Hashem, Blessed is He, has given us, and the mitzvos can be performed only in this world."

A careful reading of this selection yields several noteworthy points. The *Mesillas Yesharim* speaks of "the truest of delights," which implies that there is such a thing as "untrue delight." But how can this be? Surely each person finds different things delightful, and thus what is truly delightful for one ought not to be for all! Yet, we are told that this is not the case: There is only one "true delight" — delighting in one's closeness to Hashem.

Furthermore, *Mesillas Yesharim* begins by mentioning both "delight" (תַּעֲנוּג) and "pleasure" (עִידוּן), and then states that the place for true delight is the next world. But he does *not* say this about pleasure. From this we can derive a tremendous novelty — that the *pleasure* of being close to Hashem is meant to be enjoyed in *this* world, not the next!

R' Shlomo Wolbe explains that there are indeed two types of pleasure and delight in this world. Those that are connected to physical urges and desires are false and fleeting, and do not constitute true "delight" or "pleasure," for they actually serve to distance a person from the true goal — closeness to Hashem. However, those pleasures connected to the spiritual side of man — such as the pleasure of performing mitzvos correctly — because they are truth will serve to bring man closer to Hashem. Each mitzvah performed moves a person further along the path that leads to the ultimate goal — the greatest pleasure possible in this world, which is delighting in Hashem.

HALACHAH OF THE DAY

We continue our discussion of the prohibition against *sechitah,* "extracting" liquids from foods or other items.

The second group of fruits and vegetables with regard to *sechitah* are those fruits and vegetables that are commonly juiced, even though their juice does not represent their most important form. It is common nowadays to drink orange or apple juice, yet these juices are not seen as the most valuable form of their fruit's use. These foods are not subject to the Biblical prohibition against *sechitah*; they are, however, subject to a Rabbinic injunction against squeezing out their juices on the Sabbath. As we will see further along in our discussion of *sechitah*, since the juicing of such fruits is forbidden only by Rabbinic decree, the Sages allowed for certain exceptions under which these fruits may indeed be squeezed on the Sabbath.

The third category is fruits and vegetables that are not commonly used for their juice. This group is entirely exempt from the prohibition of *sechitah.* Such fruits or vegetables may be pressed on the Sabbath even with the specific intent of extracting their juices. Whether or not a specific fruit or vegetable is considered commonly juiced is decided by contemporary practice. If it becomes the custom to juice a fruit that had not previously been used in such a fashion, that fruit would now fall into the second category, and be subject to the Rabbinic prohibition of *sechitah*.

Foods that have absorbed foreign liquids, for instance *challah* that has been dipped in wine, are also subject to a Rabbinic prohibition against *sechitah*. However, since this prohibition is only by Rabbinic decree, here too the Sages allowed for certain exceptions, which will be detailed below.

It emerges that food items commonly pressed for their juices (other than olives and grapes), as well as foods that have absorbed liquids, are both subject to the prohibition of *sechitah* by Rabbinic decree. The Sages, however, allowed for several exceptions to their decree. In brief, there are three exceptions: One may squeeze the liquid from a food in one of these categories if he is doing so in order to enhance the food; one may squeeze liquids from a food onto another solid food; and one may suck the liquid out of a food. We will now explain each of these exceptions in greater detail.

The Rabbinic decree against squeezing liquids from a food applies only when the intended result is to obtain the liquid. If, though, the intent is only to remove the liquid in order to enhance the flavor of the food (for example, squeezing the excess oil out of a slice of potato kugel), the Rabbinic decree does not apply, and the squeezing is permitted. [We must note that while squeezing is permitted in this situation, it should only be done immediately prior to eating, in order to avoid transgressing the prohibition of *borer*, "selecting," which will be discussed later in this work.]

We will continue our discussion of *sechitah* tomorrow.

A CLOSER LOOK AT THE SIDDUR

We begin the opening *berachah* of the *Shemoneh Esrei* by saying, בָּרוּךְ אַתָּה ה' אֱלֹהֵינוּ וֵאלֹהֵי אֲבוֹתֵינוּ אֱלֹהֵי אַבְרָהָם אֱלֹהֵי יִצְחָק וֵאלֹהֵי יַעֲקֹב, *Blessed are You, Hashem, our God, and the God of our forefathers — the God of Avraham, the God of Yitzchak, and the God of Yaakov*. The Gemara in *Pesachim* (117b, cited in *Rashi* to *Bereishis* 12:2) explains that the source of this formulation lies in Hashem's promises to Avraham that are found in the opening verses of our *parashah*. From Hashem's promise *And I will make of you a great nation* it is derived that we are to mention that Hashem is "the God of Avraham"; from the promise *and I will bless you* it is derived that we are to mention that Hashem is "the God of Yitzchak"; and from *and I will make your name great* it is derived that we are to say "the God of Yaakov."

Many commentators ask why such a seemingly repetitious formula was instituted. Surely the *berachah* could simply read, *the God of*

פרשת לך לך

MONDAY

PARASHAS LECH LECHA

Avraham, Yitzchak, and Yaakov! Why is it necessary for God to be mentioned separately in connection with each of the Avos (Patriarchs)?

The *Imrei Shmuel* (by R' Shmelke of Nikolsburg) explains that the prayer is worded in this way to make it clear that each of the Avos, on his own, arrived at the realization that only one God existed. Although both Yitzchak and Yaakov had the benefit of the tradition of Avraham, they did not rely on this alone to build their *emunah* in Hashem; rather, each of them came to the independent realization that there was only one Creator who brought everything into being. [Indeed, *R' Shlomo Wolbe* notes that each of the Avos exemplified a different aspect of Hashem's service — Avraham being the exemplar of *chesed,* Yitzchak the exemplar of *gevurah,* and Yaakov the exemplar of *tiferes* (these terms will be explained in future essays). Only the Avos reached these heights independently — which, explains R' Wolbe is why only they are called *Avos.* Not even Moshe Rabbeinu, the teacher of the Torah, merited to have Hashem described as "the God of Moshe."]

Although Hashem promised Avraham that his children after him would merit this status, Avraham's stature was still supreme. This is alluded to in the end of the aforementioned Gemara, which concludes: "One might think that the blessing should be concluded with a mention of all the Avos; the verse therefore conlcudes with Hashem's promise, *and "you" shall be a blessing.* This teaches us that we are to conclude the blessing with Avraham alone — as we indeed do, by saying, *Blessed are You, Hashem, Shield of Avraham.*

We will continue discussion of the blessing's conclusion, and Avraham's unique stature, in tomorrow's selection.

QUESTION OF THE DAY:
To which place did Avraham travel when he entered Eretz Yisrael, and why?

For the answer, see page 155.

A TORAH THOUGHT FOR THE DAY

פָּרָשַׁת
לֶךְ לְךָ

TUESDAY

PARASHAS
LECH LECHA

וַיְהִי־רִיב בֵּין רֹעֵי מִקְנֵה־אַבְרָם וּבֵין רֹעֵי מִקְנֵה לוֹט
וְהַכְּנַעֲנִי וְהַפְּרִזִּי אָז יֹשֵׁב בָּאָרֶץ

And there was quarreling between the herdsmen of Avram's flocks and the herdsmen of Lot's flocks — and the Canaanites and the Perizzites were then dwelling in the land (Bereishis 13:7).

The commentators address an obvious question: What is the connection between the two halves of this verse? Why was the quarrel between the herdsmen of Avraham and Lot intertwined with the fact the Canaanites and Perizzites were in the Land at that time?

Chizkuni explains simply that the quarrel between them arose because their herds needed more grazing land, and expansion was impossible because the adjacent grazing lands were being used by the Canaanites and Perizzites. Thus, the herdsmen of Lot and Avraham were both forced to use the same land. In a similar vein, *Ramban* explains that Avraham was afraid that their quarreling over land would alert the neighboring Canaanites and Perizzites to the large numbers of foreign-owned cattle being pastured in the land, which could result in both Avraham and Lot being driven away or attacked; *Malbim* adds that Avraham was concerned that they would unite and attack in a combined force.

However, *Rashi,* based upon the Midrash, explains differently. In his view, the quarrel arose when Lot's herdsmen grazed their cattle in the pastures of other people. Their defense for this behavior was that since Avraham had been promised the land as an inheritance, and he was childless, Lot could be considered his heir, and was entitled to graze anywhere in the land. Avraham's herdsmen rebuked them for this act of robbery, however, for, as the Torah explains, *the Canaanites and Perizzites were then in the land.* That is, although the Land had in fact been promised to Avraham's descendants, this did not give Lot (or Avraham) the right to dispossess the current residents. Therefore, the herdsmen of Lot were in the wrong. [Although, according to some views, Avraham was actually bidden to take legal possession of the land, Hashem had not yet told him to do so, and it is unclear whether Avraham ever did so (see *A Torah Thought for the Day,* Wednesday).

The Mishnah considers the ramifications of various motivations to extinguish the Sabbath lamps: הַמְכַבֶּה אֶת הַנֵּר — *One who extinguishes the* Sabbath *lamp* — מִפְּנֵי שֶׁהוּא מִתְיָרֵא מִפְּנֵי נָכְרִים וּמִפְּנֵי לִסְטִים *because he fears idolaters* [1] *or bandits,* [2] מִפְּנֵי רוּחַ רָעָה — *or because of melancholia,* [3] מִפְּנֵי הַחוֹלֶה שֶׁיִּישַׁן — *or so that a sick person may fall asleep,* פָּטוּר — in all these cases, *he is exempt.* [4] בְּחָס עַל הַנֵּר — But *if* he extinguishes the flame *to spare the lamp,* [5] בְּחָס עַל הַשֶּׁמֶן, בְּחָס עַל הַפְּתִילָה — *to spare the oil,* or *to spare the wick,* [6] חַיָּיב — *he is liable.* [7]

─────────── NOTES ───────────

1. Some religions (e.g., certain Persian sects) prohibited the lighting of lamps on the day of their festival in any place other than in their houses of worship (*Rashi*). Thus, this case is one in which a person is afraid that if the adherents of such a religion see the light from his lamp, they will persecute him.

2. In this case, a person is afraid that if bandits see the light from the lamp, they will attack him (*Rashi*).

3. In this case, the mental anguish of the sufferer is soothed by the darkness (*Rashi*).

4. In all of the above cases, the person extinguishing the lamp is exempt.

Now, the Tanna of our Mishnah follows the view of R' Yehudah, that one who performs a מְלָאכָה שֶׁאֵינָה צְרִיכָה לְגוּפָהּ, *labor not needed for its defined purpose* (the *defined purpose* of a labor is the purpose that labor served in the building of the Mishkan) violates a Biblical prohibition. [R' Shimon disputes this, and maintains that in such cases, the prohibition is Rabbinic — see Gemara 105b.] This can be seen from the fact that he concludes below that if one extinguished the light to salvage the oil or the lamp he violates Torah law (see below, note 7). Nevertheless, the person who extinguished the lamp in the three preceding cases is exempt, because he extinguished the lamp due to פִּקּוּחַ נֶפֶשׁ, *protection of life,* and such cases override the prohibitions of the Sabbath (*Rav*).

In this tractate, the term פָּטוּר, *exempt*, usually indicates that although one does not violate Torah law, one does violate a Rabbinic decree. This, however, is clearly not the case where danger to life is involved, when one is not only permitted, but obligated to do whatever is necessary to prevent loss of life. Why, then, is the term פָּטוּר used here? It is used in order to preserve stylistic consistency with the term חַיָּיב, *he is liable* (the opposite of which is פָּטוּר, *he is exempt*), which is used later in the Mishnah (*Rav*).

5. The person extinguished the earthenware lamp because he was afraid it might crack due to the intense heat of the flame (*Rashi*).

6. The person extinguished the lamp because he wished to salvage the remaining oil, or what remained of the wick, to use at a later time.

7. As noted above (see note 4), our Mishnah here follows R' Yehudah's opinion that *labor not needed for its defined purpose* is prohibited by Torah law. Hence, although in these cases the person did not perform the prohibited labor for its defined purpose in

A dissenting view:

רַבִּי יוֹסִי פּוֹטֵר בְּכוּלָּן — *R' Yose exempts* the person who extinguished the Sabbath lights *in all these* cases,[8] חוּץ מִן הַפְּתִילָה — *except* in the case of *the wick*, מִפְּנֵי שֶׁהוּא עוֹשֶׂה פֶּחָם—*for* in extinguishing the flame, he *makes [the wick] into charcoal.*[9]

———————— NOTES ————————

the Mishkan — i.e., for making charcoal — he is nevertheless liable (*Rav*). [When the Mishnah states that the person is liable, it refers to the obligation to bring a sin-offering, for it deals with a case of inadvertent transgression — e.g., the perpetrator forgot that today was the Sabbath, or that it is forbidden to extinguish a fire on the Sabbath (*Rashi* 30a).]

8. R' Yose follows R' Shimon's opinion that *labor not needed for its defined purpose* is prohibited by Rabbinic decree, not by Torah law (see above, note 4). Therefore, he maintains that in *all* of these cases there is no Biblical liability — even if there is no *protection of life* involved (*Rav* from Gemara 30a). However, even according to R' Yose, the last three cases are prohibited by Rabbinic decree (Gemara 30a).

9. In the case of an unsinged wick which was ignited expressly in order to singe it for future use, the labor that is performed is needed for its defined purpose, since his intent is to make the tip of the wick into charcoal — and this was the purpose of extinguishing fire in the Mishkan. Thus, a person who extinguishes the lamp for this purpose violates Torah law according to all opinions (*Rav*).

GEMS FROM THE GEMARA

In connection with the laws set forth in the Mishnah, the Gemara (*Shabbos* 30a) records a question that was asked of R' Tanchum of Nevi: Is it permissible to extinguish a lit candle for the benefit of a seriously ill person on the Sabbath?

This query was apparently posed before a crowd who had gathered to hear a lecture from R' Tanchum. As the Gemara proceeds to relate, R' Tanchum used the question as a springboard to deliver a homiletical discourse on a related theme. After his discourse, Rav Tanchum returned (30b) to the original question asked of him, and answered: In the Hebrew language, a candle is called נֵר , *a candle*, and a person's soul is also called "a candle" [*Mishlei* 20:27 states: נֵר ה' נִשְׁמַת אָדָם, *the candle of God is the soul of man*]. Thus, when one candle must be extinguished so that the other may survive, it is better to allow the candle fashioned by flesh and blood to be extinguished before the candle fashioned by the Holy One, Blessed is He; i.e., let a candle fashioned by man be extinguished, so that the life of a person — a "candle" fashioned by God — may be preserved.

[In fact, this is not the true legal source for the concept that one may perform labor on the Sabbath to save a life. The actual source is the verse that states וָחַי בָּהֶם, *and you shall live by them* (*Vayikra* 18:5), which teaches that any Torah law (save for the bans against idolatry, murder and illicit relations) may be violated to preserve human life. Nevertheless, Rav Tanchum had been asked this particular question before a crowd that had gathered to hear inspirational words from him. Thus, he replied to the question homiletically, in a way that would draw the hearts of his listeners to his message (*Rashi*).]

A MUSSAR THOUGHT FOR THE DAY

The quarrel between the herdsmen of Avraham and the herdsmen of Lot had tragic results. Lot separated from Avraham, and turned to settle in the fertile land of Sodom. Although he prospered initially, even rising to prominence there, the lives of most of his family, including that of his wife, were lost when Sodom was destroyed.

In his *Sichos Mussar*, R' Chaim Shmulevitz speaks of the destuctive power of *machlokes* (dispute). He cites a *Yerushalmi* which states that *machlokes* has the destructive power to overcome even righteous men. The *Yerushalmi* (*Pe'ah* 1:1) states that the men of the generation of Dovid HaMelech were righteous; however, since they were at odds with one another and spoke evil of one another, they would go out to war and fall in battle. The generation of the wicked Achav, by contrast, were virtually all guilty of idol worship; they, however, would go out to battle and return victorious, for they were at peace with one another and did not speak evil of one another. [This can be seen from the fact that no one would reveal to the wicked queen Izevel that the righteous prophet Ovadiah had hidden other prophets where Izevel could not harm them.]

Why does *machlokes* have such catastrophic results? *R' Chaim* explains that the Satan gravitates naturally to a place of strife and dissent; it is his natural habitat. In a place where peace reigns, on the other hand, the Satan cannot find any rest. This can be seen from the incident recorded in *Gittin* (52a): There was once a married couple whom the Satan would provoke into fights, and every Friday (an especially hectic time when tempers are short) they would have arguments. When the matter came to the attention of R' Meir, he kept them in his presence for three Fridays in a row, so that they would be unable to fight. In this way, he broke the Satan's grip upon the couple; and after the third consecutive Friday, they heard a voice calling out, "Woe is me, for R' Meir has driven me from my house!"

How does one avoid *machlokes*? It is said in the name of R' Yaakov Kamenetsky that the root of *machlokes* is *sin'as chinam*, groundless hate. It is possible to disagree with someone's actions, he would explain, without making the disagreement personal. Once a person makes the mistake of hating the person instead of the deed, he has crossed the line into the realm of the Satan. Moreover, even when it is permitted to hate a person, this does not mean it is permitted to hate him totally and utterly! And, R' Yaakov would say, if one hates even such a person one iota more than is permitted, he has transgressed the prohibition against groundless hate, which is the sin that caused the destruction of the second *Beis HaMikdash*. It is far better, he would conclude, to be guilty of *ahavas chinam*, groundless love, than *sin'as chinam*.

HALACHAH OF THE DAY

In cases where *sechitah*, "squeezing," is prohibited only by Rabbinic decree, the Sages permitted squeezing liquids directly onto a solid food, provided that the liquid is either being used to flavor the food, or where most of the liquid will be absorbed by the food. It is, however, forbidden to squeeze one liquid into another liquid, even if the squeezing is being done for flavoring. For example, while one may squeeze the juice from a lemon directly onto a piece of fish in order to flavor the fish, it is not permissible to squeeze a lemon into tea to flavor the tea. If one desires to flavor his tea with lemon on Shabbos, one may squeeze the lemon onto a spoonful of sugar, provided that most of the lemon juice will be absorbed by the sugar, and then add the flavored sugar to the tea.

Sucking juice from a fruit is not considered to be a form of *sechitah*. Therefore, it is permissible to hold a wedge of an orange and suck out its juice. One should refrain, however, from sucking the juice from olives or grapes (where the prohibition of *sechitah* is Biblical) while holding them. Nevertheless, one may insert an olive or grape into his mouth in order to suck out the juice while the fruit remains in his mouth. It is also permissible to dip *challah* into a liquid in order that it be absorbed, and then suck the liquid out, providing that one takes care while doing so not to squeeze out any liquid with his hands, for to do so would be in transgression of *sechitah* on the Rabbinic level, as noted previously.

In order to safeguard the prohibition of *sechitah*, the Sages forbade the consumption of juices that oozed from foods on the Sabbath, even if no active squeeezing took place. However, once again, the Sages divided fruits and vegetables into three categories with regard to this law.

Olive oil or grape juice that oozed from olives or grapes on the Sabbath may not be consumed until after the Sabbath.

Within the category of other fruits and vegetables that are commonly juiced (which are all subject to the prohibition of *sechitah* by Rabbinic decree, as noted above,) the Sages created two subgroups — fruits and vegetables that one intended to squeeze for juice, and those that one intended to eat. Fruits and vegetables that were intended for juicing (for example, oranges that were purchased for the purpose of producing orange juice), are subject to the Rabbinic decree, and therefore any juice that oozed from them on Shabbos is forbidden. On the other hand, if one purchased an orange intending to eat it, any juice that oozes from the orange may be consumed on Shabbos.

Foods not typically used for juicing are exempt from this Rabbinic decree, just as they are exempt from the prohibition of *sechitah* itself. Therefore, any juice that oozes from this type of fruit may be consumed on Shabbos.

Our discussion of *sechitah* will continue tomorrow.

A CLOSER LOOK AT THE SIDDUR

Yesterday, we noted that although we mention all three of the *Avos* in the opening *berachah* of *Shemoneh Esrei,* the *berachah* closes with just the mention of Avraham — *Blessed are You, Shield of Avraham.* Why is Avraham awarded this unique status?

The Gemara in *Berachos* (7b) states: "From the day the Holy One, Blessed is He, created the universe, there was no one who called Him 'Master,' until our father Avraham came and called him 'Master.' " Before Avraham, mankind thought that there was a multiplicity of gods, each with its own particular power and sphere of influence. Although there were other righteous people who preceded Avraham, who had acknowledged Hashem as the true God and served Him, only Avraham enthroned Hashem as the true Master of every facet of existence. For this, Avraham was established as *the* ancestor of the Jewish nation. There are three *avos* — but Hashem chose to close the blessing of *Avos* by identifying Himself as the Shield of Avraham.

The term *Shield of Avraham* is borrowed from a verse (*Bereishis* 15:1) where Hashem assures Avraham that he need not fear any retribution for having killed enemy soldiers during his war against the four kingdoms, and that his reward in the World to Come would be very great, as he had not exhausted any of his merits by attaining his miraculous victory (see *Rashi* there). In the *sefer Shaarei Orah* (§7, cited in *Beur HaChaim* by R' *Chaim Aryeh Erlanger*),

another aspect of the "shield" of Avraham is noted — the fact that Avraham himself serves as a shield for those of his descendants who may be unworthy. He writes that whenever such an unfortunate soul is brought before the Heavenly court for judgment, Avraham stands and takes responsibility for him, asking that *chesed* (undeserved kindness) be granted, in the merit of Avraham, the father of *chesed*. [Indeed, the Midrash states (*Bereishis Rabbah* 48:8; see also *Eruvin* 19a) that Avraham would not allow any Jew who had been circumcised to be punished in Gehinnom.]

Pachad Yitchak (*Rosh Hashanah*), citing *Maharal* (*Gevuros Hashem,* Ch. 6), notes that the word מָגֵן means *free* in Aramaic (see *Targum Onkelos* to *Shemos* 21:11). He connects this to Avraham's trait of *chesed,* since the Mishnah states in *Pe'ah* (1:1; we say this Mishnah before the opening blessings at the beginning of the morning prayers) that a person who does *chesed* receives the "fruits" of his good deeds in this world, while the "principal" of the reward remains intact, and is received in the World to Come. In essence, then, the rewards of this world are "free" — and thus Hashem assured Avraham that his reward was to be exceedingly great (see above). Moreover, the righteousness and devotion of Avraham created an eternal source of Divine merit for the nation that would descend from him — and it is this that gives Avraham his unique status.

QUESTION OF THE DAY:
*In Shemoneh Esrei, we use the word "Magen"
only in reference to Avraham.
Where in davening do we find it used
with reference to Yitzchak and Yaakov as well?*

For the answer, see page 155.

קוּם הִתְהַלֵּךְ בָּאָרֶץ לְאָרְכָּהּ וּלְרָחְבָּהּ כִּי לְךָ אֶתְּנֶנָּה

Arise, walk in the land through its length and breadth,
for to you I will give it (Bereishis 13:17).

Ramban discusses the meaning of the instruction contained in this verse, and offers two interpretations. In the first, he suggests that Hashem was not *commanding* Avraham to walk through the length and width of the land (indeed, it is not stated explicitly in the Torah that Avraham ever did so), but rather that Hashem was assuring Avraham that he could feel free to walk the land as he wished, without fear, for one day it would all belong to his descendants.

In his second interpretation, *Ramban* maintains that Hashem in fact instructed Avraham to walk throughout the land to legally take possession of it through the *kinyan* (legal acquisition) of *chazakah*. He explains that at the time of this instruction, Avraham was in the eastern portion of the land; when he later traveled to the land of the Philistines in the west, he thereby fulfilled this command.

With regard to whether it was possible to effect legal acquisition of the land in this manner, there is a dispute in the Gemara (*Bava Basra* 100a). Rav Eliezer indeed proves from our verse that walking through the length and breadth of a newly purchased field constitutes a legal mode of acquiring it for its new owner; for this is what Avraham was told to do in order to acquire Eretz Yisrael. The Sages, however, maintain that simply walking through a field does not acquire it unless another act of ownership (such as fencing in the property) is performed. [See further in *A Taste of Lomdus.*] In their view, Hashem commanded Avraham to walk through the land not to acquire it, but "so that it should be easier for his children to conquer it." *Rashbam* (ibid.) explains that according to the Sages, the walking was merely a *symbol* of the fact that the land would be his, and Avraham was as a landowner surveying his domain. This was done to show that his descendants would enter as heirs, not robbers, and would serve to forestall future complaints by the Satan. [*Ramban's* first explanation would seem to dovetail with the view of the Sages as well.]

R' Reuven Feinstein suggests that the Torah does not mention Avraham's fulfillment of this directive because it was an option given him by Hashem that Avraham chose not to exercise. When Avraham was later told (see 15:13) that his children would need to "sojourn in a land that was not theirs" for 400 years, he realized that claiming the land for his own would mean that the 400 years could not commence until his descendants would leave Eretz Yisrael. However, if he would *not* acquire the land, then Yitzchak would be living in a land that was not his own, and his lifetime could be counted as part of the 400 years. And indeed this proved to be the case; for the 400 years of exile began from the birth of Yitzchak, and the Jews therefore needed to be exiled in Egypt for only 210 years.

MISHNAH OF THE DAY: SHABBOS 2:6

The Mishnah considers the penalty that can befall a woman who is not careful concerning the kindling of the Sabbath lamps:

עַל שָׁלֹשׁ עֲבֵירוֹת נָשִׁים מֵתוֹת בִּשְׁעַת לֵידָתָן — *For three transgressions women die during childbirth:* [1] עַל שֶׁאֵינָן זְהִירוֹת בְּנִדָּה בְּחַלָּה וּבְהַדְלָקַת הַנֵּר — *Because they are not careful regarding* the laws of *niddah,* [2] *challah,* [3] *and the kindling of the* Sabbath *lamp.* [4]

───────────────── NOTES ─────────────────

1. Although a woman's merits may be sufficient to see her through ordinary situations, when she is in mortal peril — as is the case during childbirth — she undergoes special scrutiny to decide whether she will be granted Divine assistance to come through her labor safely. It is therefore a time when, in effect, she is more vulnerable to punishment for wrongdoing (*Rav*). [This is equally true of anyone who is in any kind of mortal peril, for it is axiomatic that the Satan prosecutes during a time of peril (see *Rashi* to *Bereishis* 42:4, and *Tanchuma, Vayigash* §1).]

2. This refers to women who were not scrupulous in their observance of the laws prescribed for the נִדָּה, *menstruant.* These laws prohibit intimacy for a woman who experienced a menstrual flow and has not yet immersed herself in a *mikveh* after the prescribed waiting time and preparations (for particulars of these laws see *Shulchan Aruch, Yoreh Deah* §183-201).

3. This refers to women who were not scrupulous in their observance of the Torah's law (see *Bamidbar* 15:17-21) that a special tithe must be separated from kneaded dough and given to a Kohen. This tithe is known as *challah.* [The many laws that govern the separation of *challah* are set forth in *Yoreh Deah* §322-330.]

4. The three mitzvos specified here each bear a special connection to women. Women are entrusted to properly observe the *niddah* laws; and since they generally have charge over domestic affairs, the taking of *challah* and the kindling of Sabbath lights usually fall in their domain as well. Therefore, it is they who are faulted if the laws are not properly observed (*Rashi* to 32a).

We learned in the Mishnah that laxity in the laws of *niddah, challah* and the kindling of Sabbath lights can precipitate death, for women in particular. The Gemara inquires why this punishment is visited upon them specifically during childbirth.

The Gemara replies allegorically, citing several proverbs that revolve around similar themes: For example, Rava says: "When the ox has fallen, sharpen the knife!" — i.e., if an ox you plan to slaughter happens to fall to the floor, sharpen the knife and slaughter it at that very moment. [An ox is most easily slaughtered when it is lying prone on the ground. Thus, if the ox is already on the ground, it is easiest to slaughter it then, rather than waiting until later.]

In this response, as well as several others, the Amoraim appropriate folk sayings to illustrate their point. The general idea is that a woman is most physically vulnerable when she is in the throes of childbirth; thus, it is at that time that she is most likely to bear the consequences of her wrongdoings (*Rashi*). [This is in line with the *Midrash Tanchuma* cited above (see *Mishnah of the Day,* note 1) — for the Satan prosecutes during a time of danger.]

Having stated that women are most vulnerable to retribution for their sins at the time of childbirth, the Gemara inquires as to when men are most vulnerable to retribution for their sins. Reish Lakish replies that it is at the moment they are crossing over a bridge. [Crossing a bridge was, especially in Talmudic times, inherently dangerous, for the bridge could break under the weight of those traveling across it.] The Gemara then asks: Are men *only* vulnerable when they pass over a bridge? Are there no other times when a man is especially vulnerable to Heavenly judgment?

The Gemara answers that what Reish Lakish meant is that they are vulnerable at times that are *like* crossing a bridge — i.e., in all comparable moments of danger. [Examples of such situations would be when one is walking near an unsteady wall, or setting out on an extended journey (*Rashi*).]

In relation to this point, the Gemara details the steps various Amoraim took to protect themselves in dangerous situations. For example: Rav would not cross a river on a boat together with an idolater, for he was concerned lest the Heavenly punishment due to the idolater might come at this very time, and that therefore Rav might be seized in a calamity along with the idolater. On the other hand, Shmuel would not cross a river upon a boat *except* together with an [non-Jewish] idolater, for he held that the Satan does not have power over two nations at the same time.

A MUSSAR THOUGHT FOR THE DAY

פרשת
לך לך

WEDNESDAY

PARASHAS
LECH LECHA

In an incident recorded in the Gemara (*Bava Basra* 16a), we find a discussion between the Satan and Hashem. The Satan is extolling the virtues of Avraham Avinu (see the Gemara there for the reason the Satan was doing this). Said the Satan: "Master of the universe. I have flown throughout all of the world, and I have not found a more righteous man than Avraham. For You said to him: *Arise, walk in the land through its length and breadth, for to you I will give it*. Yet, when his wife Sarah died, he could not find a place to bury her until he purchased it for 400 *shekels* (a vast sum of money); and even so, he did not wonder at Your ways!"

There is an obvious question to be asked here. If the Satan wanted to provide proof of Avraham's greatness and his total dedication to Hashem's service, there were seemingly many more significant deeds that he could have mentioned. When one considers Avraham's willingness to be thrown into the furnace in Ur Kasdim rather than worship idols, his leaving of his homeland at Hashem's directive, or the trial of *Akeidas Yitzchak,* the virtues mentioned here seem like rather faint praise.

The question is made even stronger when we consider exactly who the source of the praise was. After all, when it comes to gauging the difficulty of a trial, who could possibly be a better judge than the Satan himself. If the Satan considered this Avraham's greatest praise, there must be a great trial within this incident!

It is said in the name of *R' Chaim of Volozhin* that this exchange reveals a great fact about human nature — the greatest trial is the one that can go unnoticed. When a person sees that he is being tested, he can muster his strength of will and bestir himself to combat the *yetzer hara*. Such trials can be weathered by determined men. But when one is simply having a bad day, and an irritating and somewhat minor aggravation presents itself, then even the strongest of men can be faced with the almost automatic reaction of, "Does this *also* have to happen now?" Such a reaction, while seemingly trivial and almost unworthy of notice, is actually no less than a complaint against Hashem's ways.

This, explained *R' Chaim*, was the situation that confronted Avraham. Upon returning triumphantly from the *Akeidah*, he found to his grief that his beloved Sarah had died. And after crying over her and eulogizing her, he turned to bury her in her rightful place, with Adam and Chavah — only to discover that the way was barred by the children of

Cheis! Grief-stricken as he was, it would almost be expected that unbidden, the thought might cross Avraham's mind: Must I endure this as well? Did Hashem not assure me that this land would be mine? But Avraham did *not* ponder Hashem's ways. His faith was so complete that he never entertained any thought that Hashem's actions were less than perfect.

The Satan, who knows better than anyone else how men think, knew that this was an ultimate expression of *emunah* in Hashem — and that is why he chose this proof of Avraham's greatness.

HALACHAH OF THE DAY

W e mentioned earlier that the *melachah* of *sechitah* applies also to wringing liquid out of an absorbent fabric. It is forbidden to wring liquid out of a fabric in which it is absorbed. Depending on the intentions of the person who is wringing it out, this activity may fall under one (or both) of two different Biblical prohibitions. If one wrings out a fabric in order to collect the liquid, he is in violation of *sechitah*. If, however, the wringing is done in order cleanse and improve the fabric, then he is violating the melachah of כִּבּוּס, *laundering*. There is a very clear difference between these two cases. In the first case, the person desires to extract and enjoy the use of the liquid. This is analogous to *sechitah*, the *toladah* of *threshing,* where the clear intent and goal is the extraction of a desired commodity from the material in which it is encased. In the latter case, by contrast, the desired goal has nothing to do with the liquid; rather, the goal is to improve the fabric, and what happens to the liquid is merely incidental.

While the above is true of the Biblical prohibitions that apply to wringing out fabrics, even wringing out liquid absorbed in fabric with *neither* of these intentions remains forbidden by Rabbinic decree. Thus, even if the liquid will go to waste and the fabric will in no way be improved, it is still forbidden to squeeze liquid out of a fabric.

Sechitah does not apply equally to all fabrics. The Biblical prohibition of *sechitah* applies only to truly absorbent fibers such as wool, cotton, linen, and sponges. Non-absorbent materials (such as leather and the like) are not subject to *sechitah* on the Biblical level.

Nevertheless, it is forbidden by Rabbinic decree to wring out even a fabric woven of non-absorbent fibers (such as nylon); for although the fibers themselves do not absorb the liquid, the fabric traps the liquid between its fibers to an extent.

However, materials which neither absorb nor trap liquid in any way are exempt from the prohibition of *sechitah*. For example, the bristles of a nylon baby bottle brush are widely spaced and do not trap any water. Thus, such a brush is therefore not subject to any prohibition of *sechitah*.

To safeguard against the possibility of transgressing the *melachah* of *sechitah*, the Sages forbade saturating a fabric with liquid that one might then desire to wring out. For example, it is forbidden for a person to saturate a sponge or a mop with water, even if he does not intend to wring it out. [This decree does not extend to items that people do not generally bother wringing out, such as rags and paper towels.] Additionally, this decree applies only to truly absorbent materials that are subject to the Biblical prohibition of *sechitah*. Materials that only trap water between their fibers and are forbidden through Rabbinic decree may be saturated with liquid (as long as they are not then wrung out).

A CLOSER LOOK AT THE SIDDUR

In the prayer of *Hodu*, we speak of the promise that Hashem extended to the *Avos*, that the Land of Eretz Yisrael would be given to their descendants. We thank Hashem for the covenant, אֲשֶׁר כָּרַת אֶת אַבְרָהָם, וּשְׁבוּעָתוֹ לְיִצְחָק וַיַּעֲמִידֶהָ לְיַעֲקֹב לְחֹק לְיִשְׂרָאֵל בְּרִית עוֹלָם לֵאמֹר לְךָ אֶתֵּן אֶרֶץ כְּנַעַן חֶבֶל נַחֲלַתְכֶם, *that He made with Avraham, and His vow to Yitzchak; then He established it as a decree to Yaakov, to Yisrael as an everlasting covenant — saying, to you I will give the land of Canaan, the lot of your heritage.* The prayer mentions four times that Hashem promised the land to the *Avos*. He promised it to Avraham in the verse, *Arise, walk in the land through its length and breadth, for to you I will give it (Bereishis* 13:17). When Yitzchak descended to Gerar, Hashem appeared to him and said, *Sojourn in this land, and I will be with you and bless you; for to you and your offspring I will give all these lands, and I will establish the oath that I swore to Avraham, your father* (ibid. 26:3). During the dream that Yaakov had while traveling to Lavan, Hashem appeared to him and said, *the ground upon which you are lying, to you I will give it, and to your descendants* (ibid. 28:14). And after Yaakov's name was changed to Yisrael, Hashem said to him, *The land that I gave to Avraham and Yitzchak, I will give to you; and to your offspring after you I will give the land.*

Why do we mention all of these promises in the prayer? *Panim Yafos* explains that when Hashem originally promised the land of Canaan to Avraham, he told him that it would be given to his descendants, without specifying which descendants. Then, He promised Yitzchak that it would be given to his children rather than Yishmael's. To Yaakov he promised that the land would be given to his children, and not Eisav's. And before Yaakov descended to Egypt, Hashem told him that his name was Yisrael — and his children would inherit the land named after him — Eretz Yisrael.

The *Vilna Gaon* notes that in this prayer, Eretz Yisrael is referred to as חֶבֶל נַחֲלָתֵנוּ, which literally means, *the rope of our heritage.* The word *chevel* is used because in earlier times, ropes were used to measure lands when they were divided into ancestral plots. But the *Vilna Gaon* states that we can find a deeper meaning here as well. A thick *chevel* is usually comprised of three smaller cords that are twisted together (as attested to by the verse (*Koheles* 4:12): וְהַחוּט הַמְשֻׁלָּשׁ לֹא בִמְהֵרָה יִנָּתֵק, *the thrice-twisted cord will not readily separate*). The *chevel* alluded to here, he explains, is the merit of the three *Avos*, to whom Hashem promised the land.

A TASTE OF LOMDUS

According to one opinion in the Gemara in *Bava Basra* (100a), Hashem told Avraham to walk across the length and breadth of the land so that he would acquire it through the *kinyan* of *chazakah* (see above, *A Torah Thought for the Day*).

A person acquires a property through *chazakah* by performing actions that signify ownership, such as locking gates, digging ditches, or (in some opinions) walking through the property to inspect its boundaries.

Minchas Asher (*Kinyanim* §10) notes that although *chazakah* is often grouped together with other *kinyanim* (legal methods of acquisition) that can acquire real estate, it is somewhat unique. Most *kinyanim* for land and the like function by concretizing the will of the involved parties to complete a transfer of ownership. For example, when a seller writes a bill of sale for a property and gives it to the buyer, he actualizes his will to turn the property over to its new owner. And when the buyer gives the seller a down payment for the property, he thus demonstrates his willingness to accept the terms of the transaction, and to receive the property.

Chazakah is different, for it involves no transfer from buyer to seller or vice versa. Simply relating to the property to be acquired in a way that only an owner would (thus demonstrating ownership) is sufficient to accomplish the transfer of ownership, when this is done with the previous owner's approval and acknowledgment.

This distinction is at the root of a ruling of *Ketzos HaChoshen* (*Teshuvah* §25, printed at the end of *Avnei Miluim*) concerning *kinyan chazakah*. He writes that although a person's Canaanite slaves and young children may not perform other *kinyanim* (such as acquisition through payment or the issuance of a bill of sale) on a buyer's behalf, they may be sent to acquire a property by means of *chazakah* (e.g., they may be sent to lock the gates of a property). Their proprietary usage of the field for the new owner successfully acquires it for him. This may be explained in light of the above approach; for other *kinyanim* by necessity involve a transfer from buyer to seller, and thus the buyer must have a legally responsible representative. Canaanite slaves and young children do not qualify as such, and therefore cannot serve to perform those *kinyanim*. But *chazakah* requires only a demonstration of ownership. Clearly, one who sends slaves or workers to improve a property is behaving as an owner even if he has no official legal presence there! Thus, the *chazakah* can be effective even if carried out by Canaanite slaves or children.

Maharam Mintz (*Responsa* §39) points out that since *chazakah* acquires through demonstration of ownership, it is not effective while another person is demonstrating ownership simultaneously upon the property to be acquired. He therefore rules that if one is purchasing a property that has a tenant living there under lease, simply making a *chazakah* by locking the door will not acquire the property. For the tenant has rights that prevent the buyer from acting in a fully proprietary manner, and it is unclear from the act of *chazakah* that the buyer, rather than the tenant, is the owner! To illustrate — the fact that the tenant must be notified before the buyer can visit the house is proof that the buyer cannot *demonstrate* total ownership of the property. Thus, if the new buyer wants the tenant to remain in the property, he must use another form of *kinyan* to acquire the property, for *chazakah* cannot be effective (see also *Ketzos HaChoshen* 216:2).

QUESTION OF THE DAY:

The verse states that the Canaanites and the Perizzites were in the land. Who were the Perizzites?

For the answer, see page 155.

וַיֹּאמַר אֲדֹנָי ה׳ בַּמָּה אֵדַע כִּי אִירָשֶׁנָּה

And [Avraham] said: "My master HASHEM/ELOKIM!
With what shall I know that I will inherit it?"
(*Bereishis* 15:8).

The commentators struggle to explain the true meaning of this verse. It seems inconceivable that Avraham, whose faith in Hashem was so great that he allowed himself to be thrown into the furnace in *Ur Kasdim* by Nimrod, and who unquestioningly followed Hashem's call to leave his father's house, would respond to Hashem's statement that his children were to inheirit Eretz Yisrael with a request for proof! Surely Hashem's word was assurance enough!

Although the Gemara in *Nedarim* (32a) indeed counts Avraham's statement here as a shortcoming, and cites it as one of the reasons that Avraham's descendants were punished with servitude in Egypt, this still does not allow us to understand how Avraham could have doubted Hashem's word in the slightest. The commentators therefore offer several interpretations of Avraham's puzzling reply.

Rashi suggests in one approach that Avraham was apprehensive lest he or his descendants prove unworthy of such a gift. Thus, Avraham's question is to be understood not as questioning Hashem's gift, but as asking, "How do I know that my children will have the merit they need to deserve this gift? Perhaps they will sin and forfeit their rights!" (see *Mizrachi* and *Maharzav* to *Bereishis Rabbah*). According to the Midrash, Hashem answered that the Jews would always be deserving, for even if they were to sin, they could repent and seek atonement through the offering of sacrifices [similar to the ones that Avraham was shortly to offer] (see *Gur Aryeh*).

Other interpretations are based on other meanings of the verb אֵדַע that are found in Scripture. *Oheiv Yisrael* notes that this verb can mean *to afflict* (see, for example, *Shoftim* 8:16). He thus interprets Avraham's question in line with the Gemara in *Berachos* (5a) that states that Eretz Yisrael is one of the three precious gifts that Hashem gave the Jews that must be acquired through suffering. Avraham therefore asked: What manner of suffering must I undergo in order to merit receiving the land? Hashem replied that the Jews would surely be chastised (יָדַע תֵּדַע) during their exile in Egypt, and this would be the suffering they would undergo before entering the land.

HaKesav VeHaKabbalah understands אֵדַע to be related to *exalted* (as it is understood in *Tehillim* 144:3). Thus, he explains that Avraham, in his

humility, was asking: How did I become so exalted in Hashem's eyes as to deserve this great bequest? Hashem replied that it was a consequence of Avraham's true faith, and proceeded to seal a covenant with him. [Seemingly, this interpretation cannot be reconciled with the view in *Nedarim* that this statement was related to the suffering of the Jews in Egypt. See, however, *A Mussar Thought for the Day.*]

R' Moshe Feinstein notes that the word אֲדַע is used in Scripture to mean *love* (see, for example, *Bereishis* 18:19). He explains that Avraham, the paragon of kindness and mercy, was distressed by the fact that his descendants would have to wipe out the Canaanites in order to inherit Eretz Yisrael. How, asked Avraham, can I love this information that you have given me, if it means that my children must kill many thousands of people in order to inherit the land? But Hashem replied that Avraham was mistaken in feeling this distress, for those who would be destroyed were wicked people who deserved to be killed. The Midrash states that Hashem told Avraham: "I am culling the thorns from My vineyard!" Thus, the Gemara reckons this misplaced mercy as a fault, for Hashem's judgment is always just.

MISHNAH OF THE DAY: SHABBOS 2:7

The Mishnah describes the responsibilites of the householder at the time of the lighting of the Sabbath lights:

שְׁלֹשָׁה דְבָרִים צָרִיךְ אָדָם לוֹמַר בְּתוֹךְ בֵּיתוֹ עֶרֶב שַׁבָּת עִם חֲשֵׁכָה — There are *three things a man must say in his home on the eve of the Sabbath just before dark.*[1] עִשַּׂרְתֶּם — "Have *you tithed* the produce we will eat on the Sabbath?"[2] עֵרַבְתֶּם — "Have *you prepared the eruv*?"[3]

———————— NOTES ————————

1. Before the Sabbath actually arrives, a householder must remind the members of his household to complete three tasks, listed below, that must be performed before the Sabbath. Clearly, he must remind them when there is still enough time left to perform the chores. Yet he should not do so too early in the day, lest the people in the house procrastinate, and eventually forget to do them altogether. The reminders should therefore be issued "just before dark," when people are likely to perform the tasks immediately, if they have not already performed them (*Rashi*).

2. Tithing produce is not permitted on the Sabbath. Thus, if one wishes to partake of any produce on the Sabbath, the tithing must be done before the Sabbath arrives. The Mishnah therefore advises the householder to inquire just before dark as to whether the tithing has been completed.

3. This query concerns both *eruvei techumin* and *eruvei chatzeiros*. An *eruv techumin* allows a person to walk more than the usual maximum of 2,000 *amos* beyond his

הַדְלִיקוּ אֶת הַנֵּר — And, *"Kindle the Sabbath light!"*[4] סָפֵק חֲשֵׁכָה סָפֵק אֵינוּ חֲשֵׁכָה — *If there is a doubt whether it is dark* yet, *or whether it is not* yet *dark,*[5] אֵין מְעַשְּׂרִין אֶת הַוַּדַּאי — *we may not tithe* produce that has *definitely* not yet been tithed,[6] וְאֵין מַטְבִּילִין אֶת הַכֵּלִים — *and we may not immerse vessels* in the *mikveh,*[7] וְאֵין מַדְלִיקִין אֶת הַנֵּרוֹת — *nor may we kindle* the Sabbath *lights;*[8] אֲבָל מְעַשְּׂרִין אֶת הַדְּמַאי — *but we may tithe*

———————— NOTES ————————

location. This is accomplished by placing food at another location, by which one establishes his "Sabbath residence" in that place, enabling him to walk an additional 2000 *amos* from that place.

An *eruv chatzeiros* allows people to carry from their houses to an enclosed courtyard jointly owned by the occupants of more than one dwelling, and vice versa. This *eruv* is established by collecting a measure of bread before the Sabbath from each of the dwellings which open into that courtyard, and placing it in one of those dwellings for the duration of the Sabbath. This allows all the houses opening into this courtyard to be treated as owned in common by a single consortium, and removes the Rabbinic prohibition against carrying between these areas in the absence of such an *eruv* (*Rashi*). It is forbidden to set up these *eruvin* on the Sabbath, because they involve acquisitions (of either a new location of residence, or of common ownership in the houses of the courtyard), and making acquisitions on the Sabbath is Rabbinically prohibited (*Meiri*). The Mishnah therefore advises the householder to query just before dark as to whether the *eruvin* have been set in place.

4. The first two reminders: "Have you tithed?" and "Have you prepared the *eruvin*?" are formulated as questions, for it is not immediately obvious whether the produce has already been tithed or the *eruvin* have been set in place. On the other hand, this reminder — "Kindle the light!" — is formulated as an instruction, for it is immediately obvious whether or not the light has been lit. Hence, should the householder find that the lights have not been lit, he should direct that the task be performed immediately (*Rashi*).

5. The Mishnah refers here to the time period known as בֵּין הַשְּׁמָשׁוֹת, *twilight*, the transition between day and night. Legally speaking, *bein hashemashos* is a period during which it is uncertain whether nightfall has arrived. Hence, during this period on the eve of the Sabbath, the performance of some forms of labor is permitted, while the performance of other forms of labor is prohibited, for the Sabbath might have already begun.

6. Tithing definitely untithed produce (*tevel*) is prohibited on the Sabbath, because the process resembles the repair of a vessel. [In a sense, one repairs the produce by rendering it fit for consumption.] Unlike actual repair, however, there is no physical change in the produce, and therefore, the prohibition is only by Rabbinic decree (*Beitzah* 36b). This Tanna rules that during the twilight period, even Rabbinic prohibitions may apply (*Rashi*).

7. Vessels that have become *tamei* (ritually contaminated) may not be immersed in a *mikveh* so as to make them *tahor*. This, too, resembles the repairing of vessels, and is also prohibited by Rabbinic decree (*Rashi*).

8. Igniting the fire of a Sabbath light is labor that is prohibited by Torah law, and therefore forbidden during *bein hashemashos*, when it is uncertain as to whether

וְטוֹמְנִין — demai,[9] **וּמְעָרְבִין** — and make an eruv,[10] **אֶת הַחַמִּין** — and insulate hot food.[11]

────────── NOTES ──────────

it is yet the Sabbath. The *Tanna* here merely draws for us the obvious conclusion that if a Rabbinic prohibition is in force during *bein hashemashos,* then certainly a Torah law is as well (*Rashi*).

9. By Rabbinic decree, anyone who purchases produce from an unlearned person (*am haaretz*) must separate tithes, for it is doubtful that the ignorant person tithed the produce himself. Such produce is called דְּמַאי, *demai,* a contraction of the expression דָּא מַאי — *what is this?* [a reference to the doubtful status of the produce] (see *Demai* 1:1). However, since as a matter of fact most of the unlearned people *did* tithe their produce, the Sages did not treat *demai* with the same degree of stringency as definite *tevel.* This being so, the Sages did not view the tithing of *demai* to be as great a "repair" as the tithing of definite *tevel,* and they therefore allowed such tithing during *bein hashemashos,* when the arrival of the Sabbath is not yet certain (*Rashi*). [However, once night has fallen and the Sabbath has certainly begun, it is forbidden to tithe even *demai.*]

10. Our Mishnah teaches that we may establish an *eruv chatzeiros* during the period of *bein hashemashos*. Since the prohibition of carrying to and from the common courtyard or from one house to another is a Rabbinic decree that is not supported by any Biblical verse, the preparation of *eruvei chatzeiros*, which allows such carrying, is not considered a true repair, and it is therefore permitted to set an *eruv chatzeiros* in place during *bein hashemashos*. [On the other hand, the prohibition against walking more than 2,000 cubits does have a Biblical support; i.e., although the ban on walking more than 2,000 *amos* is also a Rabbinic decree, there exist certain verses in the Torah that lend support to the *concept* of limiting the range of walks on the Sabbath. Therefore, an *eruv techumin*, which serves to make such walking permissible, is considered sufficiently comparable to the repair of vessels, and it may not be set in place during *bein hashemashos* (*Rav*).]

11. The Sages prohibited insulation of a dish in cases where the insulation will increase its heat, even if the insulation is done before the Sabbath and allowed to remain in place on the Sabbath. [They were concerned that if this were allowed, some might use a mixture of hot ash and coals for this purpose, and might come to stir the coals on the Sabbath, which would be a violation of the Torah prohibition of *kindling* (see 4:1).] Moreover, on the Sabbath proper, they even forbade insulation that only *preserves* the heat without increasing it. [They were concerned that if a person coming to insulate the food on the Sabbath were to find that it had cooled, he might forgetfully heat it, thereby violating the Torah prohibition of *cooking.*]

However, during *bein hashemashos*, most pots are still hot, and there need be no concern that one coming to insulate his pot would find that the food had cooled. The Rabbis therefore allowed insulating the food during *bein hashemashos* with anything that preserves heat, provided that it does not increase the heat (*Rav*).

THURSDAY

The Mishnah speaks of the period of the day in which there is a doubt whether it is dark or it is not dark. This period is known as בֵּין הַשְּׁמָשׁוֹת [bein hashemashos], or twilight — i.e., the transition between day and night. The Gemara (34b) cites a Baraisa that explains several uncertainties that pertain to the period of bein hashemashos: It may be comprised of day and of night together, or comprised entirely of day, or comprised entirely of night. Because of these uncertainties, we place upon it the stringencies of two days — i.e., depending on the situation, we treat bein hashemashos as if it were part of the previous day, or part of the following day, or a part of both days, following whichever possibility yields the greater stringency. For example, one may not perform labor during bein hashemashos on Friday evening, for bein hashemashos may be night, and the next day [the Sabbath] may thus have already begun. By the same token, one may not perform labor during bein hashemashos on Saturday, for bein hashemashos may be day, and thus the Sabbath may not yet have ended. If one does perform melachah during either of these periods, he would be liable to bring an asham talui, the offering brought when one is uncertain if he inadvertently performed melachah on the Sabbath (Rashi).

The Baraisa, in the name of R' Yehudah, states that this period of uncertainty begins once the sun has set, and lasts as long as the eastern face of the sky is reddening. More precisely, when the bottom of the sky — the part near the horizon — has darkened, but the upper part of the sky has not yet darkened, it is bein hashemashos. But once the upper part of the sky has darkened, and has attained the same color as the bottom of the sky, it is night, and the period of twilight is over. Two other views are cited: R' Nechemyah says that once the sun sets, the period of bein hashemashos begins, and it lasts the time it takes for a man to walk a half-mil (1,000 amos); while R' Yose says that the duration of bein hashemashos is like the blink of an eye [the Gemara later (35a) states that according to R' Yose, the bein hashemashos period begins when the time-frames cited by the previous Tannaim end].

Subsequently (35b), both Rav Yehudah in the name of Shmuel and a Baraisa state that when one star is visible in the sky, it is still day; when two are visible, this signifies bein hashemashos; and the visibility of three stars signifies night. In explaining this standard, R' Yose states that we are not speaking of large stars that are visible even by day, nor of small stars that are visible only later at night, after it is fully dark, but rather, of medium-sized stars. Thus, once three stars of medium magnitude become visible in the evening sky, *bein hashemashos* has concluded and night has certainly fallen.

[Various commentators question why it was necessary to provide two different benchmarks of night — the appearance of three stars (given by the Baraisa here), and the upper sky attaining a level of darkness equivalent to that of the lower sky (given by the Baraisa above). Some explain that the Baraisa [and Shmuel] gave the sign of three stars because for most people it was too difficult to discern exactly when the upper sky became as dark as the lower sky (*Meiri*). Others, though, assert the very opposite — that the earlier Baraisa spoke of the darkening upper sky, because most people are not expert in judging exactly which stars are medium-sized (*Beur HaGra* to *Orach Chaim* 261:11).]

A MUSSAR THOUGHT FOR THE DAY

R' *Nosson Tzvi Finkel,* the *Alter* of Slabodka, would take a powerful lesson from Avraham's question, *With what shall I know that I will inherit it?* (see A Torah Thought for the Day), and Hashem's response:

"Avraham was the first of the believers. He was the first to call Hashem the Master (*Berachos* 7a). He was tested with ten trials and was found to be faithful. Of him it is said, *And he believed in Hashem* (*Bereishis* 15:6). And when Moshe Rabbeinu said of the Jews, *they will not believe me* (*Shemos* 4:1), Hashem replied: They will believe, because they are believers and the children of believers — this being a reference to Avraham (see *Shabbos* 97a). Yet, the Gemara (*Nedarim* 32a) states that Avraham was punished by having his children subjugated in Egypt for many years because he asked, *With what shall I know that I will inherit it?*

"Consider: Is it possible that Avraham doubted Hashem's word? Obviously not! Indeed, *Chazal* elsewhere have interpreted Avraham's question as an expression of his concern that perhaps his children would not merit such a gift; and Hashem replied that they would receive the land by virtue of the sacrifices (see *Taanis* 27b). Nevertheless, Avraham is faulted for the *wording* of his question. Because of Avraham's elevated spiritual level, his use of an expression which might be *misunderstood* as a request to Hashem to furnish proof for His promise was held against him in Heaven.

"The Midrash (*Tanchuma, Kedoshim* §13) comments concerning this incident: Woe to the man who says something and does not know how to say it properly! Because Avraham said *With what shall I know,* he was told, *Know that they will be sojourners in a land that is not their own for*

פָּרָשַׁת
לֶךְ לְךָ

THURSDAY

PARASHAS
LECH LECHA

400 years. As a result of this slightly ambiguous remark, Avraham's descendants were enslaved for generations to the lowly Egyptians, descendants of Canaan, who himself had been cursed to be *a slave of slaves* (*Bereishis* 9:25). That servitude would indeed coarsen the souls of Israel, until the angels would remark to Hashem, "How are these (the Jews) different from these (the Egyptians)? (see *Mechilta, Beshalach*).

"The Jews were forced to make bricks, build buildings, and work in the fields. They were forced to endure backbreaking toil, and descended to the forty-ninth level of impurity. All of this for a slight, almost unnoticeable failing, a quickly passing taint on the brightly shining faith of the father of believers.

"Only Hashem Himself in His Glory could bring the Children of Israel out of their exile — not any angel nor any other messenger. For the cause of that bitter, terrible exile was a fault so slight that only Hashem Himself, Who examines man's innermost thoughts, could determine when the time had come to correct it. Only through the revelation of Hashem Himself, in all His Glory, could the Jews repair that almost imperceptible fault hidden in the question, *With what shall I know?"*

HALACHAH OF THE DAY

We will now discuss some practical ramifications of the prohibition of *sechitah* of fabrics.

It is forbidden to use a sponge or washcloth to wash dishes, because it is inevitable that water will be wrung out of them during the washing process. It is also forbidden to use synthetic cleaning pads which are dense enough to trap water between their fibers. However, one may use a synthetic pad whose fibers are widely spaced and therefore unable to trap water.

Due to the Rabbinic decree against saturating fabrics, it is forbidden to use a sponge, mop, or garment made out of naturally absorbent material to absorb a spill. However, one may use a towel. This is because automated washers and dryers are so commonplace that most people do not bother to wring out wet towels, and the Rabbinic decree against saturation therefore does not apply to them. [This reasoning is dependent upon socioeconomic conditions, and may therefore not hold true everywhere.]

If a dirty liquid spills, one may blot the spill with a garment (not with a sponge or mop) since it is unlikely that he will wring out the garment afterwards. This is because in such a case wringing out the garment will serve no purpose at all. It will not remove any stains, nor will it remove any odors that might cling to the garment as a result of its having absorbed the spill. Since the garment will have to be washed or otherwise cleaned in any case, we are not concerned that one may come to wring it out.

Colored liquids may also be mopped up with an absorbent garment for the reason noted above. However, due to the possible violation of the *melachah* of צוֹבֵעַ, *dyeing*, it is best to use rags or paper towels to blot up such spills, since in these the coloration has no significance.

It is forbidden to clean a dirty surface with a wet rag, because while rubbing the surface, some liquid will invariably be squeezed from the material. If, however, the rag is only damp, it is permissible, since water will not be squeezed from such a rag.

This concludes our discussion of *sechitah,* and the *melachah* of *threshing.*

A CLOSER LOOK AT THE SIDDUR

This week, we will discuss the third of the Thirteen Fundamental Principles (י״ג עיקרים) enumerated by *Rambam.*

The Third Principle states:

אֲנִי מַאֲמִין בֶּאֱמוּנָה שְׁלֵמָה שֶׁהַבּוֹרֵא יִתְבָּרַךְ שְׁמוֹ אֵינוֹ גוּף וְלֹא יַשִּׂיגוּהוּ מַשִּׂיגֵי הַגּוּף וְאֵין לוֹ שׁוּם דְּמְיוֹן כְּלָל.

I believe with perfect faith that the Creator, Blessed is He, is not physical, and is not affected by any phenomena, and that there is nothing whatsoever to which He can be compared.

This third principle builds upon the foundation of the previous one, in which it is stated that we must believe that Hashem is One. As we explained last week, *Rambam* links this belief to the fact that divisibility is a trait of the physical. Here, we deal directly with the fact that Hashem is totally non-physical, and cannot be affected in any way by anything physical.

This principle, however, would seem to be at odds with all of the descriptions that we use constantly to explain Hashem's relationships with us, and ours with Him. We talk constantly of Hashem "hearing" our prayers, of Hashem "going" to a certain place; we even find a verse in the Torah (*Bereishis* 2:2) that speaks of Hashem "resting" after creating the world! If Hashem has no physical reality, how are all of these statements to be understood?

The Gemara in *Berachos* (31b) tells us that the Torah speaks to us "in the language of man." This concept includes the idea that the Torah uses

פָּרָשַׁת לֶךְ לְךָ

THURSDAY

PARASHAS LECH LECHA

terminology that we are able to understand. [The academic term for this type of usage is *anthropomorphism*.] In truth, Hashem neither hears nor speaks in a physical sense. But what He *does* "do" cannot be described accurately in a language devised by, and meant to be understood by, mortal man. Thus, we use the words that we can comprehend, to describe events that are inconceivable to us.

Rambam (*Hilchos Yesodei HaTorah* 1:9) makes the further point that although we find many descriptions of physical manifestations of Hashem used by the *neviim* (prophets), this does not run counter to the third principle, for a prophetic vision is clearly not meant to be a true picture of Hashem. [Rather, it is possible that when Hashem sent a specific vision to a certain prophet, He wished to convey a certain intention or message as to His Will, and He chose to do so by providing the prophet with that image.]

We find in the Torah that Moses asked Hashem, *Show me Your Glory* (*Shemos* 33:18). This, however, does not mean that Moses actually expressed a wish to see Hashem's "image," for Moses surely knew that no such thing existed! Rather, Moses asked to understand the Glory of Hashem's *ways*. [Indeed, many have suggested that Hashem's reply to Moses, *You will see My back, but My face may not be seen,* alludes to the fact that Hashem's workings can be understood only when viewed in retrospect, after the fact. Only Hashem knows the intricacies of His Creation.]

An important point that must be made is that the belief in the non-physicality of Hashem includes the understanding that Hashem is not subject to the concepts of space and time. Thus, Hashem cannot be said to be in (or be excluded from) a location or place. Additionally, there is nothing that Hashem does not yet know, and with regard to Him, past, present, and future are all the same. These situations are all born of physical limitations and concepts, which do not apply to Hashem. [Again, the many times that our speech does seem to use such terms are results of the inadequacy of language to convey the true order of events.]

Believing that Hashem is physical can cause a person to ascribe to Hashem corporeal limitations and even partnership, a path that is heretical, and ultimately leads to idol worship. *Rambam* (*Hilchos Teshuvah* 3:7) calls a person who harbors such a belief a *min* (however, cf. *Raavad*).

QUESTION OF THE DAY:

How are the 400 years of exile
that the Jews endured reckoned?

For the answer, see page 155.

וְלֹא יִקָּרֵא עוֹד אֶת־שִׁמְךָ אַבְרָם וְהָיָה שִׁמְךָ
אַבְרָהָם כִּי אַב הֲמוֹן גּוֹיִם נְתַתִּיךָ

And your name shall no longer be called Avram;
rather, your name shall be called Avraham,
for I have made you the father of a multitude
of nations (Bereishis 17:5).

What was the significance of the changing of Avram's name? *Rashi* explains that the original name of Avram was a contraction (known in Aramaic as *notrikon*) of the words *av* and *Aram*, which literally means *father of Aram.* This signifies Avram's status as a lord and master in Aram, his native country (see *Bereishis* 11:28). However, Hashem now wished Avram's name to proclaim his status as leader of many nations; thus, his name was changed to Avraham, which is a contraction of *av hamon goyim,* "a father of a multitude of nations." [An example of Avraham's status as the father of all nations can be found in the law stating that converts are called to the Torah as "the son of Avraham" (see also *Rambam, Commentary to the Mishnah, Bikkurim* 1:4).] Others explain that Avraham is a contraction of *av raham,* with *raham* being an ancient Arabic word meaning *multitude.*

Chizkuni notes that it is an ancient custom to change someone's name when he rises in stature, to signify that the "new" person has outgrown his old status. As an example, we find that Pharaoh changed Yosef's name to Tzafnas Pane'ach when he was promoted to viceroy of Egypt.

The Gemara in *Nedarim* (32b) finds another allusion in the changing of Avram's name to Avraham. The numerical value (*gematria*) of the Hebrew letters of Avram is equal to 243; with the addition of the *hei* to form Avraham, the total became 248. R' Ami bar Abba explained that there are 248 limbs in the human body, and Avram had attained total mastery over 243 of them. Five limbs, however, remained beyond his mastery: his eyes, his ears, and the organ of circumcision. [People often see and hear things that they do not necessarily wish to, and it is exceedingly difficult to control one's eyes and ears to the point that they never collect unwanted information. The organ of circumcision is also difficult to fully control, as the physical urges of man cannot always be easily subdued.] When Hashem gave Avraham the mitzvah of circumcision, he granted him the ability to master even these limbs, which are the most difficult to control. From that time onward, none of these limbs would act — even involuntarily — in a way that was contrary to Avraham's will. In accordance with this, his name was changed to Avraham, to reflect the fact that he was now the master of all 248 of his limbs.

Our Mishnah outlines the circumstances under which one may leave food on a stove from before the onset of the Sabbath:

בִּירָה שֶׁהִסִּיקוּהָ בְּקַשׁ וּבְגִבְבָא — If *a double-stove*[1] *was heated with straw or with stubble,* [2] נוֹתְנִים עָלֶיהָ תַבְשִׁיל — *we may place cooked food upon it* on Friday and leave it there after the Sabbath begins.[3] בְּגֶפֶת וּבְעֵצִים — However, if the double-stove was heated *with sesame-pulp or olive-pulp*[4] *or with wood,* לֹא יִתֵּן — *he may not place* cooked food upon it on Friday and leave it there after the Sabbath begins,[5] עַד שֶׁיִּגְרוֹף — *until he shovels* the coals from the double-stove,[6] אוֹ עַד שֶׁיִּתֵּן אֶת הָאֵפֶר — *or until he places ash* over the coals.[7]

The Mishnah cites a disagreement concerning this law:

בֵּית שַׁמַּאי אוֹמְרִים — *Beis Shammai say:* חַמִּין אֲבָל לֹא תַבְשִׁיל — We may place *hot water* on the double-stove, *but not cooked food.* [8]

───────────── NOTES ─────────────

1. A *kirah* is a rectangular, boxlike earthenware stove upon which two pots may be placed, with the fire burning underneath them (*Rav*). [The laws concerning other types of stoves will be discussed in subsequent Mishnayos in this chapter.]

2. Straw is the upper part of the grain stalk, which is harvested together with the grain. Stubble is the lower part of the stalk which remains attached to the ground after the the harvest (*Rashi*; other *Rishonim* reverse the two definitions).

3. Straw and stubble are rapidly consumed by fire, and therefore do not become coals. Hence, if a stove is fueled with either of these substances, there is no concern that one may come to stir coals after the onset of the Sabbath and violate the forbidden labor of *kindling* on the Sabbath. Therefore, a person may place a pot of cooked food on this stove on Friday, so that it will remain hot for the Sabbath meal (*Rav*).

4. After the oils of olives or sesame seeds have been extracted, the residue can be used for fuel (*Rav*).

5. Since wood and sesame or olive residue all form coals when burned, whenever any of these substances is used as fuel, there exists a concern that one may come to stir coals after the onset of the Sabbath, and thus violate the forbidden labor of *kindling* on the Sabbath. Therefore, the Rabbis decreed that one may not place food on Friday on a stove that was heated with one of these fuels and keep it there for the Sabbath — unless the burning fuel is treated in one of the ways the Mishnah will now specify (*Rav*).

6. If the coals are removed, there is obviously no cause for concern that he might come to stir them on the Sabbath (*Rav*).

7. Covering the burning coals with ashes serves as a reminder not to stir the coals (*Rav*).

8. Beis Shammai are of the opinion that even if coals have been shoveled away, some embers may remain, and a person may come to stir these embers. Hence, Beis Shammai were concerned that if one is allowed to leave food on the stove, he may come to stir the remaining embers (or the covered coals) since cooked food may

וּבֵית הִלֵּל אוֹמְרִים — **But Beis Hillel** disagree, and **say** חַמִּין וְתַבְשִׁיל — that the Mishnah's ruling applies both to **hot water and** to **cooked food.** Therefore, we may place both hot water and cooked food on the double-stove.

Another related dispute:

בֵּית שַׁמַּאי אוֹמְרִים — **Beis Shammai say:** נוֹטְלִין אֲבָל לֹא מַחֲזִירִין — **We may remove** the cooked food from the double-stove on the Sabbath, **but not replace** it.[9] וּבֵית הִלֵּל אוֹמְרִים — **But Beis Hillel say:** אַף מַחֲזִירִין — **We may even replace** the cooked food on the double-stove.[10]

──────────── NOTES ────────────

benefit from additional cooking. Therefore, according to Beis Shammai, cooked food may not be left on a stove under any conditions. According to Beis Shammai, only hot water may be left on a stove for the Sabbath, since water needs no additional cooking, and therefore there is no concern that he might come to stir the coals (*Rav*).

9. Not only do Beis Shammai maintain that the Mishnah's ruling applies only to hot water (and not to cooked food), but they say it applies only to *leaving* the hot water on the stove on Friday. If, however, the hot water is removed from the stove after the onset of the Sabbath, it may not be *replaced* on the stove, because that gives the *appearance* of cooking on the Sabbath (*Rav*). [It is not actual cooking, because the water is still hot when he replaces it on the stove.]

10. Beis Hillel hold that if the stove has been shoveled clear of coals, or if its coals have been covered with ash, not only may one leave both hot water and cooked food on the stove on Friday, one may even replace the hot water and cooked food upon the stove after he removed them on the Sabbath, provided he is still holding the pot in his hand and has not put it down (*Rav*). [If he lets go of the pot he may not return it to the fire because it appears as though he is placing it there on the Sabbath for the first time.]

[For an entirely different interpretation of the Mishnah, see *Gems from the Gemara*.]

GEMS FROM THE GEMARA

On the basis of a dispute between Chananyah and the Sages, the Gemara (36b) offers two very different explanations of our Mishnah. For the sake of clarity, in the commentary above we have explained the entire Mishnah according to the Sages' opinion. Let us now explain the Mishnah according to Chananyah's opinion.

As explained above, according to the Sages the Mishnah deals with the question of whether cooked food may be left on a *kirah* (double-stove) on the Sabbath. According to Chananyah, however, once food has been cooked to the level of the food of Ben Derusai [a notorious bandit who, due to the uncertainties of his profession, only allowed his food to cook one-third (*Rashi*) or one-half (*Rambam*) its normal time], it may be placed on a double-stove to remain there during the Sabbath even if the coals have been neither shoveled nor covered. In his view, our Mishnah's prohibition is not addressing leaving food upon the stove over the Sabbath (*shehiyah*), but rather *replacing* onto the stove food which had been previously removed on the Sabbath itself (*chazarah*). It is only to permit *chazarah* on the Sabbath that the coals must be shoveled or covered prior to the Sabbath. Thus, whereas according to the Sages there is no difference between the rules of leaving something on the fire on the Sabbath and replacing it after having removed it on the Sabbath (except according to Beis Shammai), according to Chananyah the rules of replacing are more stringent than those governing leaving it there in the first place.

According to Chananyah, the Mishnah is to be understood as follows:

[If] a double-stove was heated with straw or with stubble, we may replace *cooked food on it; if it was heated with olive or sesame-residue or with wood, he may not* replace *[cooked food on it] until he shovels, or until he places ash.*

According to Chananyah, the implicit ruling of the Mishnah is that pots may be *left* upon a double-stove on the Sabbath even if the coals have not been shoveled or covered. The next clause of the Mishnah proceeds to comment on this rule, by stating that according to Beis Shammai, it applies to hot water but not to cooked food, while Beis Hillel say that it applies also to cooked food.

According to Chananyah's understanding, the Mishnah concludes by noting that its earlier ruling concerning *replacing* pots on the stove is not unanimous, as it accords only with Beis Hillel, while Beis Shammai reject it.

A MUSSAR THOUGHT FOR THE DAY

We learned above (see *A Torah Thought for the Day*) that Avraham succeeded in mastering his limbs so that they never acted in a way that was contrary to Hashem's will — and Hashem eventually granted him mastery over even those limbs that are most difficult to control. How does one approach the seemingly daunting task of gaining such total control over his desires and urges?

R' Yaakov Galinsky, in speaking about this topic, made the point that control is a question of boundaries. He explained that just as there is a concept of לְמַעְלָה מִן הַטֶּבַע, something that is *above and beyond the ways of nature* (i.e., a miraculous occurrence), there is also a concept of לְמַטָה מִן הַטֶּבַע, something that is *beneath the way of nature.* This means that for every person, there is a line that he will not cross — something that he will not stoop to do.

R' Galinsky illustrated this point by citing the Gemara in *Gittin* (47a) that relates that Reish Lakish was once captured by the Lydians, a cannibalistic tribe. He made his escape by taking advantage of the fact that they would never kill and devour their captives without granting them a last request. Reish Lakish requested that he be allowed to tie up his captors and hit them with a bag (which, unbeknownst to them, contained a heavy lead ball). He thus overpowered them and slew them. Now, surely the Lydians were not so foolish as to think that allowing their captive to bind them was sensible. Why, then, did they acquiesce? Because, explained R' Galinsky, *it was incomprehensible to them* not to grant a last request — it was *beneath their way of nature,* and something that they simply could not do.

The difference between an ordinary man and a righteous one, he continued, is simply where the lines of acceptable behavior are drawn. If a person trains himself so that *under no circumstances* will he stoop so low as to speak evil of another human being, he will be protected against *lashon hara*. If a man makes up his mind that just as he finds the time to eat every day and sleep every night, he will learn *every single day*, come what may, he will reap the reward in increased *limud haTorah.*

This is a lifelong task, for as a person grows, he must strive to push his boundaries ever higher, so that more and more questionable acts are beneath him, things he would never do. We find that the Tannaim reached the level of being able to say that they never walked four *amos* without Torah or *tefillin;* this, too, is an example of a heightened standard of behavior. The higher one sets his standards, the greater the heights he can reach.

HALACHAH OF THE DAY

The next step in the agricultural process after threshing is זוֹרֶה, *winnowing.* It is therefore the next of the thirty-nine *melachos* prohibited on the Sabbath. After grain is threshed, the kernels, while having been physically detached from the stalks and husks with which they grew, are still mixed together with them in a mixture of usable and unusable materials. It is through the labor of winnowing that the unusable part of this mixture, the chaff, is removed, and the kernels are isolated and prepared for further processing. Winnowing was required for the construction of the Mishkan, since it was necessary to separate the parts of plants used for dyeing from their chaff, and also to obtain flour for the *lechem hapanim,* as explained above with respect to the earlier *melachos*.

Winnowing was accomplished by throwing the mixture of kernels and chaff into the wind, so that the chaff, being lighter than the kernels, would be blown away, while the heavier kernels would fall back to the ground to be collected. This was done with an implement known as a winnowing fork, which allowed one to heave large batches of grain and chaff into the wind at one time. The *melachah* of winnowing may therefore be defined as the separation of a desired item from an undesired item by means of the wind.

While one trangresses the Biblical prohibition of winnowing only with items that grow from the ground, there is a Rabbinic prohibition against winnowing even items that do not grow from the ground.

One transgresses the *melachah* of winnowing by using any type of implement fit for the task. This is not limited to a winnowing fork, or a winnowing machine. One can trangress this prohibition through the use of a shovel, spade, or even by throwing the mixture into the wind with his bare hands. Similarly, the *melachah* is transgressed whether the wind is produced naturally or artificially. As long as the mixture becomes separated through the action of wind, the *melachah* of winnowing is transgressed. Therefore, in addition to using the force of the wind, it is forbidden to separate items by blowing upon them, or by exposing them to the wind of a fan.

The amount of food one must winnow in order to have transgressed this *melachah* is an amount equal to the size of a dried fig.

A CLOSER LOOK AT THE SIDDUR

One of the additions to the Friday night prayers is the recital of the second chapter of *Mishnayos Shabbos*, the chapter of *Bameh Madlikin* (the study of which was concluded yesterday in the *Mishnah of the Day* section). This custom dates back to Geonic times, and is recorded in the *Siddur* of *Rav Amram Gaon.* Those who follow *Nusach Ashkenaz* (as well as *Gra*) have the custom to recite this chapter after *Kabbalas Shabbos* and before *Maariv,* while those who follow *Nusach Sefard* recite it after the *Maariv* prayers.

The different customs regarding the precise placement of the recital can be linked to the various reasons given by the commentators as to why we recite this chapter on Friday evening. *Tur (Orach Chaim §270)* explains that this chapter deals with the laws of the Sabbath lamps, and the tasks that must be done before the onset of the Sabbath; it is thus appropriate to speak of them on Friday evening. While *Tur* himself maintains that *Bameh Madlikin* should be recited after *Maariv, Beis Yosef* (ibid.) notes that according to his reasoning, it should be recited before *Maariv,* when the Sabbath has not yet begun and there is still time to perform any necessary tasks. However, others explain that the recital was moved to the end of *Maariv* so that those who were not yet finished praying *Maariv* would not be left behind at the end of the prayers.

Yet another explanation of the custom to recite this chapter of Mishnayos is that it was instituted as a public repudiation of the heretical views of the Karaites, who maintained that no flames are allowed to burn in a Jewish home on the Sabbath, even if kindled before the Sabbath. To counter this incorrect view, the Geonim proclaimed that these Mishnayos, which speak clearly of the Sabbath lamps, be read every Friday evening. [The repudiation of the position is also the reason for our custom of eating hot food (such as *chulent*) during the meal on Sabbath day — as without any flame on the Sabbath, no food would remain hot until the next day.]

After the chapter of *Bameh Madlikin* is read, we conclude the additional recital with a Baraisa that cites the teaching of R' Chanina regarding Torah scholars and the peace they bring to the world. The primary reason for reciting a Baraisa is that we wish to recite *Kaddish* afterward, and it is customary to recite a passage of Aggadah before reciting *Kaddish*. However, this particular Baraisa was chosen because the Rabbinic enactments discussed in the Mishnayos all serve to increase peace in the home. The Sabbath lamps makes the meal more festive, the *eruv* improves relationships with neighbors, and tithes help provide for others. In consonance with this theme of peace, the Sages appended this Baraisa, which praises Torah scholars for fostering peace (*She'iltos*). It has also been suggested that since the first recorded instance of greeting the Sabbath is attributed to R' Chanina (see *A Closer Look at the Siddur, Noach,* Shabbos), it was appropriate to choose from among his teachings.

QUESTION OF THE DAY:

*Besides Avram, Sarai, and Yosef,
where do we find in the Torah that
someone's name was changed, and by whom?*

For the answer, see page 155.

בְּעֶצֶם הַיּוֹם הַזֶּה נִמּוֹל אַבְרָהָם וְיִשְׁמָעֵאל בְּנוֹ
On that very day, Avraham was circumcised,
along with Yishmael his son (Bereishis 17:26).

Although an earlier verse (17:23) explicitly states that Avraham and Yishmael were circumcised on the very day of Hashem's command, the Torah repeats this for a second time. The commentators derive various lessons from this repetition:

Rashi states that we derive from this that it was the 99th birthday of Avraham, and the 13th birthday of Yishmael, when they were circumcised (see also *Mizrachi*). However, *Ramban* raises two difficulties with this intepretation. First, why would the Torah deem it necessary to tell us this? Moreover, it is clear from the ensuing chapter that Avraham's circumcision took place in Nissan (for the angel foretelling Yitzchak's birth came three days later, and Yitzchak was born one year later, during Nissan); and the prevailing Tannaic view of R' Eliezer is that Avraham and Yaakov were born in Tishrei!

Ramban himself explains that from the earlier verse it is clear only that Avraham circumcised *the members of his household* on the very day of Hashem's command. He explains that Avraham performed the other circumcisions first, fearing that if he circumcised himself first, he might become ill, and too weak to circumcise the entire household. Thus, one might have thought that after performing so many circumcisions, Avraham might decide to wait a day or two to recover from his exertions before circumcising himself (see *Radak*). Moreover, with all of his servants recuperating from their own circumcisions, Avraham would have no able-bodied people to attend him. Thus, it would have been understandable had he waited for several days for some of the member of his household to recuperate (*Abarbanel*); or, failing that, at least to delay the circumcision of his son Yishmael. The Torah therefore stresses the zeal with which Avraham fulfilled Hashem's command; even after circumcising all the members of his household, he nevertheless did not hesitate to circumcise both himself and Yishmael on that very day.

[In defense of *Rashi,* it should be noted that *Tosafos* to *Rosh Hashanah* 11b ד"ה אלא mentions a Midrash that Avraham's circumicision actually took place on Yom Kippur. The Midrash derives this from the fact that the term בְּעֶצֶם הַיּוֹם הַזֶּה used in our verse in also found with regard to Yom Kippur (see *Vayikra* 23:28). The Midrash states further that every year on Yom Kippur, Hashem "sees" the blood of Avraham's circumcision and forgives the sins of Israel, for the term בַּיּוֹם הַזֶּה is also found with respect to the atonement of Yom Kippur (ibid. 16:30). According to this Midrash, it is indeed possible that Avraham was circumcised on his birthday. Furthermore, it is possible that Rashi here is following the view of Rabbi Yehoshua (cited in Rosh Hashanah ibid.), that all three of the Avos were born in Tishrei.]

MISHNAH OF THE DAY: SHABBOS 3:2

Having discussed the laws pertaining to leaving and replacing food on the *kirah*, "double-stove," the Mishnah turns its attention to other types of stoves: תַּנּוּר שֶׁהִסִּיקוּהוּ בְּקַשׁ וּבִגְבָבָא — If *an oven*[1] *was heated with straw or with stubble,*[2] לֹא יִתֵּן בֵּין מִתּוֹכוֹ בֵּין מֵעַל גַּבָּיו — *he should not place* food *either inside it or atop it.*[3] כּוּפָּח שֶׁהִסִּיקוּהוּ בְּקַשׁ וּבִגְבָבָא הֲרֵי זֶה — *A single-stove*[4] *that was heated with straw or with stubble is* treated *like a double-stove.*[5] בְּגֶפֶת וּבְעֵצִים הֲרֵי הוּא כְתַנּוּר — But if it was heated *with sesame-pulp or olive-pulp or with wood, it is* treated *like an oven.*[6]

——————————— NOTES ———————————

1. A *tanur* is an oven that is shaped so that it is wider at the bottom than at the top, and it has an opening for only one pot to be placed upon it. As a result of this construction, it retains intense heat for a longer period than does the double-stove, and is therefore treated more stringently (*Rav*).

2. It is forbidden to leave food atop or within a *tanur*-type oven on the Sabbath. Moreover, unlike the case of the *kirah* in the previous Mishnah, in the case of a *tanur*-oven the food may not be left on or in the oven even if the oven was fueled by straw or stubble. Although straw and stubble do not create coals when burned, we are concerned that they might have left behind some small embers, which a person might come to stir [see below] (*Tiferes Yisrael*).

3. Since this prohibition applies even to an oven that was fueled by straw or stubble, it certainly applies to one heated with olive or sesame-waste or wood. Even if the coals have been swept away or covered with ash, the prohibition still applies, as the intensity of the residual heat of the oven is such that it can still cook food, and therefore there remains a concern that one may rake some remaining embers (*Tos. Yom Tov*).

4. A *kupach* is shaped like a *kirah* (i.e., its top is the same width as its bottom), but is square, not rectangular, and has room for only one pot, not two. Thus, it can become somewhat hotter than a *kirah*, but not as hot as a *tanur* (*Rav*).

5. A single-stove that was fueled with straw or stubble is treated in the same manner as a double-stove that was fueled with straw or stubble, and food that was placed upon it on Friday may be left there on the Sabbath.

6. A single-stove that was fueled with sesame or olive residue or wood is treated in the same manner as a *tanur*-oven that was fueled with these substances, and food may not be placed upon it on Friday and left there on the Sabbath.

GEMS FROM THE GEMARA

As was the case in the previous Mishnah, Chananyah has a very different explanation of our Mishnah. Once again, for the sake of clarity, we have explained the entire Mishnah in the commentary above according to the Sages' opinion. Let us now explain it according to Chananyah's opinion.

According to the Sages' understanding of the previous Mishnah, our Mishnah begins by teaching us that one may not place food in or upon a *tanur*-oven before the Sabbath *to remain* there on the Sabbath, even if the *tanur* was fueled by straw or stubble. However, according to Chananyah's explanation, the Mishnah is teaching that one may not *replace* food which has been removed from the *tanur* (*Tos.* 38b). [He may, however, leave it there in the first place.]

Subsequently, according to the Sages' explanation, our Mishnah teaches that the same rules that applied to the *kirah* double-stove (in the previous Mishnah) apply to a *kupach* single-stove that was fueled with straw or stubble. Hence, if its coals have been shoveled or covered, a pot may be left on top of it or leaning against its outer wall (Gemara 38b). On the other hand, according to Chananyah's understanding, a pot may even be replaced upon it.

Our Mishnah then teaches that if the *kupach* was fueled with olive or sesame residue or wood, its status is the same as a *tanur*-oven, and according to the Sages' explanation *shehiyah* is not permitted even if one shovels or covers the coals.

Here, too, according to Chananyah's explanation, *shehiyah* is permitted and only *chazarah* will be forbidden.

Our present-day ovens generally have their openings on the side of the oven; their heat is therefore not as intensely concentrated as that of the *tanur* of the Mishnah. Nor are they as narrow as the single-stove, which had space for only one pot. As a result, our ovens are most comparable to the *kirah*, and therefore the laws of the *kirah* apply to them (*Rama, Orach Chaim* 253:1). Similarly, the tops of our gas ranges and electric stoves are deemed the equivalent of a *kirah* (*Igros Moshe, Orach Chaim,* vol. I §93; vol. 4 §74, *bishul* §26).

The *blech* (Yiddish for tin — i.e., a sheet of metal) that many people customarily use to cover the burners of a stovetop is considered the equivalent of covering the coals with ashes.

[With respect to the dispute between Chananyah and the Sages, *Shulchan Aruch* (253:1) quotes both opinions without stating a decision. *Rama,* however, states that the custom is to follow the more lenient ruling, i.e., that *shehiyah* (leaving a pot to remain on the fire over the Sabbath) is permissible even without shoveling or covering the coals — provided the food has been cooked at least to the extent of that of Ben Derusai; replacing a pot on the Sabbath, however, is permitted only if the coals have been swept away or covered (see there for other restrictions that apply as well).]

A MUSSAR THOUGHT FOR THE DAY

Maharal discusses the *mussar* implicit in the mitzvah of circumcision that was given to Avraham:

The *orlah*, "foreskin," symbolizes a barrier to holiness. Adam HaRishon was born circumcised (see *Avos D'Rabbi Nassan* 2:5) because he was as close as a physical being can possibly be to Hashem. So great was Adam at the time of his creation, that the angels thought he was a Divine being to whom they should offer praise. Thus, he was born circumcised; there was no *orlah* intervening between him and Hashem. Even the organ that represents man's worst animal-like urges was totally harnessed to the service of Hashem.

When Adam sinned, however, he caused his nature to change. Before his sin, godliness had been natural to him, and sin had been repulsive, bizarre, and foreign. Once he disobeyed Hashem, however, he fell into the traps of illicit desire and self-justification. Suddenly, temptation became natural to him, and Hashem became distant; and when Hashem reproached him for having sinned, Adam hastened to defend himself rather than admitting his sin and repenting. After his fall, the angels had no trouble recognizing his human vulnerability.

Adam was created circumcised for he was a superior being, but by succumbing to sin, he fell prey to the natural forces that should have been his servants. Having set his sights upon earth, he could no longer look to the heavens as he was created to do. His personal failure created a barrier against the spirit, a barrier that was mirrored in his body, when the symbol of his closeness to Hashem was covered by a growth of flesh (see *Sanhedrin* 38b, where it is stated that Adam's circumcision was covered).

Because Adam's sin was the failure of mankind, the foreskin symbolizing it became a permanent part of the human body. For the twenty generations from Adam to Avraham, mankind failed to raise itself from those depths. There were righteous exceptions, like Enosh,

Mesushelach and Noach, but they were individual stars in a dismal horizon. Humanity had fallen, and it awaited someone great enough to raise not only himself, but the entire race.

Then, Avraham appeared upon the scene. Avraham — who revealed new vistas of recognition that Hashem was everywhere and controlled everything. Avraham saw Hashem everywhere — and the barriers to holiness withered away. True, mankind was still encumbered with the physical and spiritual foreskin of Adam, but Avraham demonstrated that man could surmount this obstacle. Hashem recognized this change by giving Avraham the commandment of circumcision — and the privilege of being designated the father of a nation that would carry on his mission of standing up to skeptics and scoffers, until the day that all nations would acknowledge Hashem as the true King (*Maharal, Chidushei Aggados*).

In several places, the Torah mentioned עָרְלַת הַלֵּב, *the foreskin of the heart* (see, for example, *Devarim* 10:16). This is the non-physical counterpart of the physical foreskin, man's urges and desires that attempt to bar him from achieving true service of Hashem. We remove the physical foreskin as an indelible act of allegiance, demonstrating our resolve to do the same for the spiritual barriers. Nevertheless, the Torah tells us that ultimately it will be Hashem Who will complete the removal of this spiritual foreskin (see ibid. 30:6) after we have done our utmost, and this will take place at the time of the ultimate redemption.

HALACHAH OF THE DAY

In order to distance people from the possibility of transgressing the prohibition of winnowing on Shabbos, the Sages forbade actions that, while Biblically permitted, are similiar to the labor of winnowing. For example, it is Rabbinically forbidden for one to toss a mixture up and down with both his hands in order to allow the unwanted part of the mixture to fall away, even if there is no wind to separate the unused items. Likewise, it is forbidden to toss a mixture from one hand to the other so that the unwanted material falls away in between the hands. In both of these cases, it is not the wind or any moving air current that is being employed to separate the mixture; the Biblical prohibition of winnowing therefore does not apply. The Sages, however, worried that if such activities were permitted, they might lead one to separate the components in a Biblically prohibited manner.

Our discussion until this point has been based upon the understanding that the definition of *winnowing* is using the wind to separate a mixture. The *Rama*, however, cites the opinion of the *Yerushalmi* that defines the *melachah* of winnowing as *dispersing* an item by means of the wind. This, of course, makes a critical difference in how we are to understand what may be included in this prohibition. According to the aforementioned *Yerushalmi*, one transgresses the *melachah* of winnowing even where no selection between unwanted and wanted materials is being made. As long as material is being dispersed or scattered through the power of wind, the *melachah* is being transgressed. In accordance with this view, the *Yerushalmi* states that one should not spit into the wind, because this will cause the wind to scatter the saliva — a transgression of the *melachah* of *winnowing* according to this view.

Although most *poskim* rule that the halachah does not follow the view of the *Yerushalmi*, some *poskim* advise that one should refrain from scattering by means of the wind any item that grows from the ground. Since a human being is nourished by the vegetation that grows from the ground, he too is considered "an item that grows from the ground" in regard to this halachah and so, by extension, is his saliva. One should therefore refrain from spitting outdoors if the wind will scatter his saliva. For the same reason, one should refrain from shaking out a tablecloth with crumbs on it outdoors into the wind on Shabbos. When this is done, the crumbs, which are something that grows from the ground, will be dispersed by the wind — a possible transgression of the *melachah* of *winnowing* according to *Yerushalmi*.

Use of aerosol sprays is permitted on Shabbos. This is because in the case of an aerosol spray, it is not the wind that scatters the droplets, but rather the pressure of the liquid as it is forced through the nozzle head.

A CLOSER LOOK AT THE SIDDUR

W e find the subject of Avram's name being changed to Avraham toward the end of the *Pesukei D'Zimrah* section of the *Shacharis* prayers, where we recite a selection of praises of Hashem that were proclaimed by Dovid HaMelech, the prophet Nechemiah, and Moshe Rabbeinu; these praises are then repeated in condensed form in the closing blessing of *Yishtabach* (see *Abudraham*).

The first four selected verses, beginning with *Vayevarech Dovid*, were uttered by Dovid HaMelech when he finished his designation of the materials that he set aside for his son Shlomo to use in building the *Beis*

HaMikdash. In his praise, he calls Hashem "the God of Israel" (i.e., Yaakov), because it was Yaakov who first spoke of the *Beis HaMikdash,* and who designated Mt. Moriah as its future site (see *Radak* and commentaries to *Bereishis* 28:17), and it was he who first made a vow of tithes in a time of troubles (see ibid. v. 20), an example followed by Dovid (see *Bereishis Rabbah* 70:1). Following this, Dovid declares that all the wealth and acheivements that had enabled him to reach this point were the result of Hashem's gift alone, for He is the Master of all.

The prayers then continue with praises that were proclaimed by Nechemiah, Ezra, and the Jewish people on the day following Shemini Atzeres, when the Jews, newly returned from Babylonian exile, completed their first festival season back in Jerusalem. They gathered in devotion and repentance, and echoed the sentiments expressed by Dovid nearly 500 years earlier. The selection begins by recognizing that Hashem alone is the Creator of all, and that even the mightiest of natural object are subservient to Him. It then continues by thanking Hashem for choosing Avram from among the multitudes of mankind and giving him the mission of leading humanity and forming a special nation — this being symbolized by the changing of his name to Avraham, as explained above, and by establishing an eternal covenant with him.

R' Yechezkel Levenstein noted that in these prayers we speak of two separate parts of *emunah* — faith that Hashem created the world and all that it contains, and the tradition that Hashem revealed Himself to our *Avos,* who recognized and accepted Him as the One God. R' Levenstein would remark that while studying the wonders of Creation can indeed lead a person to *emunah,* the bulwark of our faith is the tradition that we have received from the *Avos.* Study of the Creation should be used as a tool to strengthen the *emunah* which must already be ingrained within us, and not as a sole support for our faith.

QUESTION OF THE DAY:

Why was Avraham commanded to circumcise himself at the age of 99, and not earlier or later?

For the answer, see next page.

Sunday:

Hashem told Moshe concerning the sending of spies into Eretz Yisrael: שְׁלַח לְךָ אֲנָשִׁים, *Send men for yourself. Rashi (Bamidbar* 13:2) explains that while Hashem gave permission to Moshe to send the spies, the decision was left up to him.

Monday:

He traveled to the city of Shechem (see *Bereishis* 12:6). *Rashi* (ibid.) states that Avraham went there in anticipation of the future, when the sons of Yaakov would do battle against Shechem, and he went to pray for their safety.

Tuesday:

We find the term *"Magen"* used to describe all three of the *Avos* in the prayer of *Magen Avos,* which is recited after *Shemoneh Esrei* on Friday night.

Wednesday:

Ibn Ezra states that the Perizzites were actually also descendants of Canaan (although Canaan had no son by this name). They were called Perizzites from the word פְּרָזוֹ, which means *open,* for they lived in open villages, as they were peaceful people and did not need to fortify their dwelling places.

Thursday:

From the day that Yitzchak was born. Yitzchak was 60 years old when Yaakov was born, and Yaakov was 130 when he descended to Egypt. Those 190 years, plus the 210 years the Jews remained in Egypt, were reckoned as the 400 years of the exile (see *A Torah Thought for the Day*).

Friday:

Moshe changed Hoshea's name to Yehoshua (see *Bamidbar* 13:16), so that his name should contain the two-letter Name of Hashem (*yud* and *hei*), as protection against the evil plots of the spies.

Shabbos:

The Midrash states that Hashem wished Avraham to circumcise himself later in life so that elderly proselytes should not be discouraged from undergoing circumcision; but He wished him to be circumcised before he fathered Yitzchak, so Yitzchak would be conceived from pure and holy seed.

פרשת וירא

Parashas Vayeiera

| פרשת וירא | A TORAH THOUGHT FOR THE DAY |

SUNDAY

PARASHAS VAYEIRA

וַיֵּרָא אֵלָיו יהוה בְּאֵלֹנֵי מַמְרֵא וְהוּא יֹשֵׁב פֶּתַח־הָאֹהֶל כְּחֹם הַיּוֹם

*And HASHEM appeared to him in the plains of Mamre,
while he was sitting at the entrance of the tent
in the heat of the day* (Bereishis 18:1).

Rashi tells us that Hashem appeared to Avraham because it was the third day following his circumcision, the time when the pain of the procedure is most painful for adults (see below, 34:25), and Hashem wished to visit the sick. Indeed, the Gemara in *Sotah* (14a) notes that we must learn from this verse to visit the sick, just as Hashem did.

One may ask: Where is there any indication in the verse that the purpose of Hashem's appearing to Avraham was to visit the sick? Perhaps Hashem came to tell Avraham about the impending destruction of Sodom! (which is discussed in the verse below).

The commentators suggest various resolutions of this difficulty. *Chizkuni* notes that nowhere else in Scripture do we find Hashem appearing without a direct communication stated immediately thereafter. Thus, since in this case Hashem did not broach the matter of Sodom immediately, it may be inferred that Hashem's appearance here was *not* for purposes of communication, but simply for a purpose that would be accomplished through the visit itself. Thus, the Gemara in *Sotah* can infer that this indeed was Hashem's primary purpose in appearing. [Indeed, there was no need for Hashem to personally appear to inform Avraham of the pending destruction of Sodom — that could have been accomplished through an emissary, as was the news that Avraham and Sarah were to have a child.]

Another approach is advanced by *Levush,* who suggests that the true purpose of Hashem's visit is hinted at in the unusual wording used in the verse. Standard Hebrew syntax places the subject of the verb immediately following the verb; thus, the verse should seemingly have stated וַיֵּרָא ה׳ אֵלָיו, rather than וַיֵּרָא אֵלָיו ה׳. The verse as it is written translates literally as *and He appeared to him* (Avraham), *Hashem;* this is an indication, says *Levush,* that the primary purpose of Hashem's appearance was *to appear to Avraham* and visit him, and not because of any information that had to be imparted.

Sifsei Chachamim notes an additional lesson that may be gleaned from the wording of the verse. We see that Avraham is not mentioned by name in the verse; it simply states that Hashem appeared *to him.* Rashi, too, does not state that Hashem came to visit *Avraham;* rather, he states that Hashem came "to visit the sick." From this it may be seen that it was not because of the lofty stature of Avraham that a visit was appropriate; it was simply because he was ill. The mitzvah to visit the sick does not apply only to a significant personage who has taken ill; the mitzvah applies equally to any Jew. [See also below, *A Closer Look at the Siddur.*]

MISHNAH OF THE DAY: SHABBOS 3:3

The Mishnah discusses cooking on the Sabbath by means of unconventional sources of heat:

אֵין נוֹתְנִין בֵּיצָה בְּצַד הַמֵּיחַם בִּשְׁבִיל שֶׁתִּתְגַּלְגֵּל — *We may not place an egg beside a* hot *kettle* on the Sabbath *in order that it should roll,* i.e. become cooked,[1]   וְלֹא יַפְקִיעֶנָּה בְּסוּדָרִין — *nor may [a person] break [an egg] open* and fry it *upon* hot *scarves* that had become heated by the sun;[2]   וְרַבִּי יוֹסֵי מַתִּיר — *but R' Yose permits* this.[3]   וְלֹא יַטְמִינֶנָּה בְּחוֹל וּבַאֲבַק דְּרָכִים — *Nor may one bury it in sand, or in the dust of roads* that have become hot in the sun,   בִּשְׁבִיל שֶׁתִּצָּלֶה — *in order to roast it.* [4]

———————— NOTES ————————

1. A raw egg does not roll well. As the egg begins to undergo cooking or roasting, it hardens, and rolls more easily. Our Mishnah here refers to the slight degree of roasting that suffices to make the egg roll.

The kettle of which the Mishnah speaks, which is no longer on the fire but was originally heated by a fire, is known as תּוֹלֶדֶת הָאוּר, *a derivative of the fire.* The Mishnah thus teaches us that cooking, whether done by fire itself (אוּר) or by the heat of an object that was originally heated by a fire, violates the Scripturally forbidden *melachah* of cooking on the Sabbath.

2. One may not crack open an egg over scarves which have been heated by the sun in order to roast the egg. Although it is permissible to cook by the *direct* heat of the sun (חַמָּה) [e.g., by setting an egg or a glass of water in a place where it will receive the full heat of the sun's rays] on the Sabbath, cooking by the heat of תּוֹלֶדֶת הַחַמָּה, *a derivative of the sun,* is forbidden by Rabbinic decree. The reason for the decree is that the heat of a derivative, once removed from its source, is the same whether that source was a fire or the sun. The Rabbis therefore forbade cooking by the heat of a derivative of the sun, lest one come to cook by the heat of a derivative of fire and violate a Scriptural prohibition.

3. R' Yose is not concerned that people might confuse a derivative of the sun with a derivative of fire.

4. The Sages forbid cooking in sand or dust because they are derivatives of the sun. Moreover, although the heat of the sand or dust is derived from the sun, even R' Yose concedes that it is forbidden to cook with them. This is because this form of cooking is akin to הטמנה בדבר המוסיף הבל, *insulating [a pot] with a substance that increases the heat.* Insulating a pot with a substance that increases the heat, that is a derivative of fire, such as ashes, is Scripturally forbidden. Since people may come to confuse heated sand with heated ashes, and might come to insulate pots with the ash, even R' Yose agrees that these cases are forbidden (Gemara 39a, first explanation).

As we saw in the Mishnah, R' Yose is of the opinion that we do not concern ourselves with the possibility that people will confuse heat derived from the sun with heat derived from a fire (Gemara 39a). Yet, nevertheless, R' Yose concurs with the ruling of the Sages forbidding a person to cover an egg in sand or in the dust of the roads in order that it be roasted. Why is this so?

The Gemara (39a) offers two reasons for this. According to one opinion, R' Yose agrees that covering an egg in sand or road dust is forbidden because this act is akin to the prohibited act of *hatmanah b'davar ha'mosif hevel* [insulating food or a pot in a substance that adds heat — viz., ashes], which is a violation of the forbidden *melachah* of *cooking*. Even R' Yose is concerned that people may tend to confuse heated sand with heated ashes, and might come to insulate food with ash.

According to another opinion in the Gemara, we are concerned that a person wishing to roast an egg in the sand or dust may dislodge tightly packed sand or soil for this purpose. He will thus be liable for *digging*, a forbidden activity that is a sub-category of the forbidden labor of *plowing* (*Rashi*). [Alternatively, the concern according to the second opinion is that he may use sand that was not designated for use prior to the Sabbath, thus violating the prohibition against moving *muktzeh* (*Tosafos*).]

The Gemara (ibid.) notes that according to the second opinion of the Gemara — viz., that R' Yose concedes that there is a concern in this case because one may come to dislodge sand — if there is sufficient soft earth available, the egg may be covered. [According to *Rashi,* this is because there is no longer a concern that he may come to dig; according to *Tosafos,* this is because the earth is so loosely packed that the egg will sink in by itself, and he will have no need to move it.] The Tanna Kamma, of course, prohibits any cooking with a derivative of the sun, and thus even such a case is forbidden in his view (*Magen Avraham* 318:9).

QUESTION OF THE DAY:

At what time of year did the angels visit Avraham, and when was Yitzchak born?

For the answer, see page 208.

The *Chofetz Chaim* in his *Ahavas Chesed* (3:3) discusses several purposes for visiting the sick. The first matter to be addressed, of course, is that the visitor must ensure that the needs of the patient are being attended to (see further in *A Closer Look at the Siddur*). A second purpose, writes the *Chofetz Chaim,* is for the visitor to see firsthand the true condition of the ill person, so that he will be properly moved to pray on the ill person's behalf. [For this reason, the halachah states that it is preferable not to visit during the morning, when the patient will often seem better than he actually is, lest the visitor not realize the gravity of the illness, and not be motivated to pray properly. Similarly, one should not visit during times when the illness seems worse than it is, lest the visitor lose hope and fail to pray at all.] This is especially true of righteous men who visit, as their prayers are especially efficacious (indeed, the Gemara makes a point of saying that even important personages should not hesitate to visit ordinary people who are ill). And a third reason for visiting is so that the visitor can urge the patient to do *teshuvah,* and (when an illness is serious) can help him prepare for the possibility that he may not recover (such as by assisting him in setting his affairs in order). [Of course, such discussions must be undertaken with great tact and delicacy, so as not to worsen the condition of the patient or throw him into despair.]

The Gemara in *Nedarim* (40a) cites the verse in *Tehillim* (41:2): *Praiseworthy is he who contemplates the needy; on the day of evil, Hashem will deliver him.* The Gemara expounds the verse as referring to one who visits the sick, and involves himself with ensuring that their needs are met. The next verse, the Gemara says, details the reward that will be received for this mitzvah in this world (visiting the sick is one of the mitzvos for which reward is received in this world; see *A Closer Look at the Siddur*); *Hashem will guard him and restore him to life, and he will be fortunate on earth.* The Gemara explains: *Hashem will guard him* from the evil inclination; *restore him to life* by protecting him from suffering; *and he will be fortunate on earth,* as everyone will honor him.

Keren Orah (to *Nedarim* ibid.) notes that these three rewards correspond, measure for measure, with the three purposes that are fulfilled when one visits the sick. The visitor urges the patient to do *teshuvah;* thus, he is saved from the evil inclination. He must see that the patient is well tended and not in pain or need; in return, he is saved from his own suffering. And in return for disregarding social strata and visiting anyone who is in need of prayer, the visitor is rewarded with honor from all sides.

After grains have undergone the processes of threshing and winnowing, what remains is a mixture of grain kernels and certain types of waste matter that cannot be separated through these methods alone. For examples, pebbles cannot be removed from grain by winnowing, because they are too heavy to be carried away by the wind. Such waste matter would be sorted and removed by hand through the labor of בּוֹרֵר, *sorting,* which is the sixth of the thirty-nine *melachos* forbidden on the Sabbath. As we have noted above, the agricultural process was a necessary component of the building of the Mishkan, to produce either the dyes used in construction or the grain for the *lechem hapanim.*

בּוֹרֵר, *sorting,* is unique among the forbidden *melachos* of Shabbos in that it occurs with great frequency not only during food preparation, but also during the eating of the meal itself. Hardly a meal passes without one encountering some halachic difficulty pertaining to the *melachah* of *sorting.* It is therefore necessary for one to acquaint himself with the intricacies of this *melachah,* and to gain an understanding of which activities are forbidden and which are permitted, as well as the proper procedure that must be followed in various cases to avoid forbidden *sorting.*

Sorting is defined as separating one variety from another with which it is mixed. There are many different forms of sorting and separating that are included in this *melachah* and therefore forbidden. For example, while sorting an entire mixture into its individual components is clearly a violation of *sorting,* the halachah, in certain instances, also prohibits the selection of even a *single* item from a mixture. This too is a transgression of *sorting,* because that one item is being sorted from the rest of the mixture. Even removing items at random from a mixture and placing them apart from one another may also be a form of *sorting,* and thus forbidden. There are, however, some forms of separation that *are* permissible on the Sabbath, as we shall see further in our discussions of this complex *melachah.*

A CLOSER LOOK AT THE SIDDUR

When we recite a blessing over a mitzvah, it is proper to perform the mitzvah as soon as possible after reciting the blessing. For this reason, after we recite the blessing over the study of Torah at the beginning of the *Shacharis* prayers, we immediately recite a selection of excerpts from both the Written and the Oral Torah. We begin by reciting the verses that comprise the Priestly Blessings (*Bamidbar* 6:24-26), then we recite a section of a Mishnah from *Maseches Pe'ah* (1:1) that mentions Torah study, and then we recite a Gemara in *Shabbos* (127a) that lists ten mitzvos for which one receives reward both in this world and the next (unlike most mitzvos, whose reward is reserved for the World to Come), including Torah study. Among the mitzvos mentioned in that Gemara are the mitzvos of *bikur cholim,* "visiting the sick," and *hachnasas orchim,* "hospitality to guests," the two mitzvos discussed in the opening of our *parashah.*

Why is the mitzvah of visiting the sick awarded this special status?

The Gemara in *Nedarim* (39a) cites a Baraisa that states that "visiting the sick has no limit." The Gemara explains this as teaching two laws: First, that even an esteemed individual must visit a simple person who is ill; and second, that one must visit as often as necessary, even 100 times.

The Gemara (ibid.) also cites an incident where one of R' Akiva's disciples fell ill, and no one went to visit him. R' Akiva himself went to visit him, and found him lying in a dirty and dust-filled room. R' Akiva took steps to have his environment cleaned (according to some, R' Akiva cleaned the room himself), and the student recovered. When he regained his strength, he told R' Akiva: "You have brought me back to life!," whereupon R' Akiva proclaimed: "Whoever does not visit the sick is as if he has spilled blood."

From this incident we learn that the importance of visiting the sick is due, at least in part, to the vital necessity of ensuring that the patient's needs are being seen to (see *Rosh* to *Nedarim* ibid.). Such watchfulness is often critical (even in modern times), and can literally save a life.

Another aspect of visiting the sick is that simply indicating to the patient that there is someone who cares enough to visit him (especially in our days of busy schedules) will often have a therapeutic effect. The Gemara (*Bava Basra* 9b) states with regard to charity that empathizing with a poor person is deserving of greater reward than simply handing him a donation; one who visits the sick and attends to their needs can accomplish both — providing necessary charity *and* lifting the patient's spirits.

R' Shimon Schwab (in *Iyun Tefillah*) points out an ancillary benefit that devolves from visiting the sick. When one sees the suffering of an ill person, he feels more keenly the gratitude that he himself must have to Hashem for his health. R' Schwab relates that an old Rav once told him that when a person would come to him for a cure for depression, he would tell him to go to the hospital and attempt to find his own name listed as a patient in one of the wards! When the person is told (obviously) that his name is not listed in the roster of patients, he should thank Hashem fervently and joyfully for his health. This will serve to ease his depression.

Tomorrow we will discuss the particular merits of the mitzvah of *hachnasas orchim.*

וַיֹּאמַר אֲדֹנָי אִם־נָא מָצָאתִי חֵן בְּעֵינֶיךָ אַל־נָא תַעֲבֹר מֵעַל עַבְדֶּךָ

*And [Avraham] said: My Lord, if I find favor in Your eyes,
please do not pass away from Your servant (Bereishis 18:3).*

This translation of the verse follows *Rashi's* second interpretation, which is followed by a majority of the commentators. According to this approach, Avraham was addressing Hashem, and asking that His Presence not depart while Avraham went to see to the needs of the guests. Thus, the word אֲדֹנָי in the verse is sacred, as it refers to Hashem. [According to the first interpretation of *Rashi*, Avraham was addressing the three guests, imploring them not to leave without accepting his hospitality; thus, the word אֲדֹנָי is not sacred, as it refers to the guests rather than to Hashem.]

The Gemara in *Shabbos* (127a), in line with *Rashi's* second interpretation, makes the statement: "Offering hospitality to travelers is greater than receiving the Divine Presence." For we see that although Avraham, who was convalescing from his circumcision, was being visited by Hashem, he nevertheless took leave of Hashem in order to offer hospitality to the three guests.

An obvious question presents itself. True, we can learn from Avraham's behavior that offering hospitality to wayfarers is of prime importance, greater even than receiving the Divine Presence. But how did Avraham know that this was so? How did Avraham deduce that taking leave of the Divine Presence was the correct course of action in this case?

The *Slonimer Rebbe* would answer this question with a parable. Suppose a person has two friends, Reuven and Shimon. He comes to Reuven's home as a guest, and Reuven treats him with great honor, attending to his every need. In the meantime, his son comes to Shimon's house, and is treated with the same level of honor. Which of the two hosts has shown greater love and respect toward their acquaintance? It is surely Shimon. For Reuven treated his own friend with honor, while Shimon did the same for the son, who was not his own friend, simply because he was *the son* of the friend.

In the same way, explained the *Slonimer Rebbe,* Avraham extended hospitality to guests not because of who they were, but because they were Hashem's creations. Thus, he was certain that extending honor to them for this reason constituted a greater honoring of Hashem than simply remaining in His presence.

Another approach is based upon the statement in the Gemara (*Bava*

Metzia 86b) that Hashem had "withdrawn the sun from its sheath," making it abnormally hot outside, so that no wayfarers would come to disturb Avraham's rest. Avraham was able to deduce from this that Hashem's Presence was *not* a reason to desist from offering hospitality, for if it would have been, Hashem would have had no reason to make it extremely hot — Avraham would have been unable to leave His Presence in any case! Perforce, then, it was permitted to leave to attend to guests, and they had to be kept away by other means.

MISHNAH OF THE DAY: SHABBOS 3:4

The Mishnah speaks of a specific case where water was heated through a means that did not involve fire:

מַעֲשֶׂה שֶׁעָשׂוּ אַנְשֵׁי טְבֶרְיָא וְהֵבִיאוּ סִילוֹן שֶׁל צוֹנֵן לְתוֹךְ אַמָּה שֶׁל חַמִּין — There was *a deed done by the people of Tiberias, that they constructed a pipe* that would carry *cold water* and placed the pipe *into a canal of hot* spring *water* before the Sabbath, so that cold water would flow within the pipe and be heated automatically by the surrounding hot water on the Sabbath.[1] אָמְרוּ לָהֶם חֲכָמִים — *The Sages said to them:* אִם בְּשַׁבָּת — *If* the water flowed through the pipe and was heated *on the Sabbath,* כְּחַמִּין שֶׁהוּחַמּוּ בְּשַׁבָּת — *it is like hot water that was heated* manually *on the Sabbath,* וַאֲסוּרִין בִּרְחִיצָה וּבִשְׁתִיָּה — and *it is forbidden for* both *bathing and drinking;*[2] אִם בְּיוֹם טוֹב כְּחַמִּין שֶׁהוּחַמּוּ בְּיוֹם טוֹב — *if* the water flowed through the pipe and was heated *on a festival, it is like hot water that was heated on a festival,* וַאֲסוּרִין בִּרְחִיצָה וּמוּתָּרִין בִּשְׁתִיָּה — and it is *forbidden for bathing but permitted for drinking.*[3]

─────────────── NOTES ───────────────

1. Tiberias is noted for its thermal springs. Nevertheless, the local cold water was cleaner than the water of the hot springs, and was preferred for bathing. Therefore, the townspeople constructed a pipe that carried the cold water for bathing through a canal of hot springs, so the water would be heated by the hot water of the canal. The heated water then ran from the pipe into a *mikveh,* which was used by the Tiberians on the Sabbath (*Tiferes Yisrael*).

2. A Rabbinic decree forbids the use on the Sabbath of anything that was cooked on that Sabbath. Although the system in Tiberias was set up so that the water that was being heated on the Sabbath flowed automatically through the pipes running through the hot springs, the Sages nevertheless forbade the use of the water, as the heating of the water took place entirely on the Sabbath (*Rav*).

3. Since it is permitted to cook food and heat liquids on Yom Tov for consumption that day, it was permitted to drink the water that was automatically heated in the

The Mishnah discusses other cases of heated water: מוּלְיָאר הַגָּרוּף — *A miliarium*[4] *that was shoveled* clear of its coals before the Sabbath, שׁוֹתִין הֵימֶנוּ בְּשַׁבָּת — *we may drink from it on the Sabbath.* [5] אֲנְטִיכִי — How- ever, *an antichi,* [6] אַף עַל פִּי שֶׁגְּרוּפָה — *even if it was shoveled* clear of its coals before the Sabbath, אֵין שׁוֹתִין הֵימֶנָּה — *we may not drink from it* on the Sabbath.[7]

--- NOTES ---

pipes running through the hot springs. However, the Sages prohibited bathing in water that was heated on Yom Tov, even in water that was heated automatically, as in Tiberias (Gemara 39b).

4. A *miliarium* is a vessel used for heating water. It consists of a large bowl for water that is surrounded by a narrow receptacle for coals (*Rashi*). [*Miliarium* is a Greek word.]

5. Once the coals are removed, the *miliarium's* walls only retain the water's heat, but cannot increase it. [Even though the residual warmth of the *miliarium's* walls will continue to add heat to the water immediately after the coals are removed, they then gradually cool, and over a longer period, they merely keep the water warm.] We may therefore keep water in it on the Sabbath and drink from it (*Rav*). However, if the coals are not removed from their receptacle, the *miliarium* continues to add heat to the water. The water is thus being heated on the Sabbath, and it is therefore forbidden to keep water in the *miliarium* and to drink from it.

6. An *antichi* is a copper vessel with a double bottom, with space for coals between the two bottoms (*Rav*). [*Antichi*, too, is a Greek word.]

7. Since the *antichi's* coals are enclosed between the two bottoms, heat remains trapped in that space even after the coals are removed. Hence, the *antichi* adds significant heat to the water it contains even after the coals are removed. [The *miliarium*, however, does not trap heat as efficiently, as the receptacle for the coals is open, and allows heat to escape.] The water is thus being heated on the Sabbath, and it is therefore forbidden to keep water in the *antichi* and to drink from it.

GEMS FROM THE GEMARA

The Gemara (40b) rules that it is forbidden to heat up oil or water to the point that it is hot enough to cause the hand to recoil from the hot liquid (יָד סוֹלֶדֶת בּוֹ); heating either of them to this degree is consid- ered *cooking.* On the other hand, merely warming the oil or water, while not heating it up to the degree at which the hand will recoil from the liquid, is permissible. The Gemara further defines the measure of יָד סוֹלֶדֶת בּוֹ, identifying it as the degree of heat that would scald the tender skin of the belly of an infant.

Rav Yitzchak bar Avdimi then relates an incident: Once, when he followed Rebbi into a bathhouse in Tiberias on the Sabbath, he wished to place a flask of oil in a hot bathtub in order to warm up the oil. Rebbi instructed him: Take some water from the pool and place it into another vessel, and place the flask of oil into *that* vessel to warm it.

[The tubs in this bathhouse were in-ground pools (similar to modern-day *mikvaos*) into which water flowed directly from the hot springs. Since the hot-spring water was drawn directly into the tub, the tub was the first "vessel" in which the hot water was contained. Now, hot water that is in its first vessel [כְּלִי רִאשׁוֹן] is considered halachically capable of cooking. That is, when water is heated in a vessel, even after the vessel is removed from the fire, the hot water in the vessel is still treated as having the capacity to cook something that is immersed in it, or (to a lesser extent) something upon which it is poured. Rebbi considered the hot-spring water in the bathtub to be similarly capable of cooking, since it was extremely hot, and the tub was the first place in which it gathered upon coming up from its source in the ground. He therefore instructed Rav Yitzchak bar Avdimi to transfer some water to a second vessel, where it would cool off somewhat, and would no longer be considered capable of cooking the oil (*Rashi*). For although hot water in a primary vessel is deemed capable of cooking as long as the water is so hot that the hand recoils from it, once the water is transferred to a second vessel, it is deemed incapable of cooking even if it is still hot enough to cause a hand to recoil from it, because the cold walls of the vessel cause it to cool rapidly (*Tosafos*).]

The Gemara comments that from this episode we learn three lessons:

(1) that oil is subject to cooking (there is actually a Tannaic view cited in the Gemara that one is not liable for cooking if he heats oil, even if it heated to the degree that a hand will recoil from it, for the oil is not changed substantively by the warming);

(2) that a secondary vessel is not capable of cooking (as was explained above); and

(3) that warming oil in a place where it can be cooked is forbidden Rabbinically even if one does not warm the oil to the degree that the hand recoils from it (see *Ritva* ibid.). [We see this from the fact that Rebbi instructed R' Yitzchak to place the oil in a secondary vessel, even though his intent was only to warm the oil slightly, and not to warm it to the extent that a hand would recoil from it.]

A MUSSAR THOUGHT FOR THE DAY

The alacrity shown by Avraham as he ran to greet his guests is an example of the essential *middah* of *zerizus*. In Chapter 7 of *Mesillas Yesharim,* we find further discussion of this critical trait:

"As soon as a man has taken hold of a mitzvah, he must rush to bring it to a conclusion, not as though he were anxious to get rid of a burden, but with a spirit of apprehension, lest he fail to complete it properly . . .

"Whatever the righteous undertake to do, they carry out with haste. Of Avraham it is written: (*Bereishis* 18:6-7) *Avraham ran into the tent, to Sarah, and said: Hurry, [prepare] three se'ahs of meal, fine flour, knead it and bake cakes. And Avraham ran to the cattle, and fetched a calf . . .* We find similarly regarding Rivkah, when she went to draw water for Eliezer's camels: *And she hastened, and emptied her pitcher into the trough* (ibid. 24:20). And when the mother of Shimshon saw the angel of Hashem, it is stated (*Shoftim* 13:10): *And the woman hurried, and ran, and told her husband.* Commenting upon this verse, the Midrash (*Bamidbar Rabbah* 10:5) states: We may learn from here that the deeds of the righteous are always performed with alacrity; no time is lost in undertaking a mitzvah or completing its performance.

"See, then, that a man who is righteous does not act sluggishly in the performance of Hashem's mitzvos. He moves with the swiftness of a fire, and does not rest until his task is completed. Note further that just as enthusiasm begets alacrity, the reverse is also true — *zerizus* enhances one's performance of a mitzvah. For when a man is fully engaged in doing a mitzvah, he will see that as he hastens his movements, his emotions are also aroused, and his enthusiasm for the mitzvah will grow stronger. But if his performance is sluggish, his spirit will also be dull and lifeless . . .

"When one serves Hashem, it is essential that his heart should yearn for closeness to Hashem, and his soul should feel a longing for Him. Therefore, if one sees that this desire does not burn within him as it should, it behooves him to deliberately bestir himself, and consciously strive to make *zerizus* part of his nature. For the outer actions of man awaken the inner attitude; and if one avails himself to correct that which is within his control to change, he will eventually acquire even that which is beyond his direct control. As a result of his efforts, he will cause to arise within himself an inner joy, and an ardent desire to fulfill Hashem's will."

The *melachah* of *sorting* applies equally to food items and nonfood items. For example, removing pits from a slice of watermelon, bones from chicken, or sorting a deli platter into stacks of individual types of cold cuts — even if the slices are selected from the mixture at random — are all subject to questions of *sorting*. Likewise, sorting cutlery, choosing a particular *bentcher* from a pile, or selecting a specific towel from an assortment are also activities subject to the rules of *sorting*.

Liquids, too, are included in the prohibition against *sorting*. Straining a liquid to remove impurities, removing an insect from a drink, or skimming fat from soup are all activities that must be scrutinized from the viewpoint of this *melachah*.

Even the partial sorting of a mixture is prohibited as a form of *sorting*. In mixtures of food and waste material, selecting only part of the food, or removing only part of the waste, remains a violation of *sorting*, although one is still left with a mixture. It is also forbidden to remove one item from a mixture in order to facilitate the finding of another item. For example, one who wishes to find meat and beans in a cholent may not remove the potatoes in order to expose the rest of the mixture.

In summation of what we have learned so far: *Sorting* may be defined as separating a mixture into its individual components. Sorting part of a mixture, or selecting one item from a mixture, falls under the category of *sorting*. Taking items from a mixture at random and arranging them separately is also a form of *sorting*. The *melachah* applies to foods and liquids, and to nonfoods as well. In any mixture of these items, or when waste materials are mixed together with a useful item, sorting all or part of the mixture can fall under the category of *sorting*.

In all of the above-mentioned cases, items are being separated from a mixture. However, choosing an article from a group of identical items, for instance selecting an apple from a bowl of similar apples, does not constitute *sorting*. This is because in such a case, the selection has not been made from a *mixture* of *different* items.

In order to differentiate between selecting that is permissible and selecting which may be subject to the restrictions of *sorting*, we must address two questions. First, how "different" from one another must the items that are mixed together be? When are two similar items said to be of the same type, and when are they considered to be different enough to constitute a mixture? Second, to what degree must different items be mixed together in order for halachah to view them as constituting a mixture?

Tomorrow we shall explore the answers to these questions.

As we mentioned yesterday, in the beginning of *Shacharis* we list the mitzvah of *hachnasas orchim,* offering hospitality to guests, among those mitzvos for which one receives reward both in this world and in the World to Come. *R' Moshe ben Yehudah Machir* in his *Seder HaYom* explains why the mitzvah of receiving guests is singled out for this reward from among other acts of kindness:

"Although the receiving of guests falls into the general category of *gemillas chasadim* (performing acts of *chesed,* lovingkindness), it is worthy of being singled out here. For one who brings guests into his home and provides them with a place where they can relax and recover from the rigors of travel has thereby benefited them in many ways: First, he has given them shelter and a place to rest in their weariness. Second, he will provide them with food and drink, so that they can recover their strength. Third, he has saved them from the embarrassment of having to wander about in a place where they are not necessarily known, where no one will recognize them and with no place to call home.

"Fourth, one who receives guests is often providing all of these kindnesses to people whom he does not know, who have never done anything for him; thus, his acts of kindness to them are perfectly altruistic. Although they are not his friends or acquaintances, he nevertheless provides them with shelter, food, drink and whatever else they might need. This last point increases the magnitude of his mitzvah many times over, for it is clear that he is performing this kindness for the sake of the mitzvah itself (*lishmah*), and he thus deserves all the credit and reward in the world.

"A fifth point is that in some cases, the host may be in a position to do as our father Avraham did, and to use his hospitality as a catalyst to draw his guests closer to the service of Hashem. For Avraham, after he would provide the needs of his guests, would remind them that their thanks rightfully belonged to Hashem, the Provider of all. If one finds himself in a situation where he can improve the spiritual level of a guest, and succeeds in doing so, he has benefited his guest even more, for he will have sated him both physically and spiritually.

"Certainly, then, the great merit that lies in this mitzvah is clear, and the reason for its great reward is readily understandable."

QUESTION OF THE DAY:
Why did Hashem send three angels to visit Avraham?
For the answer, see page 208.

יֻקַּח־נָא מְעַט־מַיִם וְרַחֲצוּ רַגְלֵיכֶם וְהִשָּׁעֲנוּ תַּחַת הָעֵץ

*Let some water be brought, and wash your feet,
and recline beneath the tree (Bereishis 18:4).*

Rashi explains that it was the custom of some pagans to worship the dust upon their feet; since Avraham did not allow any idols in his house, he had water brought so the travelers could wash their feet before entering.

R' Michel Barenbaum, in his *sefer Sichos Mussar,* notes that the bringing of the water to the guests is different than all of the other tasks that Avraham set out to perform. When it came to providing food and drink for his guests, Avraham was lavish. He asked Sarah to provide freshly baked bread, and, according to the Gemara (*Bava Metzia* 86b), he had three animal slaughtered so that each guest could receive an entire tongue with mustard. Yet, when it came to the water, Avraham was niggardly; he instructed that only *a little* be brought. Moreover, we find that Avraham ran to fetch the food himself, and he personally instructed Sarah to prepare the bread, and Yishmael to ready the meat. Yet, the bringing of the water was delegated to a subordinate.

The reason, explained *Reb Michel,* was that the water was brought because of a suspicion that the guests might be idol worshipers. Thus, providing the water was not an *honor* extended to the guests; to the contrary, it was a necessary precaution that Avraham could not avoid. Thus, he did not invest in it the same degree of enthusiasm that he brought to the other preparations.

Reb Michel would say that from Avraham we can learn the proper application of the popular saying: When an unknown person comes before you, כַּבְּדֵהוּ וְחָשְׁדֵהוּ, *Honor him and suspect him.* Avraham, too, both honored and suspected the guests; he honored them royally, but with regard to his suspicions he contented himself with just *a little* water. So too, while sometimes we must be wary, we must temper our suspicions while increasing our respect.

Nevertheless, we find that according to other commentators, Avraham is taken to task for even this degree of suspicion. The Torah does not state anywhere that the angels actually washed their feet; indeed, the Gemara (*Bava Metzia* ibid.) relates that they retorted to Avraham: "Do you take us to be as those who worship the dust of their feet? It is *your* son (Yishmael) who will do so one day!" *Maharsha* explains that because Avraham suspected the angels of worshiping idols (a sin of which, obviously, they were

פרשת ויר א

TUESDAY

PARASHAS VAYEIRA

not guilty), measure for measure, his own son was ultimately guilty of this very sin.

[Additionally, the Gemara (ibid.) states that the reward Hashem gave Avraham's descendants for the act of providing water was diminished because he did not provide the water personally; this, too, argues that Avraham should have brought the water himself. For further discussion of this point, see *A Mussar Thought for the Day.*]

MISHNAH OF THE DAY: SHABBOS 3:5

The Mishnah discusses cases in which one heats liquid by pouring it into hot vessels that are not on a fire:

לא **הַמֵּיחַם שֶׁפִּינָהוּ** — *A kettle that was removed* from atop a flame,[1] **יִתֵּן לְתוֹכוֹ צוֹנֵן בִּשְׁבִיל שֶׁיֵּחַמּוּ** — *one may not put cold water into it in order that it be heated,* **אֲבָל נוֹתֵן הוּא לְתוֹכוֹ** — *but he may put* a large quantity of cold water *into [the kettle],* [2] **אוֹ לְתוֹךְ הַכּוֹס** — *or* he may put even a smaller quantity of cold water *into a cup* of hot water,[3] **כְּדֵי לְהַפְשִׁירָן** — *so as to warm them.*

הָאִלְפָּס וְהַקְּדֵרָה שֶׁהֶעֱבִירָן מֵרְתָחִין — *A frying pan or a pot that were removed* from the fire *while boiling,* [4] **לֹא יִתֵּן לְתוֹכָן תְּבָלִין** — *one may not add spices to them;*[5] **אֲבָל נוֹתֵן הוּא לְתוֹךְ הַקְּעָרָה אוֹ לְתוֹךְ** — *but he may put* a

— NOTES —

1. A vessel that was heated on a fire is called a כְּלִי רִאשׁוֹן *[kli rishon], a primary vessel.* When a liquid is heated in a primary vessel, it is considered capable of cooking something that is added to it, as long as it is hot enough that יַד סוֹלֶדֶת בּוֹ, *one's hand recoils from it* (see *Gems from the Gemara,* Monday). [Once the liquid is transferred to another vessel (called a כְּלִי שֵׁנִי *[kli sheni]* — *a secondary vessel*), it is no longer considered capable of cooking.] Our Mishnah teaches that even if a *kli rishon* (the kettle) has been removed from the fire, it retains its status as a primary vessel, and one may not add cold water to the water in the kettle to heat it, as this action is considered an act of cooking (*Rav*).

2. Although the hot kettle is a *kli rishon,* nevertheless a person may pour cold water into the hot kettle only if he pours in such a large amount of water that there is no way the cold water can become hot, only warm (*Rav*).

3. Moreover, since a *kli sheni* does not cook, but only warms, one may add cold water to hot water in a *kli sheni* (*Tiferes Yisrael*). [In this case, one may add even a small amount of water, as it will not be cooked in any event (*Tosafos*).]

4. In this context, *boiling* means that the liquids in these vessels are so hot that one's hand will recoil when it comes into contact with them (*Rav;* see above, note 1).

5. Since the frying pans and pots are primary vessels, the liquids that are cooked in them and remain in them retain their ability to cook something else as long as they

הַתַּמְחוּי — *but one may add* spices to hot food that is *in a bowl or in a tureen.* [6]   רַבִּי יְהוּדָה אוֹמֵר — *R' Yehudah says:*   לַכֹּל הוּא נוֹתֵן — *He may add* spices *to anything,* [7]   חוּץ מִדָּבָר שֶׁיֵּשׁ בּוֹ חוֹמֶץ וְצִיר — *except something containing vinegar or fish brine.* [8]

——————————— NOTES ———————————

remain hot enough that one's hand will recoil when it comes into contact with them. Hence, it is forbidden to add spices to these pans and pots on the Sabbath even after the pans and pots have been removed from the fire, as the spices will be cooked by the hot contents (*Rashi*).

6. Since bowls and tureens are secondary vessels, the liquids that have been transferred into them from primary vessels are no longer deemed halachically capable of cooking the spices, as we have learned. Hence, spices may be added to these vessels (*Rashi*).

7. R' Yehudah's opinion is that spices can be cooked only in a vessel that is over a fire. Consequently, they may be added even to a primary vessel that contains liquid which is hot enough to cause one's hand to recoil, as long as the vessel is no longer over a fire (*Rav*). [He agrees with the Tanna Kamma, however, with regard to other foods (*Tosafos*).]

8. These sharp substances can cause spices to become cooked in a primary vessel even after it has been removed from the fire (*Rav*).

GEMS FROM THE GEMARA

The Gemara (41b) points out that while pouring a large quantity of cold water into a hot, empty kettle will not cause the water to be cooked, it may violate the prohibition of מְצָרֵף, *hardening [the steel]* of the kettle. [Steel is hardened by heating it and then drenching it with cold water. Such hardening is forbidden on the Sabbath as a sub-category of the forbidden labor of מַכֶּה בְּפַטִּישׁ, *striking the final blow* — i.e., putting the finishing touch on an otherwise complete utensil. In our case, since the kettle was heated on the fire, it likely became so hot that its metal softened somewhat. Hence, by pouring a large quantity of cold water into the kettle, one may be hardening it (see *Rashi* and *Tosafos*).]

The Gemara initially explains that our Mishnah reflects the view of R' Shimon, who holds that something that is unintended is permitted. In this case, the person who pours the cold water into the kettle does not intend to harden the steel. [When a person performs a permissible act and as a result a second, forbidden act also takes place, this second act is classified as דָּבָר שֶׁאֵין מִתְכַּוֵּין, *something that is unintended.* The person was *aware* that the prohibited act might occur, but he did not *intend* for it to occur. According to R' Shimon one is not required to refrain from

the permissible act even though he knows that the forbidden act may result, provided he does not intend for it.] In our case, then, according to R' Shimon, one may pour a large quantity of cold water into an empty, heated kettle if his intention is merely to warm the water, even though he *might* thereby be hardening the steel.

[It is important to note that R' Shimon does not permit the performance of the permissible act if the forbidden consequence is inevitable (פְּסִיק רֵישֵׁיהּ). In our case, it is not inevitable that the kettle will be hardened, for several reasons. First, the kettle may have been fully hardened before this heating. Second, it may not have been heated sufficiently this time for it to be hardened by the cold water (*Rashba, Ritva, Ran*).]

Ultimately, however, the Gemara rejects this explanation and suggests instead that in our Mishnah the kettle that was cleared from the fire was not empty, but still contained hot water; therefore, pouring cold water into it would not harden its steel. That this is the case in our Mishnah can be deduced from the fact that the Mishnah simply states that one removed the kettle from the stove, without adding that one removed the water from the kettle — indicating that the original water still remains in the kettle. Had the kettle been empty, however, our Mishnah would hold that it would be incumbent upon a person to insure that the kettle's steel is not even hardened *unintentionally*. The Mishnah thus reflects the view of R' Yehudah, who holds that *something that is unintended* is prohibited.

A MUSSAR THOUGHT FOR THE DAY

R' *Nosson Tzvi Finkel*, in *Ohr HaTzafun*, analyzes the actions of Avraham when he was visited by the angels, and the results that followed:

Our forefather Avraham sat at the opening of the tent on the third day after his circumcision, adjusting his bandages as he anxiously scanned the horizon for guests. Hashem had caused the sun to shine at its full strength so that no guests would come to disturb his rest. Yet Avraham was upset that no one had come (see *Bava Metzia* 86b). Even the appearance of Hashem to visit him did not stop his longing for guests.

Finally, Hashem sent three angels in the guise of Arabs, worshipers of the very dust of their feet. And Avraham, though he was old and in pain, ran to greet them in the heat. He bowed before them, and begged them to accept the hospitality of his tent. He ran to the cattle to slaughter three oxen and offer each of the guests the delicacy of an ox tongue in mustard. He told Sarah to hurry and bake cakes for them. There was one single detail in which he did not involve himself personally. He did not supply the water himself, probably because he was busy preparing their meal. Thus, the verse states that Avraham said: *Let a little water be brought and wash your feet* (*Bereishis* 18:4).

Now, let us see what the Gemara states regarding this (*Bava Metzia* 86b): R' Yehudah said in the name of Rav: "Whatever Avraham did for the angels himself, Hashem did for his descendants Himself. And whatever Avraham did for them through a messenger, Hashem did for his descendants through a messenger." The Gemara goes on to explain that the food that the Jews received in the Wilderness was provided by Hashem Himself, and Hashem Himself accompanied the Jews in the Wilderness, because Avraham himself had provided food for the angels and seen them on their way. But since Avraham sent a messenger to obtain water for them, the Jews received water in the Wilderness through the device of the rock (see *Shemos* 17:6).

Let us analyze this further. What was the difference between Hashem Himself accompanying the Jews or instead having His messenger do so, which they would have merited had Avraham delegated the task of accompanying his guests to Eliezer or Yishmael? Evidently, the difference was great, for we find that Moshe told Hashem (*Shemos* 33:15): *If Your Presence does not go with us, do not take us up from here.* From this we see that it would have been preferable for the Jews to remain forever in the Wilderness and forego entry into the land of Eretz Yisrael, rather than entering the land accompanied only by an angel. This gift was the result of Avraham's personally performed mitzvah.

On the other hand, what was the result of Avraham delegating the task of bringing water to the angels? That the water in the Wilderness was provided through the medium of a rock. This, too, had far-reaching implications — for had Hashem Himself provided the water, the tragedy at the *Mei Merivah* (where Moshe struck the rock to obtain the water) would not have occurred. Moshe would have led the Jews into Eretz Yisrael; the *Beis HaMikdash* would have been built immediately, never to be destroyed, and we would not have gone into exile (see *Sotah* 14b). Because Avraham did not personally perform a single, small detail of his enormous act of kindness, all this was lost. How careful, then, must we be to perform every mitzvah in the most complete manner possible!

As we discussed yesterday, it is necessary for us to define the two parameters that must be present in a combination of items in order for there to be a problem of *sorting*. These two parameters are: The items must be of two different *types,* and they must be *mixed together.* First, we shall discuss the halachic definition of what constitutes two different "types."

Food items and waste products that are combined are considered to be a mixture of two different "types" of items, and are therefore subject to the prohibition of *sorting.* This holds true even with respect to waste products that are a natural part of the food in question. Removing the bones from a piece of chicken is a question of *sorting,* even though the bones are a naturally occurring part of the chicken. Similarly, shells, pits, and peels of fruits can all be subject to the restrictions of *sorting,* although they occur naturally as part of their respective food item. [That having been said, it is permitted to peel a fruit such as an orange on the Sabbath — we will discuss the reason for this below.]

Furthermore, even if the undesired material is a naturally occurring *edible* part of the food, it too may be subject to the prohibition of *sorting.* An example of this would be separating fats from meat. Although the fat is an edible part of the meat, since the person who is eating it desires its removal, it is viewed as being a waste product that may not be separated from the desired food without transgressing the forbidden *melachah* of *sorting.*

Mixtures of different food items, where all of the items in the mixture are equally edible and no part of the mixture can be classified as waste, may also be restricted by the *melachah* of *sorting.* If the mixture contains food items of completely different types, and one wishes to select from among them, it qualifies as a mixture of various types, and may not be separated. A bowl of mixed fruits or nuts, a salad comprised of mixed vegetables, or a stew containing meat and potatoes are all examples of mixtures of totally different types of foods. These mixtures are certainly subject to the laws of *sorting.*

QUESTION OF THE DAY:
Where else in the Torah do we find that guests were given water to wash their feet?

For the answer, see page 208.

A CLOSER LOOK AT THE SIDDUR

פָּרָשַׁת
וַיֵּרָא

TUESDAY

PARASHAS
VAYEIRA

This week, we will discuss the fourth of the Thirteen Fundamental Principles (י"ג עיקרים) enumerated by *Rambam.*

The Fourth Principle states:

אֲנִי מַאֲמִין בֶּאֱמוּנָה שְׁלֵמָה שֶׁהַבּוֹרֵא שֶׁהַבּוֹרֵא יִתְבָּרַךְ שְׁמוֹ הוּא רִאשׁוֹן וְהוּא אַחֲרוֹן,
I believe with perfect faith that the Creator, Blessed be His Name, is the first and the last.

This principle teaches us that Hashem preceded all things that were created. In the beginning, only Hashem existed; there was nothing else. He then created everything from absolute nothingness, according to His will and desire (see *Moreh Nevuchim* 2:13).

This applies not only to tangible creations, but even to time itself, which is also a creation. [Thus, the question of what existed "before Hashem" is a question that has no meaning, as the concepts of "before" and "after" existed only after time was created.]

In addition, this principle teaches us that Hashem is absolutely eternal, and nothing else shares His eternal quality. This concept is discussed many times in the Torah. *Rambam* in his *Commentary to the Mishnah* in *Sanhedrin* states that this idea is taught to us by the verse (*Devarim* 33:27) that describes Hashem as אֱלֹהֵי קֶדֶם, *the eternal God.* The Gemara (*Berachos* 10a) also derives this from an exposition of the statement uttered by Channah, the mother of Shmuel (*I Shmuel* 2:2): כִּי אֵין בִּלְתֶּךָ, *for there are none besides You.* The Gemara expounds the word אֵין בִּלְתֶּךָ as לְבַלּוֹתֶךָ, yielding the reading, *for there are none that can outlive You.* The Gemara explains that while the nature of man is such that he can create things that will outlive him, God outlives all of his works, due to His eternal nature (see *Melo HaRo'im* to *Berachos* ibid.).

We find mention of Hashem's eternity throughout our prayers as well. In *Emes VeYatziv,* which we recite after the morning *Shema* during *Shacharis,* we exclaim, אֱמֶת אַתָּה הוּא רִאשׁוֹן וְאַתָּה הוּא אַחֲרוֹן וּמִבַּלְעָדֶיךָ אֵין לָנוּ מֶלֶךְ גּוֹאֵל וּמוֹשִׁיעַ, *It is true that You are the First and You are the Last, and that other than You we have no King, Redeemer, or Savior.* In the prayer of *Yehi Chevod* in *Pesukei D'Zimrah,* we proclaim, ה' מֶלֶךְ ה' מָלָךְ ה' יִמְלֹךְ לְעֹלָם וָעֶד, *Hashem reigns, Hashem has reigned, Hashem will reign forever!* And indeed, whenever we mention the Four-Letter Name of Hashem (*yud-kei-vav-kei*) we are bidden to concentrate on the fact that it signifies that Hashem is, always was, and always will be.

Rambam states in *Hilchos Teshuvah* (3:8) that one who does not believe that Hashem was first, and created all, is considered a *min* (heretic).

וַתִּצְחַק שָׂרָה בְּקִרְבָּהּ לֵאמֹר
אַחֲרֵי בְלֹתִי הָיְתָה־לִּי עֶדְנָה וַאדֹנִי זָקֵן

And Sarah laughed within herself, saying:
"After I have withered, will I again have smooth skin?
And My master is old!" (Bereishis 18:12).

It would seem from the verse that Sarah completely discounted the possibility that she would regain her youth and bear a child. Yet, she had already experienced the renewal of her menses on that very day (it was for this reason that the fresh bread Avraham had asked her to bake was never served — see *Rashi* to 18:6). Why did she not entertain the possibility that she had indeed experienced the beginning of a miraculous rejuvenation?

Ramban addresses this question by noting that Sarah had no reason to believe that the travelers were anything other than heathen wayfarers, and she could not be faulted for not giving any great weight to their words. *Gur Aryeh* notes further that the Torah makes a point of stating that Sarah's menses had ceased (in verse 11) *after* they had supposedly resumed. This means that her *regular* menses had ceased, and thus she was justified in assuming that the one-time flow was not a resumption of the menses of her youth.

Why, then, was Sarah faulted for her laughter? *Ramban* explains that a person on the lofty level of Sarah was expected not to discount the possibility of Hashem causing a miracle, no matter what the source of the blessing. It would have been appropriate for her to respond, "Amen, would that it will be so!" Her laughter, though, indicated that she felt that such an occurrence was utterly impossible. Thus, she was chastised (see verse 14): *Is anything beyond the hand of Hashem?*

The preceding is based on the assumption that Sarah had no reason to think that she would regain her youth. However, according to an interpretation of our verse cited in the Gemara in *Bava Metzia* (87a), Sarah's skin had *already* become smooth and her beauty returned (this is apparently based on the verse's use of the past tense, הָיְתָה לִּי עֶדְנָה, which translates literally to mean, *my skin has become smooth*). Thus, she did *not* doubt that she was capable of bearing the child that had been promised to her. Indeed, *Malbim* (see also *Haamek Davar*) understands that Sarah laughed *joyfully* upon realizing that she was once again capable of childbearing.

What, then, was Sarah's fault? It was the fact that she wondered, even as she exulted at her own rejuvenation, what purpose it would serve, for Avraham had not been similarly rejuvenated. Thus, she said: "True, my youth has returned, but my husband is still old!" (see also *Kli Yakar*). To this Hashem rejoined: "Is it only you who can be rejuvenated, but not your husband? Why do you believe that one will occur but not the other?"

[It is noteworthy that when Avraham was told earlier (see *Bereishis* 17:17) that he would father a son, he also reacted with laughter; yet, he was not faulted. For a discussion of why this was so, see *A Mussar Thought for the Day;* for why Avraham did not tell Sarah of the news Hashem had given him, see *Ramban.*]

MISHNAH OF THE DAY: SHABBOS 3:6

In this final Mishnah of the chapter, we shift our focus to the subject of מֻקְצֶה, [*muktzeh*] (literally, *set apart*), objects that people do not intend to use on the Sabbath, that may not be moved about on the Sabbath by Rabbinic decree (*Shabbos* 123b). Generally speaking, anything that is neither a utensil nor a food (for either people or animals) is considered *muktzeh.* For this reason, the flame of a candle or lamp is considered *muktzeh.* Moreover, something that serves as a *base to muktzeh* (when certain conditions are fulfilled) has the status of *muktzeh* as well (such an item is known as a בָּסִיס לְדָבָר הָאָסוּר). Hence, since the oil of a lamp serves as a base to the wick, which in turn serves as a base to the flame, the oil is *muktzeh* as well.

Furthermore, since anything which was *muktzeh* at the onset of the Sabbath remains *muktzeh* for the rest of that Sabbath (even if the reason it is considered *muktzeh* is no longer applicable), the oil in a lamp which was burning at the beginning of the Sabbath remains *muktzeh* even after the flame has gone out (even though it no longer serves as a base to *muktzeh*). Similarly, oil which drips out of a lamp also remains *muktzeh,* despite the fact that the oil is no longer a base to the flame.

The Mishnah discusses laws that arise from the *muktzeh* status of such oil:

אֵין נוֹתְנִין כְּלִי תַּחַת הַנֵּר לְקַבֵּל בּוֹ אֶת הַשֶּׁמֶן — On the Sabbath, *we may not place a vessel under a lamp to catch the* dripping *oil in it,* [1]

——————————— NOTES ———————————

1. The oil in the lamp is *muktzeh.* Hence, when the oil drips into a vessel, the vessel itself becomes a *base to muktzeh,* and may no longer be moved. The Gemara (43a) calls this בִּיטוּל כְּלִי מֵהֲכָנוֹ, *nullification of the vessel's availability,* for the vessel may no longer be moved. The Rabbis viewed *nullification of the vessel's availability* as tantamount to cementing the vessel in place — which would be a violation of the forbidden labor of *building* (*Meiri*). They therefore decreed that it is forbidden to do anything to a vessel

וְאִם נְתָנוּהָ מִבְּעוֹד יוֹם מוּתָּר — *but if they placed [the vessel] under the lamp while it was yet day* (i.e., before the onset of the Sabbath), *it is permitted.* [2] וְאֵין נֵיאוֹתִין מִמֶּנּוּ — *But we may not benefit from [the oil],* לְפִי שֶׁאֵינוֹ מִן הַמּוּכָן — *since it is not something prepared* for Sabbath use.[3]

The Mishnah discusses the *muktzeh* status of lamps:

מְטַלְטְלִין נֵר חָדָשׁ אֲבָל לֹא יָשָׁן — *We may move a new lamp, but not an old one.* [4] רַבִּי שִׁמְעוֹן אוֹמֵר — *R' Shimon says:* כָּל הַנֵּרוֹת מְטַלְטְלִין — *We may move all* types of *lamps,* חוּץ מִן הַנֵּר הַדּוֹלֵק בְּשַׁבָּת — *except* for a lamp that is actually *burning on the Sabbath.* [5]

The Mishnah discusses a related law:

נוֹתְנִין כְּלִי תַּחַת הַנֵּר לְקַבֵּל נִיצוֹצוֹת — *We may place a vessel under a lamp to catch* the falling *sparks,* [6] וְלֹא יִתֵּן לְתוֹכוֹ מַיִם — *but one may not place water in [the vessel],* מִפְּנֵי שֶׁהוּא מְכַבֶּה — *because he extinguishes* the sparks.[7]

———————————— NOTES ————————————

on the Sabbath which would render it immovable, including our Mishnah's case of allowing *muktzeh* oil to drip into it (*Rav*).

2. *Rashi* explains the phrase *it is permitted* to mean that once one has gone ahead and placed the vessel under the lamp before the onset of the Sabbath, he may leave it there. *Rashi* thus indicates that it is still preferable that one not place a vessel there even before the onset of the Sabbath, because we are concerned that he may inadvertently move the vessel on the Sabbath after the oil has begun to drip into it. However, this consideration does not suffice for us to require him to move the vessel before any oil drips into it.

3. Since the oil was designated specifically for use as fuel in the lamp, it is *muktzeh,* and therefore no other benefit may be derived from the oil for the duration of the Sabbath (see *Rav*).

4. An earthenware lamp which has never been lit is usable for other purposes — e.g., for storing small items. Therefore, it may be handled and moved on the Sabbath. However, once an earthenware lamp has been lit it becomes grimy, and is no longer suitable for other purposes. Hence, a used lamp falls into the category of מוּקְצֶה מֵחֲמַת מִיאוּס, *muktzeh on account of repugnance,* and may not be moved (*Rashi*).

5. R' Shimon rejects the concept of *muktzeh on account of repugnance,* and therefore permits the moving of all lamps, even those that have been used (*Rashi*). Nevertheless, even R' Shimon concedes that a lamp may not be moved while it is still lit, because the lamp, the oil, and the wick all become a *base to muktzeh* (the flame), and may not be moved (Gemara 47a).

6. Sparks are considered intangible. Hence, the vessel in which they fall is not subject to *nullification of the vessel's availability,* and does not become immovable (*Rav*).

7. Were one to pour water into the vessel under the lamp as sparks are falling into the vessel, one would violate the forbidden labor of *extinguishing.* As a precautionary measure, the Rabbis decreed that one may not even pour water into the vessel on Friday, before the onset of the Sabbath, lest one come to do so on the Sabbath itself and extinguish sparks while doing so (*Rav, Rashi*).

GEMS FROM THE GEMARA

פרשת וירא

WEDNESDAY

PARASHAS VAYEIRA

We learned in our Mishnah that there is a prohibition to move a *base to muktzeh* on the Sabbath. In introducing its discussion of this principle, the Gemara (44a-b) initially takes the position that a person may not move a bed that someone verbally designated to be used for the storage of money on the Sabbath. At this point of the discussion, the Gemara's position is that once the bed has been designated for the storage of money — which is intrinsically *muktzeh* — the bed no longer serves a permissible function. Even if no money was ever placed on the bed, the mere verbal designation for this purpose suffices to cause the bed to be considered *muktzeh* (*Rashi*).

Subsequently, however, the Gemara challenges this ruling on the basis of our Mishnah, which rules that while we may not move an old lamp, we may move a new one. This implies that only an old lamp that has actually been used is *muktzeh,* but a lamp that has never been used is not *muktzeh* — even though it has been designated for use. Accordingly, reasons the Gemara: If even in regard to a lamp, which was made for the very purpose of being used for lighting, the rule is that as long as one did not actually light in it, it is not yet *muktzeh* and one is permitted to move it, then in the case of a bed, which was not made for the purpose of storing money but was merely designated verbally, is it not certain that it is permitted to move it as long as one did not actually store money in it?

Conceding the point, the Gemara revises its ruling, stating that it is only forbidden to move a bed that someone verbally designated to be used for the storage of money on the Sabbath if he once actually *placed* money on it — even on a weekday. [Once it was so designated and used, it may not be used even if there is no money on it on this Sabbath.]

If, however, the bed was designated for such use but no money was ever placed on the bed, it is permitted to move the bed on the Sabbath when there is no money on the bed. If the bed was never designated for this use, but it once happened that money was placed upon it, this is meaningless, and the bed may be moved on the Sabbath if there is no money on the bed now. On the other hand, if he actually placed money on the bed before the Sabbath with the intention of leaving it there, he may not move the bed even if it was never designated for the storage of money, as it is thus a *base to muktzeh.*

WEDNESDAY — PARASHAS VAYEIRA / 181

WEDNESDAY

PARASHAS VAYEIRA

We find in the Torah that Sarah is taken to task for her reaction to the statement by the guests that she would bear a son. Yet, we find earlier (*Bereishis* 17:17) that Avraham, too, laughed when Hashem told him that Sarah would bear him a son. Why was Sarah taken to task, when Avraham was not?

Rashi (to ibid.) explains that while Avraham laughed jubilantly, Sarah laughed scornfully. He points to the differing translations used by *Targum Unkelos;* concerning Avraham, *Unkelos* renders וַיִּצְחָק as וַחֲדִי, *and he rejoiced,* while concerning Sarah, he translates וַתִּצְחַק simply as וְחַיְּכַת, *and she laughed* [derisively].

Another approach is taken by *Malbim,* who is of the opinion that neither Sarah nor Avraham was taken to task for their laughter; for indeed, even Sarah's laughter was the laughter of joy, as we explained above (see *A Torah Thought for the Day*). In his view, it was Sarah's concern that Avraham had not been rejuvenated as she had (as evidenced by her statement, *but my master is old!*) that was subject to criticism. According to this view, it is clear why Avraham was not chastised.

From *Chizkuni,* however, it is clear that Avraham, too, should not have laughed. He explains the reaction of Hashem to Sarah's laughter and not to Avraham's with a parable: It is comparable to a wise woman who wished to rebuke her daughter-in-law. Instead of addressing her directly, she directed the rebuke to her daughter, and the daughter-in-law understood the indirect message. Here, too, Hashem rebuked Avraham indirectly, in order to spare his feelings.

Midrash HaGadol, expanding on this theme, states that when one gives *mussar,* it is proper to rebuke the lesser person rather than the greater. For if the lesser is rebuked, the greater will surely realize that the rebuke applies to him as well; but if the greater person is rebuked, the lesser person may assume that the criticism is justified only when directed against a great person, and does not apply to him.

QUESTION OF THE DAY:

Where else in Tanach do we find that a couple was blessed with a child in return for their hachnasas orchim?

For the answer, see page 208.

Items of the same general species are more difficult to separate by type. As a rule, if the items differ in function or differ significantly in taste, they are then viewed as being different types of items and therefore pose a problem of *sorting* when they are combined. For example, a bowl of mixed Macintosh and Granny Smith apples, or a tray of boiled and roasted chicken would constitute a mixture from which one may not select due to the constraints of *sorting*. Since the two food items — although of the same general species — differ significantly in their taste, they are considered two different types of foods, and therefore form a mixture subject to the laws of *sorting*.

As we learned yesterday, items that are of the same general type, yet have different functions, are also considered to be different types, and are therefore subject to the *melachah* of *sorting* if they are mixed together. An example of this would be a combination of soup spoons and tea-spoons. While both items are eating utensils — indeed, they are both spoons — the function of a soup spoon is not the same as the function of a teaspoon. Since they have two clearly delineated individual functions, they are deemed two different types of items, and sorting them is forbidden.

In general, items that are of the same type but differ only in size, are considered to be of one type. Therefore, a combination of such items would not constitute a mixture in regard to the *melachah* of *sorting*. However, it must be noted that this is true only in cases where the difference in size does not translate into a difference in function. In the case of the spoons mentioned above, the only difference between the two spoons is one of size; yet, it is that size difference that effects the difference in function which is key to their halachic status when mixed. The same rule would apply to different-size plates — once again, the difference in size changes the function of the individual items, and marks them as "different" from one another.

When speaking of food items, size rarely changes the function of food. While one may prefer a larger apple to a smaller one, both fruits are food items designated for consumption. There are times, though, when size does indeed change a food's function. For example: The difference between matzah and matzah meal is in truth only a difference of size. While both are food items prepared for human consumption, they clearly have different functions. It is therefore forbidden for one to remove pieces of matzah that have become mixed into matzah meal.

As we discussed earlier, *Ramban* states that Sarah was faulted for not responding to the blessing of her guests that she would have a child by saying, "Amen, would that it will be so!" This underscores one of the basic concepts that must always accompany our prayers — nothing is ever beyond the power of Hashem to accomplish. He is All-Powerful and can do as He wishes in any circumstance.

The Gemara (*Berachos* 10a) expresses this sentiment with a pithy aphorism: אֲפִילּוּ חֶרֶב חַדָּה מוּנַחַת עַל צַוָּארוֹ שֶׁל אָדָם אַל יִמְנַע עַצְמוֹ מִן הָרַחֲמִים, *Even if a sharp sword rests upon a person's neck, he should not hold himself back from [praying for] mercy.* No matter how dire the circumstances, the chance is always there that Hashem will hear the prayer and reverse the evil decree.

History is replete with instances where Jewish individuals and even the Jewish nation seemed to be in danger of imminent destruction. But Hashem does not slumber nor does He sleep; and He listens always for our prayers.

Indeed, the greater part of our prayers is not made up of requests, but rather of praises of Hashem. This is because we must first acknowledge that He is the One Who can answer our requests, before we direct them to Him. We find this formula repeated in the *Shemoneh Esrei* as well, where we begin with the praises of the first three blessings before we begin to request our needs.

The Gemara (*Yevamos* 64a) tells us: All of the *Avos* and the *Imahos* were physically incapable of bearing children, and miracles had to be performed so that they could have children. Why did Hashem do this? Because Hashem desires the prayers of the righteous.

Indeed, we find in *Hallel* the following descriptive praise of Hashem: *He transforms the barren wife into a glad mother of children* (*Tehillim* 113:9). *Radak* there explains: Hashem exercises complete control over all of nature. This control is most vividly demonstrated when He suddenly transforms a barren woman into a mother, and so Dovid HaMelech chose this as an an example of Hashem's power.

When we come to our prayers secure in the knowledge that Hashem can provide all of our needs, it elevates the very essence of our *avodas halev* — the *service of the heart,* that is *tefillah.*

A TORAH THOUGHT FOR THE DAY

פרשת
וירא

THURSDAY
PARASHAS
VAYEIRA

כִּי יְדַעְתִּיו לְמַעַן אֲשֶׁר יְצַוֶּה אֶת־בָּנָיו וְאֶת־בֵּיתוֹ
אַחֲרָיו וְשָׁמְרוּ דֶּרֶךְ יהוה לַעֲשׂוֹת צְדָקָה וּמִשְׁפָּט
לְמַעַן הָבִיא יהוה עַל־אַבְרָהָם אֵת אֲשֶׁר־דִּבֶּר עָלָיו

For I have loved him (Avraham),
because he commands his children and his household after him
that they should keep the way of HASHEM, doing charity and justice;
in order that Hashem might then bring upon Avraham
that which He had promised him (Bereishis 18:19).

This translation of the verse follows *Rashi,* who translates the verb יְדַעְתִּיו as connoting *love* (this usage of the verb ידע is found else-where in the Torah as well; see, for example, *Bereishis* 4:1). According to *Rashi,* the verse is Hashem's explanation of why He wished to inform Avraham of Sodom's impending destruction. Hashem reasoned: Avra-ham is so beloved to Me that I intend him to become a great nation, and a source of blessing to the people of the earth. How, then, can I conceal such an important event from him? The verse continues by explaining *why* Avraham was deserving of that special love — because he ensures that his descendants will follow in his footsteps, practicing charity and justice. And how does he do so? By teaching his children of the rewards that will be bestowed upon them by Hashem if they follow in His ways.

Targum Onkelos, however, understands the word יְדַעְתִּיו in the usual sense. Thus, he renders the opening of the verse: *For I know about him (Avraham) that he will command his children and household after him etc.* According to this interpretation, the verse flows a bit differently: Since I know that Avraham will ensure that his children will follow in My ways, it is clear that they will merit the reward that I have promised him. *Rashbam* sums up the thrust of this point: Since his descendants will remain righteous, they will eventually settle in the Land of Eretz Yisrael. And if that is the case, how can I destroy part of his inheritance without first informing him?

According to either of these interpretations, it is clear that Hashem attached primary importance to the fact that Avraham would impress upon his children the supreme importance of keeping the ways of Hashem. *R' Reuven Feinstein* notes that this special ability of Avraham is clearly seen in the preceding passage, when Avraham went to receive his guests. The verse states (18:7) that Avraham ran to the cattle and took a calf, which he gave to "the youth" to prepare. Who was this "youth"? *Rashi* tells us that it was none other than Yishmael, and that

Avraham included him in the preparations to train him in the performance of mitzvos. Now, consider — Yishmael had been circumcised three days earlier, just as Avraham had been. He was ill and in pain. Yet, Avraham did not indulgently allow him to remain in bed; rather, he impressed upon him the importance of attending to the guests even in such circumstances. Possibly, it was this display of *chinuch* which was the ultimate proof that Avraham would be successful in transmitting his beliefs and ideals to his descendants. [See further in *A Mussar Thought for the Day.*]

MISHNAH OF THE DAY SHABBOS 4:1

It is forbidden to insulate pots before the Sabbath by wrapping them in substances that add heat to the food. The Mishnah enumerates those substances which are included in this prohibition:

בַּמֶּה טוֹמְנִין, וּבַמֶּה אֵין טוֹמְנִין — If a pot with hot food was removed from a stove on Friday, and we want to preserve its heat, *with what may we insulate* [it], *and with what may we not insulate* [it]? אֵין טוֹמְנִין לֹא בְגֶפֶת — *We may not insulate, neither* by wrapping the pot *with sesame-pulp or olive-pulp,*[1] וְלֹא בְזֶבֶל לֹא בְמֶלַח וְלֹא בְסִיד וְלֹא בְחוֹל — *nor with manure, nor with salt, nor with lime,* בֵּין לַחִים בֵּין יְבֵשִׁים

————————— NOTES —————————

1. The pulp of pressed sesame seeds or olives, as well as the other substances listed in our Mishnah, radiate heat, and therefore can readily be confused with hot ash mixed with live coals. Hence, lest someone come to use hot ash mixed with live coals to insulate his food — which, in turn, may lead to his raking the coals in order to hasten the cooking, a violation of the *melachah* of *cooking* — the Rabbis forbade the use of all such substances for *hatmanah* (literally, *hiding* — i.e., insulating the hot food to preserve its heat). Moreover, the Rabbis even forbade a person to use these substances to insulate hot food on Friday, before the onset of the Sabbath (*Rav*). [The prohibition of *hatmanah* applies even to foods that are completely cooked, even though one will certainly not come to rake coals to hasten the cooking in such a case. This is because of the principle known as לֹא פְּלוּג, *non-differentiation* — i.e., when the Rabbis issue a decree, they apply the decree even in individual cases where the reason for the decree may not apply (*Tiferes Yisrael; Rashi* 34b).]

[Note that even substances that do *not* raise the temperature of the food may not be used to insulate pots on the Sabbath itself, for the Sages were concerned that one coming to insulate his pot on the Sabbath might find that the food had already cooled, and forgetfully reheat it over the fire. The distinction made in this Mishnah between substances that raise the heat of the food and those that do not is relevant only to whether these substances may be used to insulate *before* the Sabbath.]

nor with sand, whether wet or dry; [2]   לֹא בְתֶבֶן וְלֹא
בְזַגִּים וְלֹא בְמוֹכִים וְלֹא בַעֲשָׂבִים בִּזְמַן שֶׁהֵן לַחִים — *not with*
straw, nor with grape skins, nor with flocking, [3] *nor*
with grasses, when they are moist, [4]   אֲבָל טוֹמְנִין בָּהֶן
בִּשֶׁהֵן יְבֵשִׁין — *but we may insulate* hot food *with them*
when they are dry.

טוֹמְנִין בִּכְסוּת וּבְפֵרוֹת בְּכַנְפֵי יוֹנָה וּבִנְסֹרֶת שֶׁל חָרָשִׁים וּבִנְעֹרֶת
שֶׁל פִּשְׁתָּן דַּקָּה — *We may insulate* the hot pot by wrapping it *with*
clothing, with produce, [5] *with pigeon feathers,* [6] *with carpenters'*
sawdust, or with fine flax combings. [7]   רַבִּי יְהוּדָה אוֹסֵר בְּדַקָּה וּמַתִּיר
בְּגַסָּה — *R' Yehudah prohibits* insulation with *fine* combings, *but per-*
mits insulation with *coarse* combings. [8]

———————————— NOTES ————————————

2. Not only may we not use these substances when they are damp and thus tend to
radiate a great deal of heat, but they may not be used as insulation even when dry, for
they still tend to generate some heat (*Rav; Rashi*).

3. Flocking includes any tufts of unprocessed soft material such as cotton, soft wool,
or shreds of worn-out clothing (*Rav; Rashi*).

4. All of the substances in this second grouping — viz., straw, grape skins, flocking
and grass — may not be used to insulate hot food before the Sabbath, but this is so
only when they are moist (*Rav*). This is because these substances cause the temperature of the insulated food to rise only when they are damp, not when they are dry.
[For a discussion of whether this is true only in a case involving the original, natural
moisture of these substances, or even if they became dry and then were moistened
artificially, see *Gems from the Gemara.*]

5. Such as wheat or beans (*Rashi; Meiri*).

6. Other feathers may be used for *hatmanah* as well (*Meiri; Tiferes Yisrael*). Pigeon
feathers are cited only as an example because they were the most commonly used
feathers in Mishnaic times (*Shenos Eliyahu*).

7. Fine flax combings are the splinters that fall from the flax when it is combed out
(*Tiferes Yisrael*). [As the Tanna Kamma permits *hatmanah* even with fine flax comb-
ings, he certainly permits *hatmanah* before the Sabbath with coarse ones (*Meiri*).
Indeed, several commentaries delete the word "fine" (*Rif; Rosh; Tiferes Yisrael*).

8. R' Yehudah's disagreement with the Tanna Kamma concerns only the flax combings. He agrees with the Tanna Kamma, however, that both coarse and fine sawdust
may be used to insulate before the Sabbath (*Rav* from Gemara).

QUESTION OF THE DAY:

Why did Avraham pray that Sodom be saved only
if there were ten righteous people in the city?

For the answer, see page 208.

The Mishnah taught that we may not insulate with straw, grape skins, flocking, or grasses, when they are moist. The Gemara (49a) analyzes this ruling, inquiring whether the Mishnah meant to forbid the use of these substances only when they are moist on their own account — i.e., with their own natural moisture — or whether it also meant to forbid their use when they are moist because of an external factor — even if their natural moisture is gone.

The Gemara seeks to resolve this issue on the basis of the inclusion of flocking in this list. The Gemara assumes that flocking is not naturally moist; thus, it must be that our Mishnah forbade the use of these substances even when they are moist because of an external factor. However, the Gemara rejects this proof, explaining that the Mishnah refers to wool pluckings that come from between the thighs of the sheep, where the wool is naturally damp from the sweat of the animal.

The Gemara attempts another proof from a Baraisa, in which R' Oshaya taught that one may insulate with dry clothing and with dry produce, but not with moist clothing or with moist produce. It would seem obvious that the moisture here is an external factor, for how is it possible for clothing to be moist naturally?

Nevertheless, the Gemara rejects this proof as well, since it is possible that the clothing in question was spun from the aforementioned wool pluckings that come from between the thighs of the sheep, which were still naturally moist. The question thus remains unresolved.

[According to most commentators, the premise of the Gemara's discussion is the assumption that these substances might cause the temperature to rise only when they are damp on account of their natural moisture. Accordingly, if the original moisture of these substances had dried out and they subsequently became moist due to external factors, these materials would be suitable for insulating (*Rav; Rif; Rambam Commentary*).

[In our texts of the *Rambam* (*Hil. Shabbos* 4:1), he states that we may not use "grape skins, flocking or grasses, when they are moist *even* if the moisture is their own," implying that external moisture would cause an even greater increase of heat. However, it would seem that *Rambam* in *Hilchos Shabbos* is at variance with his own *Commentary to the Mishnah* here, for he states therein that *only* if they are naturally moist are they prohibited (*Tiferes Yisrael*). However, old manuscripts of *Rambam's Hilchos Shabbos* omit the word *even,* thus reconciling his statements there with his commentary (see *Rambam,* Frankel ed., pp. 25, 734).]

A MUSSAR THOUGHT FOR THE DAY

As we mentioned above (see *A Torah Thought for the Day*), Avraham's practice of *chinuch,* ensuring that his children would keep the ways of Hashem, was a highly prized virtue. It behooves us, therefore, to analyze just why Avraham was so successful in this important task.

A critical clue can be gleaned from a careful reading of the verse. Hashem stated (according to *Rashi's* translation of the verse) that He loved Avraham because Avraham *commands his children and his household after him that they should keep the way of Hashem, doing charity and justice.* Seemingly, the words *after him* (אַחֲרָיו) are superfluous. The verse should simply have stated that Avraham commanded his children and his household to keep the way of Hashem! What is being added by the words *after him*?

These words teach us an essential fact of *chinuch* — children are taught not by words, but by example. "Do as I say, not as I do" may be a clever slogan, but it is never effective in teaching. Children who see that the rules and values they are being asked to follow are ignored by the very person who teaches them will not attach any value to the lessons. And why should they? If the parent — who is the most important role model a child can ever have — cannot be bothered to learn Torah or perform mitzvos properly, the child receives a clear message that it obviously cannot be that important to do so — and the lesson is doomed from its very inception.

Avraham, however, commanded his children and household to follow *after him* — to tread the path that he himself lived. When Avraham lay ill, recovering from his circumcision, and guests came to his door, he did not wait for younger, fitter people to fulfill the mitzvah he so treasured. He arose himself, sick and in pain — and he challenged his son Yishmael to do the same. This is true *chinuch,* for when a child sees that a parent is willing to expend time and effort to do something, the message is clear — that thing is important, and worthy of effort. By leading from the front, Avraham personified successful *chinuch.*

HALACHAH OF THE DAY

A significant difference in quality between two similar items also must be taken into consideration in regard to defining items as different with respect to the *melachah* of *sorting.* How do we define a significant difference? If the difference between the two items in question

is so extensive as to make the inferior-quality item seem to be "waste" as compared to the higher-quality one, this difference is then significant enough to cause the combination to be considered a mixture. For example, if one has before him a cluster of grapes in which some are overripe and soft, while the others are ripe and firm, this is a mixture subject to the restrictions of *sorting*. While the soft grapes are still edible, in the presence of the ripe grapes they are seen as waste matter, which would be eaten only if necessary.

Now, in order for there to be a question of *sorting* when separating one type of item from another type of item, the items must be *mixed* — that is, they must be combined in such a way as to form what the halachah considers to be a mixture. If the two types of items are merely next to each other, but not considered mixed together, selecting either of the two types of items is not a violation of the *melachah* of *sorting*.

We will now discuss this criterion further. What constitutes a mixture in the eyes of halachah? How, and to what degree, must items be mixed together for the *melachah* of *sorting* to apply?

The precise degree to which items must be mixed to be halachically deemed a mixture is not clearly discussed in the Gemara. Because of this, the *poskim* take a very stringent stance with regard to this question. As a result of this stringency, the following general rule can be applied: In any situation where objects are found in close physical proximity to one another, to the degree that they are no longer perceived as individual items by someone viewing them, but rather as an assortment, the resultant combination is now considered to be a mixture, and is subject to the restrictions of *sorting*. This is true even if the individual items comprising the mixture can still be readily discerned one from the other should one attempt to do so. Since the individual items are no longer *perceived* as remaining apart and isolated, but rather, the entire collection of objects is viewed as a combination, with each item looked at as a part of the greater mixture, the halachah follows this perception, and views the grouping as a mix. Accordingly, removing items from this combination can constitute *sorting*.

This constitutes the general rule that governs the question of whether a combination is considered a mixtures. However, it does not tell the entire story. There are several different types of mixtures recognized by halachah; and, as we shall see, there are leniencies that apply to some types of mixtures and not to others. For this reason, we will begin tomorrow's discussion by describing various types of mixtures described by halachah.

In our daily prayers, we do not find any requests of Hashem that He show us the proper manner to train our children in the ways of Hashem. This is perhaps because, as discussed earlier, the surest way to train is by example; thus, if we act as we should, our children will have been taught well. Nevertheless, we do find instances in the prayers where we beseech Hashem for children who will be righteous, and children who are Torah scholars. The most prominent example is the prayer that is part of *Birchas HaTorah,* the blessings we recite at the beginning of the *Shacharis* prayer thanking Hashem for choosing us as His nation and giving us His Torah. We ask: *May we and our offspring, and the offspring of Your entire nation, the House of Israel, all of us, together, know Your Name and study Your Torah for its own sake.* [Some versions state *our offspring and our offspring's offspring,* on the basis of a Gemara (*Bava Metzia* 85a) which states that once Torah has been the focus of a family for three generations, the Torah will always seek to return there; our version omits the extra words, as it intends the word *offspring* to include both children and grandchildren (*Gra, Berachos* 11a).]

Another such request can be found in the prayers of *Yekum Purkan,* which are said after the Torah reading and before the *Mussaf* prayers on the Sabbath. We ask that Hashem grant us *children who will live and endure; children who will neither interrupt nor cease from the words of the Torah.* And in some versions of the prayer said when the Torah scroll is removed from the *Aron Kodesh* (בְּרִיךְ שְׁמֵיהּ, *May His Name be blessed . . .*), we find the prayer: *May it be Your will that You give me sons who shall carry out Your will.*

Mishnah Berurah (47:10) states: The prayers of a mother and father should be constantly fluent in their mouths, to pray that their children should grow up to be Torah scholars, righteous people possessed of good *middos;* one should be especially careful to have this in mind when saying the blessing of *Ahavah Rabbah* (the blessing that immediately precedes the morning recitation of the *Shema,* wherein we ask Hashem to grant us success in understanding and disseminating His Torah), and also while saying the sentence: *may we and our offspring* etc. during *Birchas HaTorah* (see above).

Mishnah Berurah adds that when one is reciting the prayer of *U'va LeTzion* at the end of *Shacharis* — in which we ask Hashem to imbue our hearts with love and fear of Him, so that we may do His will and serve Him wholeheartedly, *so that we do not struggle in vain nor produce for*

פרשת וירא

THURSDAY

PARASHAS VAYEIRA

futility — one should have in mind that his children should be worthy and righteous. This last directive, in a way, is the most revealing, for it starkly states the essential truth — if we do not succeed in teaching our children to follow in our ways, we have indeed struggled in vain.

A TASTE OF LOMDUS

As we discussed above, the concept of *chinuch* — *educating a child to perform mitzvos* — is first illustrated in the Torah when Avraham includes Yishmael in making preparations for his guests. Although a child is not required to perform mitzvos before he or she reaches maturity, the directive of *chinuch* obligates parents to accustom their children to live a life centered around serving Hashem. In this way, the responsibility to do mitzvos does not take a child by surprise upon his or her attainment of legal majority, as it is already a familiar and meaningful part of the child's existence by the time mitzvah performance becomes mandatory.

Each mitzvah should be introduced to the child from the time he is mature enough to fulfill it properly. The Gemara in *Maseches Succah* (42a-b) lists the points of development at which a child is required to begin to perform various mitzvos. For example, a child who knows how to wave a *lulav* in the proper manner is obligated to perform the mitzvah of *lulav* (i.e., the taking of the Four Species). When he is old enough to properly enfold himself in a *tallis,* he is obligated in the mitzvah of *tzitzis.* When he is old enough to properly care for *tefillin* (and prevent them from entering unclean places) his father must buy him *tefillin.*

Netziv (Meromei Sadeh to 42a) points out that the Gemara's comments concerning *lulav* are quite puzzling. Earlier, the Gemara had observed that one successfully fulfills the Torah's commandment to take the Four Species on Succos as soon as he lifts the *lulav* bundle [containing the *hadassim* and the *aravos*] along with the *esrog. Naanu'im,* or *wavings,* the Gemara (*Succah* 37b) explains, are merely a supplementary aspect of the mitzvah. A person who does not perform *naanu'im* nonetheless fulfills the basic Biblical commandment. Why, then, does the Gemara obligate a child to begin his training in the mitzvah of *lulav* only after he is able to *wave* it? Shouldn't *chinuch* in this area of halachah begin from the moment a child is able to pick up the *lulav* bundle and the *esrog?*

Netziv's question also applies to the Gemara's description of the appropriate age for a child to begin to wear *tzitzis.* Although part of the daily mitzvah of donning a *tallis* with *tzitzis* indeed includes enfolding the *tallis* around the head and body, many opinions maintain that a person fulfills the basic mitzvah of *tzitzis* from the moment he puts the garment on and wears it in a normal way (as one does every day with a *tallis katan*). Why, then, does the Gemara obligate a child in *tzitzis* only when he is able to wrap himself in a *tallis*?

Netziv and others (see *Chidushei HaGriz al HaShas, Arachin* 2b), explain that a parent's *chinuch* obligations begin only when the child is able to perform mitzvos in the exact manner in which he will actually carry them out when he grows up. While it is true that an adult who lifts the *lulav* bundle without waving it, or wears his *tallis* without enfolding himself in it, fulfills the basic mitzvah, training a child to do this would not fulfill the purpose of *chinuch*. *Chinuch's* purpose is not merely to *include* a child in mitzvah performance. The idea behind *chinuch* is that the child should become *familiar* with performing mitzvos; and this is accomplished by having the child perform them in the manner that they will be carried out when the child is grown up.

Netziv's contemporary, *Bikkurei Yaakov* (657:3), adds another point. He explains that *Chazal* purposely did not institute *chinuch* for partial mitzvos, out of fear that people would grow up thinking that the way they learned to perform the mitzvos as children is the preferred way. This would cause them to spend their lives doing incomplete and imperfect mitzvos.

R' Yechezkel Abramsky (*Chazon Yechezkel, Chagigah* 1:3) addresses *Netziv's* question from a totally different perspective. He explains that only properly waving the *lulav* and enfolding oneself in a *tallis* demonstrate that the child appreciates that these actions are being done to fulfill a purpose called a mitzvah. Young children happily grab any unusual object, and most enjoy wrapping themselves in blankets. Therefore, if one tries to instruct a child to lift a *lulav* or wear a *tallis* at too young an age, he will not realize that he is performing a mitzvah, rather than just playing a new game. He will not recognize these actions as separate from, or beyond, his normal activities. It is only when the child becomes mature enough to make distinctions between mundane and sacred actions and objects [as evidenced by his ability to follow the proper *naanu'im* patterns (see *Orach Chaim* 657:1 and *Vilna Gaon* §1 from *Yerushalmi*) or appropriately wrap his body in a *tallis* and hold his *tzitzis* while reciting the *Shema* (see *Rama, Orach Chaim* 17:3)], that he shows his grasp of the concept that this action is different from the regular pattern of his life. When he reaches this stage, he is able to understand a mitzvah, and only at this point is he able to begin the process of *chinuch* education for a life of *avodas Hashem*.

הִנֵּה־נָא הָעִיר הַזֹּאת קְרֹבָה לָנוּס שָׁמָּה וְהִוא מִצְעָר
אִמָּלְטָה נָא שָׁמָּה הֲלֹא מִצְעָר הִוא וּתְחִי נַפְשִׁי

*Behold, please, this city is near enough to
escape there and it is small; I shall flee there.
Is it not small? And I will live (Bereishis 19:20).*

T he verse relates that Lot requested of the angels that he be allowed
to flee to the city of Tzoar, rather than to the mountains where Avraham resided. *Rashi* explains that Lot was afraid that were he to return to
Avraham's location, any merits he possessed would pale next to the righteousness of Avraham, and he would be exposed as a sinner and killed.
[*Pesikta Rabbasi* adds that Lot argued that Avraham had already asked
him to separate himself from his camp (see above, 13:9).] Moreover, since
the city of Tzoar was a relatively young city (as *Rashi* explains, it was
settled a year after Sodom was established), its sins had not yet reached
the point where it could not be saved. The angels acquiesced, and allowed
Lot to proceed to Tzoar, which was not destroyed.

One might wonder: How is it that Lot was able to save Tzoar with a
simple request, while Avraham prayed for the cities in vain? Surely,
Avraham's prayers should have carried greater weight!

Some Midrashim address this question by saying that, in truth, Tzoar
was not saved, in a strict sense, for all of its inhabitants were killed; it was
only the physical city itself that was left intact. According to this approach,
Lot and his daughters ultimately left Tzoar because they were afraid to live
in a city filled with corpses (see 19:30). However, this is not universally
accepted; many commentators explain that Lot and his daughters left
Tzoar because they were afraid that Tzoar's reprieve would last for only
one year, when Tzoar would be the age that Sodom was upon its destruction (*Ohel David*); or that it would be spared only for long enough to allow
Lot to regroup and then leave (*Ramban*). Thus, the question remains —
why was Lot able to save the inhabitants of Tzoar, while Avraham was not?

From *Sifsei Chachamim* it seems that Tzoar was actually saved in the
merit of Avraham, not that of Lot. Although it was Lot who made the
request, his point was that he would not survive unless Tzoar was saved;
and since Lot was to be saved in Avraham's merit, his merit served to
protect Tzoar as well. When Avraham prayed for the cities, however, he
did not ask Hashem to save the cities in *his* merit; he merely requested
that they be spared in the merit of any righteous people who inhabited
them. Since no such people existed, his prayers could not save the cities.

For another approach, see *A Mussar Thought for the Day.*

As we learned in the previous Mishnah, it is forbidden to insulate a hot pot with substances that add heat to the food, even if this is done before the Sabbath. The Mishnah enumerates substances that may be used to insulate pots before the Sabbath (because they do not increase the heat of the food), but which may be subject to another problem — the prohibition to move *muktzeh* items on the Sabbath:

וּמַטְמְנִין בַּשְּׁלָחִין — *We may insulate* hot pots *with pelts,*[1] בְּגִזֵּי צֶמֶר וְאֵין אוֹתָן — *and we may move them* on the Sabbath;[2] מְטַלְטְלִין אוֹתָן — we may also insulate *with wool shearings, but we may not move them* on the Sabbath.[3] כֵּיצַד הוּא עוֹשֶׂה — If one did insulate with wool shearings, *what should he do* to remove the pot from its *muktzeh* wrapping?[4] נוֹטֵל אֶת הַכִּסּוּי וְהֵן נוֹפְלוֹת — *He should remove the lid, and [the shearings] fall* away of their own accord.[5]

──────────── NOTES ────────────

1. Pelts are animal hides from which the hair has not been removed (*Rav; Tos. Yom Tov*).

2. It would seem that an unfinished pelt should be categorized as *muktzeh,* and it should therefore be forbidden to move the pelts. [Hence, if a person were to use pelts to insulate food, he should not be allowed to move the pelts to get to the food.] Nevertheless, although the pelts have not been fashioned into a usable utensil, they may be moved about — even for purposes other than covering hot food — because they can be, and sometimes are, used as a rug upon which to recline (*Rav; Rashi*).

3. Wool shearings are generally reserved to be made into thread. Since in using them one runs the risk of their becoming soiled or otherwise damaged and consequently unfit for their primary purpose of thread, they are normally not used for any other purpose. They are therefore categorized as *muktzeh* due to [potential] loss of money, and may not be moved (*Mishnah Berurah* 259:3). [This is so even where they have previously been used to cover food, since it is still expected that they will be spun into thread. If, however, one *permanently* designates them for *hatmanah,* they are no longer *muktzeh,* and may be moved about (*Rav*).]

4. How can he remove the food without moving the *muktzeh* shearings? (*Rav; Rashi*).

5. Moving the shearings by means of lifting the lid and causing them to slide off is known as טִלְטוּל מִן הַצַּד, *indirect movement* of *muktzeh,* and is permissible. [This exemption to the general ban of moving *muktzeh* is explained at length in Ch. 21.] Moreover, although the wool shearings are being supported by the lid, the lid does not become a base to the shearings (and thus a base for *muktzeh,* which is then itself treated as *muktzeh* — see above, mishnah 3:6), for the lid's primary purpose is to cover the pot, not to hold up the shearings (*Rav; Rashi*). However, the lid may be picked up by its handle only if the handle of the lid is exposed. One may not grope through the shearings to get at the handle, since this would constitute direct

FRIDAY

PARASHAS VAYEIRA

After explaining how to remove the lid, the Mishnah proceeds to discuss the proper procedure for removing the food from the insulated pot:

רַבִּי אֶלְעָזָר בֶּן עֲזַרְיָה אוֹמֵר: קֹפָּה מַטֶּה עַל צִדָּהּ וְנוֹטֵל — R' **Elazar ben Azaryah says: He tilts the** entire **box,** which contains the shearings and the pot, **onto its side, and removes** the food by pouring out the amount he requires. He then leaves the rest of the food in the pot for the next meal. He should not lift the pot out of the box, שֶׁמָּא יִטֹּל וְאֵינוּ יָכוֹל לְהַחֲזִיר — **lest he remove** the pot **and be unable to replace** it.[6] וַחֲכָמִים אוֹמְרִים נוֹטֵל וּמַחֲזִיר — **But, the Sages say: He may remove** the pot from the box **and replace** it.[7]

The Mishnah continues discussing the laws of insulating with substances that do not add heat:

לֹא כִסָּהוּ מִבְּעוֹד יוֹם, לֹא יְכַסֶּנּוּ מִשֶּׁתֶּחְשַׁךְ — If he **did not cover** the pot of hot food **when it was yet day,** before the onset of the Sabbath, **he may not cover it after dark.** [8] כִּסָּהוּ וְנִתְגַּלָּה — But **if he did cover it** before dark **and it became uncovered** after dark, מֻתָּר לְכַסּוֹתוֹ — **he may cover it** again.[9]

מְמַלֵּא אֶת הַקִּתוֹן — **One may fill a bottle** with cold water or a cooked food that has become cold, וְנוֹתֵן לְתַחַת הַכַּר אוֹ תַחַת הַכֶּסֶת — **and place it under a cushion or under a bolster,** to keep it cold, even on the Sabbath.[10]

——— NOTES ———

movement of the *muktzeh* shearings (*Shulchan Aruch* 259:5). Nevertheless, he may insert a reed or stick through the shearings to get to the handle and thereby lift off the cover (*Magen Avraham* 259:5). Alternatively, he may tip the receptacle which contains the pot and the shearings until the shearings fall away and expose the handle (*Ran*).

6. If he removes the pot, and the shearings on both sides fall into the cavity, he will not be permitted to move them aside when he will want to replace the pot with the remaining food (*Rav; Rashi*).

7. The Sages agree with R' Elazar ben Azaryah that if the shearings *do* collapse, it is prohibited to rearrange them in order to restore the cavity. They disagree only in that they do not view the possibility that the cavity will collapse as a sufficient reason to forbid the removal of the pot from the box (*Rav*).

8. This covering constitutes *hatmanah,* which may never be done on the Sabbath proper, even with substances that do not raise the level of the heat [see the previous Mishnah, end of note 1] (*Rav; Rashi*).

9. Just as one may remove a pot from its *hatmanah* and then replace it, so may one replace the lid of a pot that has become uncovered on the Sabbath (*Tosafos* 5la).

10. Since it is not usual to insulate cold foods, the Rabbis did not prohibit it (*Rav*).

The Gemara (50a) states in the name of Rava that our Mishnah's ruling that wool shearings may not be moved applies only if the shearings were not permanently designated for insulating; but if one permanently designated them for insulating, they are not *muktzeh,* and may be moved.

The Gemara then cites an even more lenient opinion, that merely *using* the wool shearings once for *hatmanah* relieves them of their *muktzeh* status. And the fact that the ruling in our Mishnah indicates otherwise — for we see from our Mishnah that wool shearings may not be moved when they have been used for insulation — poses no difficulty, for our Mishnah speaks of wool shearings that came from a warehouse, i.e., shearings that a merchant stocks on his shelves for sale. Such shearings, even if removed from the shelves, are destined to be returned there. They therefore remain *muktzeh* unless they are expressly designated for *hatmanah.* Ordinary shearings, on the other hand, lose their *muktzeh* status even if they were used for insulation only once.

[Rava's ruling here seems to conflict with Abaye's ruling (on 48a) that flockings remain *muktzeh* even *after* being used for insulation. Given that the Gemara does not point out that Rava here disputes Abaye above, we must say that Abaye, too, was referring specifically to flockings from a warehouse (*Tosafos,* 48a). Alternatively, we can say that flockings are more valuable than wool shearings. Thus, while one who uses wool shearings for insulation even just once is apt to continue using them for this purpose, one who uses flockings for insulation is likely to return them afterwards to their primary purpose of making felt (*Rosh*).]

Subsequently, the Gemara discusses how other *muktzeh* items may be released from their *muktzeh* status. For example, the Gemara cites Rav Yehudah, who says that a person may bring a basketful of earth into his house before the Sabbath and use it for all his needs on the Sabbath — e.g., to cover unsightly filth or saliva on the floor of his house. However, Mar Zutra in the name of Mar Zutra Rabbah attests that this leniency of Rav Yehudah applies only if the person set aside a corner of the house for the storage of the earth (i.e., he piled it up in one corner, and did not spread it out on the ground). However, if he scattered it over the ground of the house, where it will be trodden upon by the residents of the house, it becomes subordinate to the ground and remains *muktzeh.* [According to this understanding, simply bringing the earth into the house is not considered an act performed upon the earth (which would remove its *muktzeh* status), because doing so only changes the earth's location; it does not make the earth *intrinsically* more suitable for covering filth (*Tos. HaRosh*).]

The *mashgiach* of Ponevezh, in his *sefer Yad Yechez-kel,* addresses the question of why Lot's prayer to save Tzoar was more efficacious than Avraham's. He cites a Midrash (*Bereishis Rabbah* 50:1) that offers a simple but powerful answer: Lot had provided food and lodging for the angel whose job it was to destroy Tzoar, so the angel owed him a debt of *hakaras hatov* (gratitude). This caused the angel to be disposed to grant Lot's request. [It should be noted that this Midrash obviously follows the view espoused by *Radak* here that angels sometimes have the power and authorization from Hashem to modify their instructions according to their own judgments and assessments of particular circumstances — cf. *Ramban* here.]

How great, then, is the power of *hakaras hatov*! As a result of a meal and a place to stay, Lot was given power over the angels to accomplish that which Avraham could not.

R' Daniel of Kelm, in developing this theme, noted that the prophet Elisha blessed the woman of Shuneim with a son, and later, after the son died, brought him back through his prayers (see *II Melachim,* Ch. 4). And why did he do this? Because the woman had provided him with a place to stay whenever he would be in the vicinity. His *hakaras hatov* for her hospitality created the obligation to perform miracles on her behalf!

Indeed, said *R' Daniel,* it can even be said that the angels' blessing to Avraham and Sarah — both aged and childless together for many years — was occasioned by the hospitality that was shown to them when they came to visit. Although the miracles necessary to bring this about were certainly considerable ones, the *hakaras hatov* of the angels rendered them obligated to strive toward ensuring that this blessing would be fulfilled. [Obviously, the promise that Yitzchak would be born existed independently of the angels' obligation; nevertheless, the fact that the angels issued their blessing upon this occasion shows us the extent of the obligation that can be engendered by *hakaras hatov.*]

QUESTION OF THE DAY:
Why did Lot's wife turn into a pillar of salt?

For the answer, see page 208.

As we learned yesterday, while the *poskim* view as a mixture any combination of items within which the separate components of the mixture have to some degree lost their individual identity due to their physical proximity, the halachah does recognize differences between various types of mixtures. Let us explain:

With respect to the *melachah* of *sorting,* we may categorize mixtures into three types: "Random" mixtures, "attached" mixtures, and "piled" mixtures. We will now analyze these different types of mixtures.

A "random" mixture is one in which different types of items are intermingled so that they lose their individual identity somewhat. This includes cases in which the separate ingredients are not readily discernible, for instance a well-cooked *cholent,* as well as those in which the different items are more easily recognized, such as a bowl of cut-up fruits. In either one of these cases, the combined items are no longer seen as individual units; they have instead combined to become part of a larger grouping. Items that have not been combined totally at random, but have been arranged in close proximity to one another in order to form a single unified grouping — for example, a deli platter comprised of different cuts of meat — also fall into this category of mixtures.

The next category of mixtures is the "attached" mixture. When two halachically different types of items are attached to one another, they are considered to be mixed at the point at which they are attached. Meat and its fat, a fruit and its peel, or an egg and its shell — all of these are considered attached to one another at the point at which they meet. This is true even though the two items in question are clearly delineated one from the other. Since they are attached, the halachah views them as being mixed where they meet.

The third category mentioned above is the "piled" mixture. This type of mixture is one in which large items are either piled one on top of another, or arranged next to one another. In such cases, since we are dealing with large items, it is more difficult for the items in question to lose their individual identity to the group. Yet, these items are still seen as being mixed, since they have been stacked together in one unified group. Examples of this category would be a stack of different-size plates, a pile of assorted types of towels, or various types of linens.

To summarize: A combination of different types of items is seen as a mixture when each component of the mixture has lost its individual identity to some degree, and is now perceived as part of a larger group.

Additionally, items that are not actually mixed, but rather are attached to one another, are also considered to be mixed at the point of contact, and are therefore subject to the restrictions of *sorting*.

A CLOSER LOOK AT THE SIDDUR

The Friday night *Maariv* prayer, from the beginning of the prayer until the end of the second blessing after the *Shema* (the *berachah* of *Hashkiveinu*) is identical to the weeknight *Maariv*. The closing of the blessing, however, is changed on Friday night (as well as on the eve of a Yom Tov). During the weekdays, we ask Hashem to safeguard our goings and comings for life and for peace, from now and for all eternity, and close with the blessing, בָּרוּךְ אַתָּה ה׳ שׁוֹמֵר עַמּוֹ יִשְׂרָאֵל לָעַד, *Blessed are You Hashem, Who safeguards His nation Israel forever*. On the Sabbath, however, we conclude by repeating a request found earlier in the blessing: *And spread over us the shelter of Your peace* (this follows *Nusach Ashkenaz; Nusach Sefard* reads: *and spread over us a shelter of mercy, life and peace*). And we close the prayer with an expanded blessing: בָּרוּךְ אַתָּה ה׳ הַפּוֹרֵשׂ סֻכַּת שָׁלוֹם עָלֵינוּ וְעַל כָּל עַמּוֹ יִשְׂרָאֵל וְעַל יְרוּשָׁלָיִם, *Blessed are You, Hashem, Who spreads the shelter of peace upon us, and upon His entire nation Israel, and upon Yerushalayim*.

Abudraham explains that our weekday request for protection is unnecessary on the Sabbath, based on the Midrash (*Midrash Tehillim* § 10) that the Sabbath provides its own protection. Accordingly, he says, we substitute a request that Hashem spread His peaceful shelter over us (the text of this request is found in *Yerushalmi Berachos* 4:5). [The repeat of the request to be sheltered in Hashem's peace is a result of the general rule that the conclusion of a prayer and its closing blessing should be similar in content.]

Anaf Yosef explains that this request is appropriate for the Sabbath and festivals rather than for the weekdays, for the "peace" that we are praying for is a result of the closeness to Hashem that is a result of the holiness of these days.

While some versions of the *siddur* (such as *Nusach Teiman*) remove the request for protection from the body of the blessing as well as from the conclusion, our versions retain it within the blessing itself. *Ba'er Heiteiv* (*Orach Chaim* 267:2) suggests that this is due to our fear that we do not manage to observe the Sabbath as completely as we should, and that therefore we may not merit the protection spoken of in the Midrash. Thus, we pray for Hashem's protection even on the Sabbath.

וַיְהִי אַחַר הַדְּבָרִים הָאֵלֶּה וְהָאֱלֹהִים נִסָּה אֶת־אַבְרָהָם . . .
וַיֹּאמֶר קַח־נָא אֶת־בִּנְךָ אֶת־יְחִידְךָ אֲשֶׁר־אָהַבְתָּ אֶת־יִצְחָק

And it happened after these things that HASHEM
tested Avraham . . . and He said: Please take your son,
your only one, whom you love, Yitzchak . . . (Bereishis 22:1-2).

The commentators dwell at great length upon the *nisayon* (trial) of the *Akeidah,* in which Avraham was bidden to offer his son Yitzchak as a *korban* before Hashem. As the Torah relates, Avraham unquestioningly proceeded to travel to Har HaMoriah to do as he was bidden; ultimately, Hashem told him not to sacrifice Yitzchak, but bade him offer a ram in his stead.

Rambam (*Moreh Nevuchim* 3:24) explains that the *Akeidah* teaches two great principles of our faith. First, it portrays the extent that one must fear Hashem and obey Him . . . At the age of 100, Avraham was finally rewarded with a child who, he is promised, will become the father of a great nation. How intensely he must have hoped for this to come to pass! Yet, as soon as he was commanded to slaughter him, he set aside all considerations, and undertook to fulfill Hashem's command; not because of fear that he would be punished if he disobeyed, but because it is man's duty to love and fear Hashem.

[It is noteworthy that in *Derashos HaRan* (§9) it is suggested that when Hashem told Avraham to sacrifice Yitzchak, he specifically asked Avraham to agree to forgo the fulfillment of the blessing that his children would be a great nation!]

For this reason, *Rambam* explains, once Avraham proved his readiness to sacrifice Yitzchak, the angel told him (22:12): *For now I know that you are a God-fearing man.* His action had proved the extent of his fear of Heaven, and would serve as an example to all of proper service of Hashem.

The second purpose of the *Akeidah,* writes *Rambam,* was to demonstrate by Avraham's example how a prophet must unquestioningly confirm the principles of the truth of prophecy — regardless of how difficult it is to perform the commandment. Avraham's compliance with the command to bring up his beloved Yitzchak to the altar to be slaughtered would have been impossible if Avraham did not believe utterly in the truths of the prophetic visions he received.

Abarbanel adds that a third purpose of the *Akeidah* was to teach unequivocally the concept of הִשָּׁאֲרַת הַנֶּפֶשׁ, *eternity of the soul.* Without this belief, Avraham could not have undertaken slaughtering his son and heir, leaving himself bereft in this world. It was only because he recognized the existence of the World to Come that he was able to do so, with the understanding that whatever the implications of his act were to be in this world, they would be only transitory.

A thorough discussion of the *Akeidah* is beyond the scope of this work; it is treated by almost every major commentary on *Chumash*. Indeed, the passage of the *Akeidah* has become part of our daily prayers (see further in *A Closer Look at the Siddur*). It is not an overstatement to say that the actions of Avraham and Yitzchak during this period shaped the destiny of the Jews for eternity.

MISHNAH OF THE DAY SHABBOS 5:1

The Torah forbids the owner of an animal to let it do work on the Sabbath. Accordingly, one may not allow one's animal to carry a burden four *amos* within a public domain, or from a private domain to a public domain, and vice versa. However, gear that is essential for controlling the animal is not considered a burden, and the animal may go out with it on the Sabbath. Our Mishnah distinguishes between essential and non-essential gear:

בַּמֶּה בְהֵמָה יוֹצְאָה — *With what* gear *may an animal go out* into a public domain, וּבַמֶּה אֵינָהּ יוֹצְאָה — *and with what* gear *may it not go out?* יוֹצֵא הַגָּמָל בְּאַפְסָר — *A camel may go out with a halter;* [1] וְנָאקָה בַּחֲטָם — *and a female dromedary* may go out *with a nose ring;* [2] וְלוּבְדְּקִים בִּפְרוּמְבִּיָא — *and a Libyan ass* may go out *with a bit;* [3] וְסוּס בְּשֵׁיר — *and a horse* may go out *with a collar.* [4] וְכָל בַּעֲלֵי הַשֵּׁיר יוֹצְאִין בְּשֵׁיר

———————— NOTES ————————

1. A halter is used to lead an animal. It consists of a length of rope whose end is tied around the animal's mouth. Since it serves to control the animal, it is not deemed a burden, and it may be worn by a camel [and certain other animals] in a public domain on the Sabbath (*Rambam Commentary*).

2. A female dromedary is faster than an ordinary camel, and is more apt to break away. It therefore requires a more powerful restraint than does the camel (*Rashi; Tiferes Yisrael*).

3. Donkeys from Libya are even more powerful than camels, and the curb normally used for a camel is insufficient to control the Libyan ass. They are therefore controlled by a bit that consists of a harness enclosing the head and jaws (*Rashi*). [Domestic donkeys may not go out with a bit, since they are milder in manner than the Libyan strain, and do not require such great restraint (*Shulchan Aruch* 305:3, see *Taz*).]

4. This refers to a band placed around the animal's neck. To this band is affixed a ring, into which is inserted a rope or strap by which the animal is led (*Rashi*).

וְנִמְשָׁכִין בְּשֵׁיר — *And all* animals *that* typically *wear a collar* for adornment, such as hunting dogs or other smaller animals, *may go out with a collar, and may be pulled by* a rope attached to *the collar.* [5]

The Mishnah records other laws concerning an animal's collar. These laws are not related to the Sabbath: וּמַזִּין עֲלֵיהֶן — When purifying these collars from *tumah* contracted from a corpse, *we may sprinkle* the ash-water of the *parah adumah upon them* even while they are in their place on the animal's neck,[6] וְטוֹבְלָן בִּמְקוֹמָן — *and we may* also *immerse them* in a *mikveh* while they are *in their place* on the animal's neck.[7]

——————————— NOTES ———————————

5. *Rashi* explains that this collar is worn as an ornament, and is therefore permitted. *Tosafos,* however, maintain that an animal would not be permitted to go out with an ornamental collar. Rather, this collar is worn so that if the animal attempts to run away, it can be seized by the collar. Since the collar serves to control the animal, it is not considered a burden.

6. Persons, or utensils designated for use by humans, that contract ritual contamination from a corpse are *tamei* [ritually contaminated] for seven days. They are ritually purified in the following manner: A hyssop is immersed in the water prepared with ashes of a *parah adumah* — a red cow (see *Numbers* 19:1-22) — and the water is sprinkled on the man or utensil on the third and seventh days of a week-long period, after which they are immersed in a *mikveh* and become *tahor* after sunset of that day.

[Although normally utensils that are made for an animal are not susceptible to *tumah*, since the collar discussed here serves the person's purpose of leading the animal, it is considered designated for use by humans. Hence, contact with a corpse renders it *tamei*, and it requires purification (*Rav; Tos. Yom Tov* from Gemara 52).] The Mishnah here teaches us that the cleansing water may be sprinkled on the collar even while it is on the animal, and we need not be concerned that the sprinkling water may first fall on the animal [rendering it unfit for use in cleansing according to some opinions], or that he may intend to sprinkle the water on the animal and only inadvertently hit the collar [which is invalid according to other opinions] (*Tos* 52a; *Tiferes Yisrael, Meleches Shlomo, Parah* 12:3).

7. We need not be concerned that the collar may be fastened too tightly to the animal and thereby prevent the water of the *mikveh* from coming between the collar and the animal's neck (*Tos. Yom Tov*).

QUESTION OF THE DAY:
How old was Yitzchak at the time of the Akeidah?

For the answer, see page 208.

The Gemara (51b) considers whether an animal may go out with an excessive restraint that it does not require — e.g., an ordinary camel with a nose ring (that is required only for the more powerful female dromedary). In the course of its discussion, the Gemara cites a Baraisa in which the Tanna Kamma rules that a wild beast (a *chayah*) may not go out on the Sabbath with a collar of rope, while Chananyah rules that the beast may go out with a collar of rope or with anything that restrains it.

The Gemara analyzes this Baraisa and concludes that it refers to a cat. Thus, the issue of excessive restraint is the subject of the dispute: The Tanna Kamma holds that since an ordinary cord is enough for a cat, a rope collar is considered excessive and therefore a burden, while Chananyah holds that an excessive restraint is never considered a burden.

The Gemara then cites a legal decision rendered by Rav Huna bar Chiya said in the name of Shmuel, that the law follows Chananyah.

Later (52a), however, the Gemara demonstrates that Shmuel's decision is not universally accepted, and that Rav's view is that an excessive restraint is indeed classified as a burden. In the course of its analysis of Rav's position, the Gemara challenges it from a Baraisa that rules that if the owner of a *parah adumah* tied a leash to it, it is nevertheless valid (to be burned and processed into the ash used for purification from corpse *tumah* — see note 6 to the Mishnah above). Now, a *parah adumah* is valid only if it has never carried a burden; and since a leash is an excessive restraint for a cow, according to Rav who maintains that an excessive restraint is a burden, the *parah adumah* should *not* be valid!

Three Amoraim advance solutions in defense of Rav:

(1) Abaye says that the Baraisa refers to a case where the owner is leading the *parah adumah* from city to city: Since a cow tends to go to its regular resting place, when taking it to a different city one must hold onto it to prevent it from turning back. In such a circumstance, a leash is not an excessive restraint.

(2) Rava says that a *parah adumah* is different from all other cows, because a cow that meets the requirements of a *parah adumah* is extremely rare, and therefore very precious. Therefore, if a completely red calf was born to one's herd, one would guard it with extreme care. In this instance, a rope halter is not considered an excessive restraint.

(3) Ravina says that the Baraisa refers to a rebellious cow: When used for a cow of a particularly rebellious nature, a rope halter is not deemed an excessive restraint.

A MUSSAR THOUGHT FOR THE DAY

פרשת
וירא

SHABBOS
PARASHAS
VAYEIRA

The question is often asked: Why is the *Akeidah* viewed as uniquely *Avraham's* trial? While Avraham was indeed being tested, surely the *Akeidah* was a great trial for Yitzchak as well! Yitzchak, when told of his father's purpose, acquiesced wholeheartedly; indeed, his conduct during those fateful three days leading up to his ascent to the altar teaches us lasting lessons in proper service of Hashem. Avraham and Yitzchak were partners in approaching the *Akeidah*. Why, then, is the trial aspect of the *Akeidah* not ascribed to both? Since it was Yitzchak's life that was being requested, should the trial not be described as least equally as his?

When this question was asked of the *Alter* of Novaradok, *R' Yoseif Yoizel Horowitz,* he replied: "It is harder to live like a Jew than to die like a Jew."

Rabbi Nosson Scherman would explain the Alter's words as follows: True, Yitzchak faced the challenge: Was he ready to offer his life? But once he stood up to that challenge, his trial would be over. He would not have to deal with the aftermath of his trial. He would ascend to Har HaMoriah, and remain there, having surrendered his life in the service of Hashem — retiring from the scene in a blaze of glory. Although the supreme sacrifice of one's life is not to be taken lightly, such acts of heroism are not uncommon in human experience. Even ordinary people can rise to such greatness; surely Yitzchak would not be expected to do less.

The challenge facing Avraham, however, was that after he would carry out Hashem's command, he would have to go on living. He would have to face an unbelieving world, and his wife Sarah. He would have to continue opening his home to wayfarers and entertaining guests, though they would now most likely be afraid to accept hospitality from the barbarous old man who had killed his own son. He would have to find a way to continue spreading the ways of *chesed* to a world that would regard him as the greatest of hypocrites. And he would always wonder if his sin of failing to marry off Yitzchak in a timely manner had caused this unspeakable tragedy. Yitzchak had to *die* as a Jew; but Avraham had to bear the infinitely harder burden of carrying on, and continuing to *live* like a Jew.

HALACHAH OF THE DAY

As we mentioned at the outset of our discussion of the *melachah* of *sorting,* this is a *melachah* that is encountered with great frequency every Shabbos. With that having been said, it is also true that most selecting that one may desire to do on Shabbos can be done in a permissible

fashion — one need only acquaint himself thoroughly with the guidelines and rules of *sorting* in order to know the proper procedure that must be followed in each case. We have already identified which types of mixtures are subject to the restrictions of *sorting*. Now, we may begin to discuss the methods one is permitted to use to make selections from such mixtures.

There are three conditions that must be met in order for selecting to be permitted on Shabbos. These three conditions are as follows: First, one must remove the "food" from the "waste," and not the "waste" from the "food." [As we have learned previously, in this context the term "food" means any useful substance that one desires to remove from the mixture, as opposed to "waste," which refers to the undesired substance mixed in with the "food." Thus, one must remove that which he wishes to use, not that which he wishes to discard.] Second, the removal must be done by hand, as opposed to by means of a utensil such as a strainer (this will be discussed further below). Third, the selection can be performed only if the item(s) being removed from the mixture will be used immediately.

Let us now expand on each of these three conditions. One may select from a mixture of food and waste only by taking the food and leaving behind the waste. For example, a cluster of grapes comprised of ripe, desirable grapes and soft, undesirable ones, is a mixture subject to the restrictions of *sorting*. Accordingly, one may not remove spoiled grapes from a cluster — that would be an act of *sorting*. He may, however, proceed by selecting the desirable grapes, eating them, and leaving the undesirable ones behind. Similarly, if one has a mixture of foods from which he wishes to select one type — for example, a bowl of mixed nuts from which he wishes to eat cashews — he must select and eat the cashews, rather than remove the other nuts and leave the cashews behind to eat. In this case, the cashews — the desired component of the mixture — are the "food," while the rest of the nuts are viewed as "waste."

Whenever a person is choosing one item from among other items, the same rule applies. The item that is desired for immediate use is considered "food," and the unwanted items are viewed as "waste." Accordingly, one must select the desired item and leave the unwanted items behind. For example, if one has before him a pile of assorted cutlery from which he needs spoons for immediate use, he may not remove the forks and knives, thereby isolating the spoons. Rather, he must select and remove the spoons that he needs, leaving behind the mixed forks and knives.

Tomorrow, we will continue exploring the methods by which selecting can be done in a permissible manner.

A CLOSER LOOK AT THE SIDDUR

פרשת
וירא

SHABBOS

PARASHAS
VAYEIRA

In addition to assuming a central role in the prayers of the *Yamim Nora'im* (High Holy Days), the passage of the *Akeidah* is recited daily by many, after the blessings at the beginning of *Shacharis* and before the passages of the *Korbanos*. [In a sense, of course, Yitzchak was the very first *korban!*] *Abarbanel* states the case for the inclusion of this passage in one's daily prayers very strongly: "In Hashem's eyes, this passage constitutes the very reason for the existence of the Jewish nation. It has therefore become part of our daily prayers, and must be studied more thoroughly than other passages . . ."

Shulchan Aruch (*Orach Chaim* 1:5) states: "It is a good practice to recite the passage of the *Akeidah* [in one's daily prayers]." *Mishnah Berurah* (ibid. §13) explains: It is not merely enough to say the verses without contemplation; rather, one should think into what he is saying, and come to appreciate the majesty of Hashem . . . Citing *Taz,* he states that there are two reasons to recite the passage of the *Akeidah*: to recall in our prayers the merits of the Patriarchs, who were tested so severely and responded so magnificently; and to subdue our evil inclination with the constant knowledge that we must always be ready to sacrifice our very lives in Hashem's service, just as Yitzchak was ready to do.

After the passage of the *Akeidah* is said, we recite a special prayer asking Hashem to suppress any anger He may feel toward his nation, in the merit of Avraham's suppression of his natural filial mercy when he went to sacrifice his beloved son Yitzchak; and we close the prayer with a plea that Hashem remember the covenant that He established with each of the *Avos*, even in times of Divine displeasure. We do so by citing the verse that appears in the Torah in the midst of Hashem's listing the terrible punishments that will befall sinners, in the curses of the *Tochachah* (*Vayikra* 26:42): *I will remember My covenant with Yaakov, and also My covenant with Yitzchak, and also My covenant with Avraham I will remember; and I will remember the land.*

Ohel Yaakov notes that this verse not only reassures the Jews of Hashem's support, but also reminds them why they are held to a higher standard — precisely because they are the children of the *Avos*. This, too, is a lesson that must be absorbed from the *Akeidah*; we are descended from spiritual giants, and must do our best to live up to the deeds of our ancestors.

Sunday:

Yitzchak was born on Pesach. There is a difference of opinion as to whether the angels appeared on Pesach of the prior year (the most commonly accepted opinion), or in Tishrei (see *Rosh Hashanah* 11a-b with *Tosafos* and *Maharsha*).

Monday:

An angel is sent to perform only one function. One (Michael) was sent to foretell Yitzchak's birth; one (Gavriel) to overthrow Sodom, and one (Rephael) to heal Avraham [later, Rephael was given another mission — to rescue Lot] (*Rashi* to 18:2).

Tuesday:

Lot offered the angels water to wash their feet (19:2), and Eliezer and his men were offered water by Lavan (24:32).

Wednesday:

Elisha blessed the righteous woman of Shuneim who provided a place for him to stay whenever he would pass by, and she bore a child (see *II Kings* 4:16).

Thursday:

Several answers are suggested: (1) Avraham knew that Noach, his three sons, and their wives could not save the world, even by adding Hashem Himself (Who is everywhere) for a total of nine. He therefore knew at least ten were necessary (*Rashi*). (2) Avraham thought that Lot, his wife, and their four married daughters and their husbands were all righteous, so he assumed that there were at least ten righteous people in the city (*Daas Zekeinim*). (3) Avraham would indeed have continued to pray, but the Divine Presence departed from him, and he understood that he was to cease in his prayers (*Haamek Davar*).

Friday:

According to the Midrash, Lot's wife did not want the guests, and deliberately revealed their presence by going to the neighbors and asking for salt for the guests. [According to *Ibn Ezra,* the salt refers to the salt and sulfur that rained down upon Sodom; she was engulfed by the salt.]

Shabbos:

According to most opinions, Yitzchak was 37 years old. This is derived from the fact that Sarah died immediately after the *Akeidah,* and she was 127 at the time of her death; since she bore Yitzchak at the age of 90, he was 37 when she died, which was right after the *Akeidah.*